PEARSON EDUCATION
AP* TEST PREP SERIES
AP U. S.HISTORY
FOR

AMERICA PAST AND PRESENT

Ninth
Advanced Placement* Edition

Michael K. Barbour
St. Brendan's College

Anthony Jones
Houston County High School

Len Rabinowitz
Ashland High School

Gordon Utz
Stratford Senior High School

Longman

Boston   Columbus   Indianapolis   New York   San Francisco   Upper Saddle River
Amsterdam   Cape Town   Dubai   London   Madrid   Milan   Munich   Paris   Montréal   Toronto
Delhi   Mexico City   São Paulo   Sydney   Hong Kong   Seoul   Singapore   Taipei   Tokyo

*Advanced Placement, Advanced Placement Program and AP are registered trademarks of the College Entrance Examination Board, which was not involved in the production of, and does not endorse, this product.

Printed in the United States of America

10 9 8 7 6 5

Longman
is an imprint of

www. PearsonSchool.com/Advanced

ISBN 10: 0-13-136910-5
ISBN 13: 978-0-13-136910-8

CONTENTS

About Your Pearson Test Prep Series   1

Part I: Introduction to the AP* U.S. History Examination   3

Dos and Don'ts of the AP* Exams   5

AP* Topics Correlation to America Past and Present   15

Part II: Topical Review with Sample Questions and Answers and Explanations   21

CHAPTER 1
New World Encounters   23
  Native American Histories Before Conquest   23
  A World Transformed   23
  West Africa: Ancient and Complex Societies   24
  Imagining a New World   24
  The French Claim Canada   24
  The English Enter the Competition   24
  Irish Rehearsal for American Settlement   25
  An Unpromising Beginning: Mystery
    at Roanoke   25
    Multiple-Choice Questions   25
    Free-Response Question   26
  ANSWERS AND EXPLANATIONS   26

CHAPTER 2
New World Experiments: England's Seventeenth-Century Colonies   29
  Breaking Away   29
  The Chesapeake: Dreams of Wealth   29
  Reforming England in America   30
  Diversity in the Middle Colonies   30

  Quakers in America   30
  Planting the Carolinas   31
  The Founding of Georgia   31
    Multiple-Choice Questions   31
    Free-Response Question   32
  ANSWERS AND EXPLANATIONS   32

CHAPTER 3
Putting Down Roots: Opportunity and Oppression in Colonial Society   35
  Sources of Stability: New England Colonies of the
    Seventeenth Century   35
  Challenge of the Chesapeake Environment   35
  Race and Freedom in British America   36
  Rise of a Commercial Empire   36
  Colonial Factions Spark Revolt, 1676–1691   36
    Multiple-Choice Questions   37
    Document-Based Question   38
    Free-Response Question   42
  ANSWERS AND EXPLANATIONS   42

CHAPTER 4
Experience of Empire: Eighteenth-Century America   45
  Growth and Diversity   45
  Spanish Borderlands of the Eighteenth Century   45
  The Impact of European Ideas on
    American Culture   46
  Religious Revivals in Provincial Societies   46
  Clash of Political Cultures   46
  Century of Imperial War   47
    Multiple-Choice Questions   47
    Free-Response Question   49

ANSWERS AND EXPLANATIONS   49

CHAPTER 5
The American Revolution: From Elite Protest to Popular Revolt, 1763–1783   51
Structure of Colonial Society   51
Eroding the Bonds of Empire   51
Steps Toward Independence   52
Fighting for Independence   52
The Loyalist Dilemma   53
Winning the Peace   53
Multiple-Choice Questions   53
Free-Response Question   54
ANSWERS AND EXPLANATIONS   54

CHAPTER 6
The Republican Experiment   57
Defining Republican Culture   57
Living in the Shadow of Revolution   57
Social and Political Reform   57
The States: Experiments in Republicanism   57
Stumbling Toward a New National Government   58
Strengthening Federal Authority   58
"Have We Fought for This?"   58
Whose Constitution? Struggle for Ratification   59
Multiple-Choice Questions   59
Free-Response Question   60
ANSWERS AND EXPLANATIONS   61

CHAPTER 7
Democracy in Distress: The Violence of Party Politics, 1788–1800   63
Principle and Pragmatism: Establishing a New Government   63
Conflicting Visions: Jefferson and Hamilton   63
Hamilton's Plan for Prosperity and Security   63
Charges of Treason: The Battle over Foreign Affairs   64
Popular Political Culture   64
The Adams Presidency   65
The Peaceful Revolution: The Election of 1800   65
Multiple-Choice Questions   65
Document-Based Question   67
Free-Response Question   71
ANSWERS AND EXPLANATIONS   71

CHAPTER 8
Republican Ascendancy: The Jeffersonian Vision   75
Regional Identities in a New Republic   75
Jefferson as President   75
Jefferson's Critics   76
Embarrassments Overseas   76
The Strange War of 1812   77
Multiple-Choice Questions   77

Free-Response Question   78
ANSWERS AND EXPLANATIONS   78

CHAPTER 9
Nation Building and Nationalism   81
Expansion and Migration   81
A Revolution in Transportation   81
Emergence of a Market Economy   82
The Politics of Nation Building After the War of 1812   82
Multiple-Choice Questions   83
Free-Response Question   84
ANSWERS AND EXPLANATIONS   84

CHAPTER 10
The Triumph of White Men's Democracy   87
Democracy in Theory and Practice   87
Jackson and the Politics of Democracy   88
The Bank War and the Second Party System   88
Heyday of the Second Party System   89
Multiple-Choice Questions   89
Free-Response Question   90
ANSWERS AND EXPLANATIONS   90

CHAPTER 11
Slaves and Masters   93
The Divided Society of the Old South   93
The World of Southern Blacks   93
White Society in the Antebellum South   93
Slavery and the Southern Economy   94
Multiple-Choice Questions   94
Free-Response Question   95
ANSWERS AND EXPLANATIONS   95

CHAPTER 12
The Pursuit of Perfection   97
The Rise of Evangelicalism   97
Domesticity and Changes in the American Family   97
Institutional Reform   97
Reform Turns Radical   98
Multiple-Choice Questions   98
Free-Response Question   99
ANSWERS AND EXPLANATIONS   99

CHAPTER 13
An Age of Expansionism   101
Movement to the Far West   101
Manifest Destiny and the Mexican War   101
Internal Expansionism   102
Multiple-Choice Questions   103
Free-Response Question   104
ANSWERS AND EXPLANATIONS   104

CHAPTER 14
The Sectional Crisis 107
The Compromise of 1850 107
Taylor Takes Charge 107
Political Upheaval, 1852–1856 108
The House Divided, 1857–1860 108
Multiple-Choice Questions 109
Document-Based Question 110
Free-Response Question 115
ANSWERS AND EXPLANATIONS 115

CHAPTER 15
Secession and the Civil War 119
The Storm Gathers 119
Adjusting to Total War 119
Fight to the Finish 120
Multiple-Choice Questions 120
Free-Response Question 122
ANSWERS AND EXPLANATIONS 122

CHAPTER 16
The Agony of Reconstruction 123
The President Versus Congress 123
Reconstructing Southern Society 123
Retreat from Reconstruction 124
Reunion and the New South 124
Multiple-Choice Questions 125
Free-Response Question 126
ANSWERS AND EXPLANATIONS 127

CHAPTER 17
The West: Exploiting an Empire 129
Beyond the Frontier 129
Crushing the Native Americans 129
Settlement of the West 130
The Bonanza West 130
Multiple-Choice Questions 131
Free-Response Question 132
ANSWERS AND EXPLANATIONS 132

CHAPTER 18
The Industrial Society 135
Industrial Development 135
An Empire on Rails 135
An Industrial Empire 135
The Sellers 136
The Wage Earners 136
Multiple-Choice Questions 137
Free-Response Question 138
ANSWERS AND EXPLANATIONS 138

CHAPTER 19
Toward an Urban Society, 1877–1900 141
The Lure of the City 141

Social and Cultural Change, 1877–1900 141
The Stirrings of Reform 142
Multiple-Choice Questions 142
Free-Response Question 143
ANSWERS AND EXPLANATIONS 144

CHAPTER 20
Political Realignments in the 1890s 147
Politics of Stalemate 147
Republicans in Power:
The Billion-Dollar Congress 147
The Rise of the Populist Movement 147
The Crisis of the Depression 148
Changing Attitudes 148
The Presidential Election of 1896 148
The McKinley Administration 149
Multiple-Choice Questions 149
Free-Response Question 150
ANSWERS AND EXPLANATIONS 150

CHAPTER 21
Toward Empire 153
America Looks Outward 153
War with Spain 153
Acquisition of Empire 154
Multiple-Choice Questions 155
Free-Response Question 156
ANSWERS AND EXPLANATIONS 156

CHAPTER 22
The Progressive Era 159
The Changing Face of Industrialism 159
Society's Masses 1659
Conflict in the Workplace 160
A New Urban Culture 160
Multiple-Choice Questions 161
Free-Response Question 162
ANSWERS AND EXPLANATIONS 162

CHAPTER 23
**From Roosevelt to Wilson in the Age
of Progressivism** 165
The Spirit of Progressivism 165
Reform in the Cities and States 165
The Republican Roosevelt 166
Roosevelt Progressivism at Its Height 166
The Ordeal of William Howard Taft 166
Woodrow Wilson's New Freedom 167
Multiple-Choice Questions 167
Document-Based Question 168
Free-Response Question 172
ANSWERS AND EXPLANATIONS 172

CHAPTER 24
The Nation at War 175
  A New World Power 175
  Foreign Policy Under Wilson 175
  Toward War 175
  Over There 176
  Over Here 176
  The Treaty of Versailles 177
    Multiple-Choice Questions 177
    Free-Response Question 178
  ANSWERS AND EXPLANATIONS 178

CHAPTER 25
Transition to Modern America 181
  The Second Industrial Revolution 181
  City Life in the Jazz Age 181
  Politics of the 1920s 182
    Multiple-Choice Questions 182
    Free-Response Question 183
  ANSWERS AND EXPLANATIONS 184

CHAPTER 26
Franklin D. Roosevelt and the New Deal 187
  The Great Depression 187
  Fighting the Depression 187
  Roosevelt and Reform 188
  Impact of the New Deal 188
  End of the New Deal 188
    Multiple-Choice Questions 189
    Document-Based Question 190
    Free-Response Question 196
  ANSWERS AND EXPLANATIONS 197

CHAPTER 27
America and the World, 1921–1945 201
  Retreat, Reversal, and Rivalry 201
  Isolationism 201
  The Road to War 201
  Turning the Tide Against the Axis 202
  The Home Front 202
  Victory 202
    Multiple-Choice Questions 203
    Free-Response Question 204
  ANSWERS AND EXPLANATIONS 204

CHAPTER 28
The Onset of the Cold War 207
  The Cold War Begins 207
  Containment 207
  The Cold War Expands 208
  The Cold War at Home 208
  Eisenhower Wages the Cold War 208
    Multiple-Choice Questions 209
    Document-Based Question 210
    Free-Response Question 216

ANSWERS AND EXPLANATIONS 217

CHAPTER 29
Affluence and Anxiety 221
  The Postwar Boom 221
  The Good Life? 221
  Farewell to Reform 222
  The Struggle over Civil Rights 222
    Multiple-Choice Questions 222
    Free-Response Question 223
  ANSWERS AND EXPLANATIONS 224

CHAPTER 30
The Turbulent Sixties 227
  Kennedy Intensifies the Cold War 227
  The New Frontier at Home 227
  "Let Us Continue" 228
  Johnson Escalates the Vietnam War 228
  Years of Turmoil 228
  The Return of Richard Nixon 229
    Multiple-Choice Questions 229
    Free-Response Question 230
  ANSWERS AND EXPLANATIONS 231

CHAPTER 31
To a New Conservatism, 1969–1988 235
  The Tempting of Nixon 235
  The Economy of Stagflation 236
  Private Lives, Public Issues 236
  Politics and Diplomacy after Watergate 236
  The Reagan Revolution 237
  Reagan and the World 238
    Multiple-Choice Questions 239
    Free-Response Question 240
  ANSWERS AND EXPLANATIONS 240

CHAPTER 32
To the Twenty-First Century 243
  The First President Bush 243
  The Changing Faces of America 243
  The New Democrats 244
  Clinton and the World 245
  Republicans Triumphant 245
  Challenges of the New Century 245
    Multiple-Choice Questions 246
    Free-Response Question 247
  ANSWERS AND EXPLANATIONS 247

Part III: *Sample Tests with Answers and Explanations* 249

Sample Practice Test 1 251

Sample Practice Test 2 275

About Your Pearson Test Prep Series

Pearson Education is the leading publisher of textbooks worldwide. With operations on every continent, we make it our business to understand the changing needs of students at every level, from kindergarten to college.

This gives us a unique insight into what kind of study materials work for students. We talk to customers every day, soliciting feedback on our books. We think that this makes us especially qualified to offer this series of AP* test prep books, tied to some of our best-selling textbooks.

We know that as you study for your AP* course, you're preparing along the way for the AP* exam. By tying the material in the book directly to AP* course goals and exam topics, we help you to focus your time most efficiently. And that's a good thing!

The AP* exam is an important milestone in your education. A high score will position you optimally for college acceptance—and possibly will give you college credits that put you a step ahead. Our goal at Pearson Education is to provide you with the tools you need to excel on the exam … the rest is up to you.

Good luck!

Part I

Introduction to the AP U.S. History Examination*

This section provides an overview of the format of the Advanced Placement* Exam in U.S. History, introduces the types of questions you will encounter on the exam, and provides helpful test-taking strategies. It also explains how the exam is evaluated and provides a list of dos and don'ts for excelling on the exam. In addition, a correlation chart is provided that shows where key information commonly tested on the examination is covered in *America Past and Present*. Review this section carefully before trying the sample items in the following parts.

Dos and Don'ts of the AP* Exams

Early Preparation

To do well on the national AP* U.S. history exam you will have to take personal responsibility for your own review and early preparation. Begin your preparation weeks before the exam. Do this preparation on your own time outside of your AP* U.S. history classroom. There are many aids available to assist you in this preparation, for example:

- The College Board provides an excellent testing resource in the form of general advice Web site for students taking the Advanced Placement* U.S. History Examination. You can access the Web site at:

  http://collegeboard.com/student/testing/ap/about.html

- Many professionally developed preparation handbooks are available through any competent bookstore and are usually priced around ten dollars.
- Your teacher might provide you with a study guide for the AP* U.S. history exam, especially if that teacher has been teaching the course for many years.
- Your own notes taken during the course of the year are a valuable resource. Old tests and essays can tell you where your weaknesses are located and where you need to concentrate your study.
- Search the Web for teacher Web sites with self-testing practice quizzes.

You should begin your review for the AP* U.S. exam several weeks before the actual date, usually about early March. Pace your study so you do not overly burden yourself. Take some of the released exams that are available from the College Board or the simulated exams available from the preparation handbooks. Some preparation handbooks contain several versions so you can test yourself two or three times with different exams. Focus on areas where you detect a weakness in your knowledge such as colonial era or Reconstruction. Many teachers have posted diagnostic tests on school or personal Web sites for their students that you can take and to uncover your weaknesses. Do a search in your favorite search engine to locate these Web sites.

Students who have disabilities that might impact the exam should contact their teacher, counselor, or campus AP* coordinator to determine if modifications are appropriate. These modifications must be documented and established long before the exam date.

A particularly rich resource for students would be the College Board's Released Exam for U.S. History. This is an actual administered exam and you can practice with it. It also contains valuable information of all sorts. It is available at the College Board Web site for AP* U.S. history at: apcentral.col-legeboard.com. You will also find essay questions, both document based and free response, from the past several years posted on the AP* Central site along with grading rubrics and samples student essays.

Format of the National Advanced Placement* Exam in U.S. History

As the test date approaches your school will make arrangements for you to pay the appropriate fees, file the appropriate forms, and arrive at the established location of the exam on the day indicated. It is wise to arrive at least a quarter to a half hour earlier than the time set by the testing authority so that you are settled in before preparations for the exam begin. The U.S. history exam is usually given in the morning.

Make sure you had a good breakfast before the exam, but avoid anything excessively heavy. You are permitted to bring a bottle of water with you to the exam at most exam sites.

Bring with you to the exam some photo identification such as a driver's license, a school ID card, etc. You will have to identify yourself as you check in. Bring your social security number and your school code. Your school code is available from your counselor.

Bring several sharpened #2 pencils and at least a couple of new, tested dark ink pens. Dark blue or black pens are the best to use. It is not wise to write your essays in pencil. Also avoid colored inks. At the national exam the readers are reading your composition in a large area under lighting that make light pencil or bright colored ink less easy to read. Place no artificial impediments in front of your reader like a composition that is difficult to read.

Do not bring highlight pens or colored markers or colored ink pens. A proctor will instruct you to put them away. You will not be allowed to take any other materials like correction fluid, dictionaries, books and extra paper into the testing area, so do not bring them.

Personal laptop computers will not be allowed except for those who have received prior permission due to established special needs. Portable CDs or any recording device will not be allowed in the testing area. Do not bring cellular phones, as they will be viewed with suspicion. Beepers, blackberries or personal digital assistants (PDAs) are also banned for test security reasons.

It is advisable to bring a watch to check your own time. If the testing area has several wall clocks, you could become confused. Time yourself and avoid depending upon the proctor. You do not want to arrive at the end of the multiple-choice or essay section and discover the allotted time will end five minutes before you expected. Do not bring a watch that beeps or has an alarm. If you disrupt the examination session with noise or other distractions, you might be invited to leave.

The exam is three hours and five minutes long and is broken down into the multiple-choice section, given first, and the essay section. A short break of perhaps ten minutes usually is given between the two sections. Do not talk to your fellow students about the exam or the multiple-choice questions you have just taken and most especially do not talk to any AP* U.S. history teachers in the area as that would be a breach of security that could invalidate your school's scores for everyone.

You will be required to sign a protocol in which you pledge not to discuss the multiple-choice questions at any time. Do not post any questions you remember on a personal Web site. Students who have done so in the past have had their score invalidated and faced legal consequences. Do not discuss the essay questions with your teacher for at least 48 hours following the exam.

Section I of the AP* U. S. History Examination—the Multiple-Choice Questions

The 80-question multiple-choice section must be completed within 55 minutes and counts as half of your score. The questions will test both your analytic skills and your abilities at recall. The multiple-choice section will be comprehensive for the entire year. You will have to be familiar with the entire scope of U.S. history to do well on this section. There is no replacement for good, hard study for this portion of the exam. What your teacher has given you in class has laid a foundation for the test, but you will be responsible for fleshing out the details in your mind. You will have to prepare yourself outside of class time on your own.

Section II of the AP* U.S. History Examination—the Free Response (Essay) Questions

In Section II of the AP* U.S. history exam you will be required to write three essays, one document-based essay (DBQ) and two shorter free-response essays. There is no choice concerning the DBQ, but a certain amount of choice will be allowed with the two shorter essays.

Following a short break after the multiple-choice section, you will begin the free-response section of the exam lasting for 130 minutes. This block of time will be for you to divide as you wish except for a 15-minute preparation period at the beginning when you will be allowed to open the essay test booklet, but not the answer booklet. During this preparation period you can examine all of the essay questions, the documents for the DBQ, and formulate your initial response to the DBQ. *Do not open the answer booklet.* You can take notes in ample spaces among the documents in the DBQ booklet. It is advisable to devote much of this time to brainstorming for outside facts useful with the DBQ question, extract facts from the documents that you think you can use, and write a rough outline of the essay response along with a proposed thesis statement. Most students tackle the DBQ first, but once you are allowed into the answer booklet you can really write your essays in any order you wish.

After the 15-minute preparation period you will be advised that you have 45 minutes to answer the DBQ. You may use your time as you wish, but you are strongly advised to follow the recommendations of the College Board. Their advice is based upon the proven results of hundreds of thousands of students over many years. Your proctor will advise you when to begin the essays. Watch your time carefully and pace yourself, even if the proctor is writing times on a display board of some kind. Do not open your answer booklet early or you will commit a serious security breach.

In the second portion of the essay section you will be allowed a choice between two alternative questions in Part B and two alternative question in Part C. Spend no more than 35 minutes on each part of this portion of the essay section. In each grouping select the question with which you feel most comfortable. Remember that in both the DBQ and the free-response essays you must demonstrate a significant knowledge of U.S. history and this is accomplished by using outside facts in substantial amounts. One of the worst errors frequently committed by students sitting for the exam is to depend entirely upon the documents for their facts for the DBQ essay.

You may expect that the DBQ and the free-response essay taken together will be comprehensive for the entire span of U. S. history. Even with choices, you will have to respond with essays that cover the whole time frame of U.S. history.

The proctor of the exam should give you fair warning of the approaching end of the essay section. Do not attempt to work beyond the time allotted or you will commit a serious security breach that may invalidate your examination. During both the multiple-choice section and the essay section of the exam, neither give nor receive communication with any other student in the testing area. Recent national cheating scandals have made officials particularly sensitive to potential security breaches. You do not wish to attract attention with questionable behavior. Disruptive behavior will probably result in your expulsion from the testing site.

Evaluation of Your Free-Response Essays

After being returned to the offices of the Educational Testing Service which handles the evaluation of the AP* exams for the College Board, your essays will be blind-coded and sent to the designated evaluation site in early June where several hundred college instructors and high school teachers gather to read the essays. Essays are not really graded, but are actually ranked in comparison against each other. The "readers" are highly experienced individuals drawn from a wide variety of teaching environments. These readers are given intensive training in ranking your essays against the thousands of others they will see. Many of the readers are themselves experienced Advanced Placement* U. S. history teachers. A significant portion of the readers are college and university history instructors. Multiple checks and balances are employed to make certain every essay produced by every student is given a fair and equitable evaluation. A different reader will evaluate each of your essays.

General Information on Essay Writing

It is important to realize that your essay is evaluated at the college level, but it is also considered a rough draft. Errors in spelling and punctuation will not detract from your performance rating unless they interfere with the reader's understanding of your essay. Be legible with your handwriting. Your essay will have to reach college level writing, so consider the following standards:

- Does the essay contain a thesis statement that clearly addresses and deals with the question? [thesis statement defined below]
- Do arguments within the essay support the thesis and lead toward a viable conclusion?
- In the case of document-based questions, are substantial numbers of the documents used appropriately and in a way that clearly supports the position of the thesis?
- Is outside information used appropriately and in sufficient quantity to support the position of the thesis?
- Does the essay analyze rather than describe as it attempts to prove the position of the thesis? [analysis defined below]
- Does the essay end with a clear restatement of the thesis in a way that affirms what the writer was attempting to prove?

Understanding Your Audience: There are many styles of writing. What you have learned in your English courses will probably not fit the essay questions presented in Advanced Placement* U. S. history. You need to understand that the audience and purpose are different. Neither your English nor your AP* U.S. history teacher is wrong. For AP* U.S. history the best comparison is to consider that you are like a lawyer presenting a case before a jury. You must muster a set of arguments that support your position (the thesis statement). You must draw your arguments from the evidence available, document-based facts and/or outside information. You must convince a jury that your position is correct; the jury is your reader at the national exam. You are engaged in an activity that is more like a debate than creative literature. Flowery statements and fanciful language do not fit well into the purpose and audience for which your arguments are intended.

Outline Your Answer: At the beginning of both the document-based question and the two short free-response essays it is a good practice to outline your answer by breaking the question down into its primary parts and jotting down ideas that you can discuss relating to each of the issues of the question. After that, list the outside facts that you can use to support those positions and finally, comb the documents for facts to use with your outside facts. This kind of prior organization will definitely lead to better evaluations for your essays. You are allotted 15 minutes for this purpose with the DBQ and five minutes each for the shorter free-response essays.

Thesis Statement: For many students this is one of the most important and least understood parts of a good essay. A thesis statement comes at the beginning of your essay in a short introductory paragraph where you basically tell the reader the position you will attempt to prove.

In order to create a good thesis statement, you must understand exactly what the question is asking you to do and then you craft your thesis to address each of the major issues presented by the question. In this situation a simple repetition of the question will not be considered a good thesis statement. You have to create a thesis that tackles the issues of the question and states what you plan to prove regarding those issues. A good introductory paragraph and thesis statement will also suggest briefly how you plan to prove your position.

When you have finished your introductory paragraph/thesis statement, you basically have a roadmap that points the direction your essay will travel, marks the turning points of your trip, and tells the reader the conclusion you plan to reach. Writing the essay at that point becomes much easier to do for you—just connect the points on the map.

Together the thesis statement and the introduction must address the central issues of the question in a clear way. Each paragraph that follows must contain only information used in support of that thesis. Nothing should appear in your essay that is not essential to support that thesis statement. A good essay will end with a strong, short conclusion that restates the thesis.

Definition of Analysis Level Writing

Analysis level writing is also a very difficult concept for many students to grasp. Earlier in your academic career, especially in grade and middle school, you were able to achieve high grades by simply writing down everything you knew about the general topic of the question. If the question concerned the causes of the Civil War, you wrote down everything you knew about the causes of the Civil War. The more you knew and wrote down, the higher your grade would be. This is no longer true. A little later in middle school and early high school an essay with a better description would earn the top score, but this is also no longer true. You have now reached a point where you will be expected to write at the level of analysis.

Analysis level writing is simply using substantial amounts of facts to prove positions that support the ideas advanced in your thesis statement. Your essays will be judged on the quality and accuracy of your arguments in support of the position you have taken. Now you must answer more than the "what and when" by moving on to prove the "how and why."

Example of Analysis Level Writing

Analysis is the use of a fact at a higher order than just citation or description. To cite a fact is to prove that you know it. Using a fact with analysis demonstrates that you understand that fact and know how to use it to prove something significant regarding the issues of the question or your thesis statement.

Here is a simple citation of a fact:

"The sinking of the RMS *Lusitania* in 1915 with the loss of American civilian lives was seen by President Wilson as a violation of American neutral rights. This would be a major event in a chain which drew the United States into World War I on the British side."

Here is that same fact used with analysis:

"By 1915 both Britain and Germany had violated American neutral rights, but President Wilson responded more dramatically to events such as the sinking of the RMS *Lusitania* because American lives were lost whereas British violations involved only property rights. The death of women and children had a much greater impact on American public opinion than the seizure of a few cargoes. The emotional impact of events like the sinking of the RMS *Lusitania* would gradually draw the United States into conflict with Germany and an alliance with Britain."

Notice that in the first example the writer simply cited the fact that the *Lusitania* had been sunk and this drew the U.S. into the First World War. This first writer has faithfully answered the "what and when."

The second writer has move beyond the "what and when" by explaining why the sinking of the *Lusitania* drew the U.S. into this war and provided the "how and why." Notice that the sample of analysis level writing also contains more facts at a greater depth. The difference between the two samples of writing is what defines analysis level writing.

Definition of a Document-Based Question (DBQ)

A document-based question is in effect a mini-research paper with the research materials provided. You are expected to exhibit an acceptable knowledge of U.S. history by presenting outside information in your answer and incorporating with that a substantial number of facts from the documents. In addition to the question, there will be between 12 to 16 short documents in the DBQ booklet. Two or three of those documents will probably be graphics in the form of political cartoons, charts and graphs, maps, photos, poster, or paintings. The better essays almost always use the graphic documents. The rest of the documents will be short and text-based. Your answer must directly address the main issues of the question and propose a thesis or position that you will prove within your essay.

Definition of a Free-Response Question—Short Essay

These are standard essay questions much like those you have previously received in social studies classes. You must exhibit an acceptable level of knowledge of U. S. history by presenting facts that support the position you have taken in your thesis statement. You will have to select one question from a group of two possibilities and then a second question from another group of two questions. Together with the DBQ, you can expect these essays to cover the whole span of U. S. history.

Answer the Entire Question

It is vital that you examine each question very carefully and are absolutely certain that you are answering every part of the question. The most common error at the national exam is to answer only part of the question while ignoring equally important segments which the student overlooked as they began writing their response. A partial answer will only receive a partial evaluation. An equally common error is for a student test-taker to answer the wrong question. This usually results when the student does not read the question carefully. An example would the student who, when asked to discuss gender and racial issues of the 1920s, writes down everything they know about diplomatic, political, legislative, and social history of the 1920s. That student will receive a low evaluation because they have not answered the question that was posed.

Length of Essays

Students constantly want to know how long their essays must be in order to obtain a good evaluation. There really is no definitive answer to the question. You must address all the issues of the question with your essay. To make you comfortable, consider that most good DBQs usually run between three to five handwritten pages in length while most short free-response essays run between two and four handwritten pages. That is not a rule written in stone, just a guideline.

A Rapid Checklist of Dos and Don'ts

Pre-Exam Preparation

■ Do begin individualized study for national exams several weeks before the exam date

■ Do get a good night's sleep before the exam. Have a good, light breakfast. Arrive early for the exam.

■ Do double check your supplies before you leave for the exam site. Make certain you have the necessary pens, pencils, and watch.

■ Do not bring back packs or large bags into the exam site. Leave cellular phones and other electronic equipment at home. Do not bring correction fluid, highlighters, or colored pens or pencils.

■ Do bring at least two or three sharpened #2 pencils and two-three dark blue or black pens.

■ Do bring a photo ID such as your driver's license. Bring your social security number and school code.

Writing Skills

■ Do make serious effort to right legibly—scratch outs, messy smudges, difficult to read handwriting can hurt your evaluation.

■ Do try to keep your essay in an organized appearance—arrows pointing to pieces of text in the margins or across the page are distracting and hard to follow.

■ Do not use abbreviations or symbols that are not clearly understood by others.

■ Do not use colored pens—Do use only dark blue or black ink.

■ Do not use pencil for writing essays—it is harder to read.

■ Do not use highlight pens on your essay.

■ Do not use flowery statements and fanciful language—keep your arguments as clear and as straightforward as possible.

■ Do outline your answer during the preparation period given at the beginning of the essay section.

■ Do not add materials to your essay that are not directly in support of your thesis position—unrelated facts or arguments will not help your essay.

Introduction and Thesis Statement

■ Do define key terms if they fit and help explain your essay.

■ Do break the question down into its key or core issues before formulating your thesis.

■ Do aim your thesis statement directly at the core issues of the question.

- Do not cite documents in the introduction/thesis statement paragraph—save citations for the body of your essay.
- Do place your thesis statement at the end of your introductory paragraph.

Document Usage

- Do not use a document you do not understand. Don't try to fake it.
- Do use as many documents as you can—50 to 75 percent is a good rule of thumb.
- Do use the graphic documents such as political cartoons, maps, graphs, and charts. Search the graphic documents for information you can use in your essay.
- Do not use the DBQ documents in the order they were printed or refer to them as "In Document A…".
- Do cite documents both by title as in "The Wilmot Proviso was an attempt…" and by the usual form of (Doc. A) at the end of the sentence in which they were used.
- Do not quote the documents; instead, synthesize the materials into your own words. The weakest essays tend to use many quotes.
- *Analysis Skills*
- Do use facts, document-based and outside, to prove arguments that support your thesis.
- Do not express a personal opinion—keep to the facts to prove your points.
- Do use substantial amounts of facts to support your thesis position, draw your facts from both outside sources and from the documents.
- Do aim every argument and every sentence toward supporting your thesis position.
- Do close with a good conclusion that restates your thesis position.

AP* United States History Topics Correlated to America Past and Present, Ninth AP* Edition

AP* Topics	*America Past and Present*, Ninth Edition
1. Pre-Columbian Societies	**Chapter 1**
▪ Early inhabitants of the Americas	pp. 4–6
▪ American Indian empires in Mesoamerica, the Southwest, and the Mississippi Valley	pp. 4
▪ American Indian cultures of North America at the time of European contact	pp. 8–10
2. Transatlantic Encounters and Colonial Beginnings, 1492–1690	**Chapters 1, 2, 3**
▪ First European contacts with Native Americans	pp. 8–10
▪ Spain's empire in North America	pp. 19–21
▪ French colonization of Canada	pp. 2–22
▪ English settlement of New England, the Mid-Atlantic region, and the South	pp. 25–26, 31–44, 45–46, 46–52
▪ From servitude to slavery in the Chesapeake region	pp. 62–63
Religious diversity in the American colonies	pp. 35–36, 37–38, 39–41, 46–48
Resistance to colonial authority: Bacon's Rebellion, Glorious Revolution, and the Pueblo Revolt	pp. 69–73
3. Colonial North America, 1690–1754	**Chapters 2, 3, 4**
▪ Population growth and immigration	pp. 81–84
▪ Transatlantic trade and the growth of seaports	pp. 92
▪ The eighteenth-century back country	pp. 80–82
▪ Growth of plantation economies and slave societies	pp. 61, 63, 66–67
The Enlightenment and the Great Awakening	pp. 90–92, 93–95
Colonial governments and imperial policy in British North America	pp. 96–98, 109–110, 113–115, 117, 120
4. The American Revolutionary Era, 1754–1789	**Chapters 4, 5, 6**
▪ The French and Indian War	pp. 102–103
▪ The Imperial Crisis and resistance to Britain	pp. 98–99
▪ The War for Independence	pp. 123, 125–131
State constitutions and the Articles of Confederation	pp. 141–145, 153, 157–158
The federal Constitution	pp. 141–142, 155
5. The Early Republic, 1789–1815	**Chapters 6, 7, 8, 9**
▪ Washington, Hamilton, and shaping of the national government	pp. 162–169, 174–176, 195–196
▪ Emergence of political parties: Federalists and Republicans	pp. 160, 162, 168–172, 174–181 202–203
▪ Republican Motherhood and education for women	pp. 139–140

    ■ Beginnings of the Second Great Awakening   pp.282–285
         Significance of Jefferson's presidency   pp. 188–193, 197–199
         Expansion into the trans-Appalachian West;
             American Indian resistance   pp. 137, 144–147, 185–186
             Growth of slavery and free Black communities   pp. 137–139, 187, 196–197
    ■ The War of 1812 and its consequences   pp. 201–204, 212–213

6. Transformation of the Economy and Society in Antebellum America Chapters 9, 11, 13, 14

    ■ The transportation revolution and creation of
       a national market economy   pp. 222–227, 232
    ■ Beginnings of industrialization and changes
       in social and class structures   pp. 226–227
    ■ Immigration and nativist reaction   pp. 325–327, 340
    ■ Planters, yeoman farmers, and slaves in the cotton South   pp. 258–263, 267–278

7. The Transformation of Politics in Antebellum America   **Chapter 10**

    ■ Emergence of the second party system   pp. 239–241, 249–255
    ■ Federal authority and its opponents: judicial federalism,
       the Bank War, tariff controversy, and states' rights debates   pp. 240–242, 249–251
    ■ Jacksonian democracy and its successes and limitations   pp. 241–243, 249

8. Religion, Reform, and Renaissance in Antebellum America   **Chapter 12**

    ■ Evangelical Protestant revivalism   pp. 281–285
    ■ Social reforms   pp. 288–291
    ■ Ideals of domesticity   pp. 285–288
    ■ Transcendentalism and utopian communities   pp. 295–297, 300
         American Renaissance: literary and artistic expressions   pp. 237–239

9. Territorial Expansion and Manifest Destiny   **Chapters 9, 10, 13**

    ■ Forced removal of American Indians to the trans-Mississippi West   pp. 422—425
    ■ Western migration and cultural interactions   pp. 307–309, 312–314, 323
    ■ Territorial acquisitions   pp. 308–313, 320
    ■ Early U.S. Imperialism: the Mexican War   pp. 314–320

10. The Crisis of the Union   **Chapters 14, 15**

    ■ Pro- and antislavery arguments and conflicts   pp. 332–336, 345, 348–349
    ■ Compromise of 1850 and popular sovereignty   pp. 333–336
    ■ The Kansas-Nebraska Act and the emergence
       of the Republican Party   pp. 337–339
    ■ Abraham Lincoln, the election of 1860, and secession   pp. 349–351, 358, 360–363

11. Civil War   **Chapters 15, 16**

    ■ Two societies at war: mobilization, resources, and internal dissent   pp. 363–367
    ■ Military strategies and foreign diplomacy   pp. 365, 370–374, 378–381
    ■ Emancipation and the role of African Americans in the war   pp. 374–378
    ■ Social, political, and economic effects of war
       in the North, South, and West   pp. 381–383

12. Reconstruction   **Chapter 16**

    ■ Presidential and Radical Reconstruction   pp. 384–389
    ■ Southern state governments: aspirations, achievements, failures   pp. 397–404
         Role of African Americans in politics, education,
             and the economy   pp. 386–389, 401
    ■ Compromise of 1877   pp. 409

Impact of Reconstruction		pp. 397–408

13. The Origins of the New South — **Chapters 16, 18**
- Reconfiguration of southern agriculture: sharecropping and crop lien system — pp. 398, 413
- Expansion of manufacturing and industrialization — pp. 412
- The politics of segregation: Jim Crow and disfranchisement — pp. 393, 413–415

14. Development of the West in the Late Nineteenth Century — **Chapters 17, 18**
- Expansion and development of western railroads — pp. 418, 425, 428–429, 444–446, 448–450
- Competitors for the West: miners, ranchers, homesteaders, and American Indians — pp. 419–422, 430–440
- Government policy toward American Indians — pp. 422–425
- Gender, race, and ethnicity in the far West — pp. 418, 440–441
  - Environmental impacts of western settlement — pp. 418–419, 440–441

15. Industrial America in the Late Nineteenth Century — **Chapters 18, 19, 20**
- Corporate consolidation of industry — pp. 447–454
- Effects of technological development on the worker and workplace — pp. 454–455, 458
  - Labor and unions — pp. 461–464
- National politics and influence of corporate power
- Migration and immigration: the changing face of the nation — pp. 470–471, 474–475
- Proponents and opponents of the new order, e.g., Social Darwinism and Social Gospel — pp. 485–488

16. Urban Society in the Late Nineteenth Century — **Chapters 19, 20**
- Urbanization and the lure of the city — pp. 466–468
- City problems and machine politics — pp. 475–476
- Intellectual and cultural movements and popular entertainment — pp. 476–480, 481–485

17. Populism and Progressivism — **Chapters 20, 22, 23**
- Agrarian discontent and political issues of the late nineteenth century — pp. 502–508
- Origins of Progressive reform: municipal, state, and national — pp. 485–490
- Roosevelt, Taft, and Wilson as Progressive presidents — pp. 476, 544, 571–572, 577–588
- Women's roles: family, workplace, education, politics, and reform — pp. 480–490, 548–549
- Black America: urban migration and civil rights initiatives — pp. 483–485, 492–495, 550–551

18. The Emergence of America as a World Power — **Chapters 21, 24, 25**
- American imperialism: political and economic expansion — pp. 522–527
- War in Europe and American neutrality — pp. 598–603, 604–607
- The First World War at home and abroad — pp. 607–609, 612–618
- Treaty of Versailles — pp. 618–621
- Society and economy in the postwar years — pp. 621

19. The New Era: 1920s — **Chapter 25**
- The business of America and the consumer economy — pp. 623–626
- Republican politics: Harding, Coolidge, Hoover — pp. 639–642
- The culture of Modernism: science, the arts, and entertainment — pp. 626–627, 628–631
- Responses to Modernism: religious fundamentalism, nativism, and Prohibition — pp. 634–639
- The ongoing struggle for equality: African Americans and women — pp. 627–628, 632–634

20. The Great Depression and the New Deal　　　　　　**Chapter 26**

- Causes of the Great Depression　　　　　　　　　pp. 647–651
- The Hoover administration's response　　　　　　pp. 653–654
- Franklin Delano Roosevelt and the New Deal　　pp. 654–666, 672
  Labor and union recognition　　　　　　　　　　pp. 663
- The New Deal coalition and its critics from the Right and the Left　　pp. 660–662
- Surviving hard times: American society during
  the Great Depression　　　　　　　　　　　　　pp. 651–653, 672

21. The Second World War　　　　　　　　　　　　**Chapters 27, 28**

- The rise of fascism and militarism in Japan, Italy, and Germay　　pp. 678, 680
- Prelude to war: policy of neurality　　　　　　　pp. 678–680
  The attack on Pearl Harbor and United States
  declaration of war　　　　　　　　　　　　　　pp. 684–685
- Fighting a multifront war　　　　　　　　　　　pp. 687–688
- Diplomacy, war aims, and wartime conferences　pp. 694–695
- The United States as a global power in the Atomic Age　pp. 704

22. The Home Front During the War　　　　　　　**Chapter 27**

- Wartime mobilation of the economy　　　　　　pp. 688–689
- Urban migration and demographic changes　　　pp. 689–692
- Women, work, and family during the war　　　　pp. 690–692
  Civil liberties and civil rights during wartime　pp. 690–692
  War and regional development
  Expansion of government power　　　　　　　　pp. 699

23. The United States and the Early Cold War　　**Chapters 28, 29**

- Origins of the Cold War　　　　　　　　　　　pp. 702–704
- Truman and containment　　　　　　　　　　　pp. 704–705
- The Cold War in Asia: China, Korea, Vietnam, Japan　pp. 709–712
  Diplomatic strategies and policies of the Eisenhower
  and Kennedy administrations　　　　　　　　pp. 718–721, 724–725, 747, 751
- The Red Scare and McCarthyism　　　　　　　pp. 714–718
- Impact of the Cold War on American society　　pp. 712–715

24. The 1950s　　　　　　　　　　　　　　　　**Chapters 28, 29**

- Emergence of the modern civil rights movement　pp. 738–742
- The affluent society and "the other America"　　pp. 727–730
- Consensus and conformity: surburbia and middle-class America　pp. 727–730
- Social critics, nonconformists, and cultural rebels　pp. 734–735
- Impact of changes in science, technology, and medicine

25. The Turbulent 1960s　　　　　　　　　　　　**Chapters 30, 31**

- From the New Frontier to the Great Society　　pp. 751–753, 756–759
- Expanding movements for civil rights　　　　　pp. 753–755
- Cold War confrontations: Asia, Latin America, and Europe　pp. 748–749
- Beginning of Détente　　　　　　　　　　　　pp. 777–778
- The antiwar movement and the counterculture　pp. 765–767

26. Politics and Economics at the End of the Twentieth Century　**Chapters 30, 31, 32**

- Election of 1968 and the "Silent Majority"　　pp. 772–776, 778–779
- Nixon's challenges: Vietnam, China, Watergate　pp. 777–780
- Changes in the American economy: the energy crisis,

deindustrialization, and the service economy   pp. 781–784
- The New Right and the Reagan revolution   pp. 792–795
- End of the Cold War   pp. 810

27. **Society and Culture at the End of the Twentieth Century**   **Chapters 30, 31, 32**
- Demographic changes: surge of immigration after 1965, Sunbelt migration, and the graying of America   pp. 812–817
- Revolutions in biotechnology, mass communication, and computers   pp. 783
- Politics in a multicultural society   pp. 812–817

28. **The United States in the Post-Cold War World**   **Chapter 32**
- Globalization and the American economy   pp. 832–833
- Unilateralism vs. multilateralism in foreign policy   pp. 828–830
- Domestic and foreign terrorism   pp. 825, 828
- Environmental issues in a global context   pp. 783–784, 830

Part II

Topical Review with Sample Questions and Answers and Explanations

Use these practice questions to arm yourself thoroughly for all kinds of test items you will encounter on the AP* exam. Answers and explanations are provided for each question for your further review. Additional review items address additional important topics, for further study or in-class discussion. Answers to these items are not provided in this guide.

CHAPTER 1

New World Encounters

During the sixteenth century the Spanish, French, and English explored the Americas, displaced Native American cultures, and established colonies in the Western Hemisphere. These changes forced both cultures to adapt and change, though Native American cultures often suffered the most in these early exchanges.

Native American Histories Before Conquest

Humans occupied part of the Western Hemisphere thousands of years before the European discovery of America. Environmental conditions spurred ancient settlement as glaciers moved south and uncovered a **land bridge** connecting Asia and North America, across which came the Paleo-Indians.

- **The environmental challenge: food, climate, culture,** and especially **global warming** ended the Ice Age, allowing Native American cultures to expand their populations and where they lived. As food sources changed due to the **Agricultural Revolution**, so did their cultures, and soon they developed semi-agricultural societies of considerable sophistication.

- **Many of these sophisticated cultures**, especially in the Southwest and the Ohio and Mississippi River Valleys in North America, had disappeared just before the arrival of the Europeans. **Cahokia**, a Native American city near present-day St. Louis, rivaled European cities in size and sophistication.

- **The Aztecs** developed a complex and successful empire in central Mexico. **Tenochtitlan**, the center of Aztec culture, contained as many as 250,000 inhabitants.

- **Eastern Woodland cultures** formed along the Northeast Atlantic coast and into the Eastern Great Lakes. Native Americans formed diverse and mobile communities of hunters, gatherers, and farmers.

A World Transformed

Native Americans were profoundly changed by contact with the Europeans. They often sought mutually beneficial trading arrangements with the foreigners, who typically misunderstood native ways. While some adopted European religion, others tenaciously held onto their own world view.

- **Creative adaptations** included resolving communication problems as well as cultural conflicts. Native peoples resisted most European attempts to "civilize" them but readily assimilated parts of the material culture into their own. Iron tools were more accepted than Christianity by many Native Americans, frustrating the European settlers, and making it seem that Indians were their main obstacles to settlement.

- **European trade goods** quickly became part of Native American material culture, and their efforts to gather furs for trade altered the ecological balance in much of the New World. This growing dependence caused increasing conflicts between Indians and Europeans, as well as between different tribal groups. Many Native Americans who were not killed in battle died as a result of diseases brought to the Americas by the Europeans (the **Columbian Exchange**).

West Africa: Ancient and Complex Societies

A variety of intricate and sophisticated cultures dominated sub-Saharan West Africa at the time of the European colonization of the New World. Complicated trade routes stretched across the African continent, tying together diverse cultures. The **Portuguese** explored the coast of West Africa and began trading in slaves, beginning the massive forced migration of black Africans to the Americas. By 1650, most West African slaves were destined for the New World.

- **Europe on the eve of conquest** at the end of the latter Middle Ages saw strong monarchs centralizing power in the form of modern nation-states. The **Renaissance** and the invention of the printing press aided in the expansion of new ideas and new technologies in Europe.

Imagining a New World

With explorers like Christopher Columbus leading the way, **Spain** established the largest colonial empire in the New World.

- **The Conquistadores** were independent adventurers that led the Spanish movement in carving out a colonial empire.
- **After initial forays for riches**, Spanish government officials brought some order, class and caste distinctions, and Catholicism to the empire of New Spain. More than 400,000 Spaniards migrated to the New World by 1650.

The French Claim Canada

Later, the **French**, without much support from the Crown, settled parts of North America, primarily exploiting the valuable fur trade. The French often worked and lived more cooperatively with the Native Americans to trade with them as well as convert them to Christianity.

The English Enter the Competition

England began to venture out into the North Atlantic in the latter fifteenth century, in search of better fishing areas and, possibly, a short route to Asia, the mythical **Northwest Passage.**

- **The birth of English Protestantism** during the Protestant Reformation and the desire of **Henry VIII** for a male heir prompted a break with the Catholic Church and the establishment of the Church of England. The resulting turmoil delayed England's entry into the New World.
- **Elizabeth I** settled the religious debates and established in England a stronghold of Protestantism.
- **As English nationalism** increasingly became associated with Protestantism, the English longed for victories over Catholic Spain.

Irish Rehearsal for American Settlement

In the latter sixteenth century, the English established an ongoing pattern for colonization in Ireland.

▪ **English conquest of Ireland** was used as a testing ground for their theories of colonial rule. Irish cultural differences justified their theories.

An Unpromising Beginning: Mystery at Roanoke

An English pioneer of colonization, **Sir Humphrey Gilbert**, tried unsuccessfully to plant an outpost of the English nation in North America. Later, **Sir Walter Raleigh** similarly tried and failed to establish a settlement on **Roanoke Island, Virginia** which subsequently disappeared without a trace.

Multiple-Choice Questions

1. The first migrants to the New World came from
   (A) Western Europe.
   (B) Asia.
   (C) Africa.
   (D) Australia.
   (E) Southeast Asia.

2. The peopling of America was made possible some 30,000 years ago because of
   (A) a long period of global warming.
   (B) the domestication of horses.
   (C) new canoe technology.
   (D) bitter intertribal wars in Asia.
   (E) the onset of the Ice Age.

3. By the time of the arrival of Europeans, approximately how many separate languages were spoken by Native Americans?
   (A) 50
   (B) 350
   (C) 450
   (D) 500
   (E) All spoke variations of a single language.

4. The people of the Great Plains did not obtain horses until 1547 because
   (A) horses were not indigenous to the Americas.
   (B) horse populations had died out due to disease.
   (C) the early natives hunted and killed off the population.

(D) both B & C
(E) all of the above

5.

The item in this picture is an example of
(A) complex values of Southwest Cultures.
(B) complex values of Northwest Coastal Cultures.
(C) complex values of Southeast Cultures.
(D) complex values of South American Cultures.
(E) complex values of Eastern Woodland Cultures.

6. Which of the following North American plant had a drastically positive impact on both European and African diets?
(A) maize
(B) beans

(C) squash

(D) tomato

(E) pepper

7. Columbus originally was determined to prove that
   (A) a westward water route to China existed.
   (B) the world was not flat.
   (C) the continents of North and South America existed.
   (D) the lost continent of Atlantis was actually part of South America.
   (E) the world was smaller than scientists believed at the time.

8. Geographically, the French claimed and settled
   (A) the Southwest.
   (B) the Atlantic seaboard.
   (C) the Mississippi Valley and Canada.

(D) Brazil.

(E) the Southeast.

9. What sixteenth-century European upheaval had a profound impact upon England's settlement of the New World?
   (A) the Crusades
   (B) the War of the Roses
   (C) the Hundred Years' War
   (D) the experience of the Marian exiles
   (E) the Reformation

10. Who developed strong arguments for England's continued efforts at colonizing the New World, despite early failures?
    (A) Humphrey Gilbert
    (B) Walter Raleigh
    (C) Francis Drake
    (D) Richard Hakluyt
    (E) Arthur Barlow

Free-Response Question

> *Describe the effect of European exploration and colonization on African and Native American cultures. How did each group react to these confrontations of societies?*

ANSWERS AND EXPLANATIONS

Multiple-Choice Questions

▌ **1. (B) is correct.** The first migrants crossed a land bridge between Asia and North America.

▌ **2. (E) is correct.** The Ice Age caused receding waters, exposing a land bridge between Asia and North America. Early migrants were most likely pursuing large mammals for hunting.

▌ **3. (B) is correct.** Although concrete evidence is sketchy at best it is estimated that there were around 350 separate native languages in the Americas. These languages were mainly caused because of geography.

▌ **4. (D) is correct.** Archeologists have found evidence that the horse was an indigenous animal to the Americas, but the horse did become extinct because of combination of factors including the changing climate, disease, and overhunting by natives. The European explorers reintroduced the horse onto the American continents around 1547.

▌ **5. (C) is correct.** This is an Effigy Jar of the Mississippi Nation. They are primarily a Southeastern Tribe. This jar displays the advanced culture because of the details involved in the jar.

■ **6. (A) is correct.** Maize was taken back to the "Old World" by Columbus. This was one of the most significant changes in European and African diets after this point. Significant improvement in health and nutrition is evidenced on both continents.

■ **7. (A) is correct.** Columbus was almost obsessed with the idea that one could travel west to reach the east. Based on early explorer's journals and tales, Columbus was convinced a shorter route existed. He was rejected multiple times before the Spanish queen agreed to finance the voyage.

■ **8. (C) is correct.** The French were slow to enter the Age of Exploration. Three decades after Columbus, the French King Francis I still was convinced there was a short water route to China by sailing to the north of North America. Jacques Cartier stumbled onto Canada on one such exploration.

■ **9. (E) is correct.** The Protestant Reformation reached England in the form of King Henry VIII and his quest for an heir. The result was a schism with the Catholic Church, the creation of the Church of England and much turmoil throughout the kingdom.

■ **10. (D) is correct.** Richard Hakluyt, the Younger, publicized explorers' accounts of the New World. Although Hakluyt never visited America, his vision of the New World shaped English public opinion.

Free-Response Essay Sample Response

Describe the effect of European exploration and colonization on African and Native American cultures. How did each group react to these confrontations of societies?

Although the reasons varied by nation, all European nations' desires for exploration revolved around three central themes. Those themes were the quest for gold and spices, the desire to spread Christianity, and a desire to utilize new technologies. This then had a huge impact on all three continents. Each continent had negative and positive consequences.

Positive consequences included trading of crops between continents thus stabilizing the diets and nutrition of each continent. Another positive consequence was the exchange of and growth of cultures through diffusion. Negative consequences were African slavery, annihilation of Native American populations and cultures and the damage of two continents' ecosystems.

CHAPTER 2

New World Experiments: England's Seventeenth-Century Colonies

In the seventeenth century, different and sometimes disparate groups of English settlers established several colonies in North America.

Breaking Away

Some Englishmen migrated to the New World for economic reasons, leaving poverty and seeking land. Others came seeking religious opportunity or to avoid strife and conflict in England.

- **King James I and his son Charles I** fought constantly with the elected members of **Parliament**. Charles attempted to rule the country without Parliament's oversight, causing a call for constitutional reform and the **English Civil War** (1640–1649), followed by the **Restoration** period and the **Glorious Revolution** of 1688.

The Chesapeake: Dreams of Wealth

In the early to mid-seventeenth century, the English established two successful but diverse colonies around the Chesapeake Bay—**Virginia and Maryland.**

- **Entrepreneurs in Virginia,** namely the London Company, built **Jamestown** in Virginia. This **joint-stock company** experienced trouble because of a hostile environment, because colonists did not work for the common good, and because of unclear goals.
- **To save the colony,** Captain John Smith took over the management of the town and imposed military order. The London Company also restructured the government and sent more people to populate the colony.
- In Virginia, **John Rolfe** developed a milder variety of tobacco than the Indians had been cultivating, creating an export to European smokers. **Tobacco as a commercial crop** was the key to the eventual success of Virginia. London Company directors further attracted settlers by giving land grants (**headrights**), establishing local government (**House of Burgesses**), and bringing women to the colony. In 1624, King James I declared Virginia a royal colony.
- **Maryland.** In the 1630s, Sir George Calvert and his son Cecilius, the Lords Baltimore, acquired a royal grant to settle a colony north of Virginia, which was named Maryland in honor of the queen. The second **Lord Baltimore** insisted on religious toleration, but this proprietary colony still faced much sectarian trouble during the early days.

Reinventing England in America

Calvinist religious principles played an important role in the colonization of New England. A small group of Separatists, or **Pilgrims**, first went to Holland and then settled the "Plymouth Plantation." There these new settlers tried to replicate the villages and communities of England.

▌ **In the 1630s, Wealthy Puritans**, wanting to escape the tyranny of King Charles I, established the **Massachusetts Bay Colony**. Under the leadership of **John Winthrop**, they attempted to create a better society in the New World by purifying themselves and the Church from within.

▌ **The Massachusetts Bay** embraced rigorous economic and political institutions. Bound by a common purpose and religious goals, the colony flourished. Many villages in the colony used **democratic town meetings** to solve local political problems, and unlike in Virginia, the town became the center of public life.

▌ **Religious Dissent** came to Massachusetts Bay when some of the leaders of the colony disagreed with the laws and theology of the legal authorities, and were expelled—there was no promise of religious freedom. Two of these, **Roger Williams and Anne Hutchinson**, were forced to leave the colony. Four colonies—**New Hampshire, New Haven, Connecticut, and Rhode Island**—were established as a result of people leaving Massachusetts Bay. They left for religious reasons as well as economic reasons.

Diversity in the Middle Colonies

The key to the Middle Colonies—New York, New Jersey, Pennsylvania, and Delaware—was diversity, both within and among the several colonies.

▌ **The Dutch colony of New Netherland** had been settled not only by the Dutch but also by Finns, Swedes, Germans, and Africans. England easily wrested the colony from the Dutch and established **New York**. This diversity and the huge area meant bureaucratic problems for the Crown.

▌ **New Jersey** was originally a proprietary colony owned by Lord Berkeley and Sir George Carteret, and was split into two colonies when a group of Quakers bought land there. New Jersey never prospered in the way that New York did, and struggled with much internal political discord as well as conflicts with the Crown and other colonies.

Quakers in America

Because they were persecuted in England, the Quakers came to the New World and settled **Pennsylvania**.

▌ **Quakers** turned away from **Calvinism** and its beliefs of original sin and eternal Predestination. In Quaker theology, everyone possessed an "Inner Light" that offered salvation.

▌ **William Penn**, a Quaker convert, tried to establish a complex society based on Quaker principles. Its complexity caused lasting problems. Penn and other Quakers promoted the colony aggressively throughout the colonies and Europe. The colony welcomed people of all faiths and nationalities, making Pennsylvania a remarkably diverse colony.

Planting the Carolinas

The area south of the Chesapeake known as the **Carolinas** evolved differently compared with Virginia or Maryland.

- **The English** settled the land south of Virginia as a result of the **Restoration** of King Charles II. He offered the area as a reward to a few of his followers.
- **Anthony Ashley Cooper, later the Earl of Shaftesbury** was largely responsible for success in the Carolinas due to the migration of wealthy families from Barbados. In 1729, the land was divided into **North and South Carolina** and made a royal colony. It possessed a more diverse agricultural base, and while there was political conflict, the colonies soon prospered and grew.

The Founding of Georgia

The colony of Georgia resulted from a utopian vision of **General James Oglethorpe.** He settled the land south of Charleston in order to give hope to the debtors imprisoned in London, and at the same time, occupied land claimed by both England and Spain. Oglethorpe's utopian goals soon faded, and Georgia struggled in its early years.

Multiple-Choice Questions

1. Which one of the following was NOT a factor that stimulated English migration to the New World?
   (A) religious disagreements in England
   (B) poverty or fear of falling into poverty
   (C) a desire for land ownership
   (D) rapid population growth
   (E) government laws that forced the migration of the poorer classes

2. Unlike Virginia, Maryland was established
   (A) as a commercial center.
   (B) as a frontier outpost to secure the area from the French.
   (C) by French *Huguenots.*
   (D) as a religious sanctuary for persecuted Catholics from England.
   (E) by a commercial trading company.

3. The major difference in the founding of the colony of Georgia was
   (A) it was a royal colony in which the king paid the governor's salary.
   (B) religious differences between England and its colonists.
   (C) an act of aggression and defense from the Spanish.

   (D) the colony was not heavily populated by natives.
   (E) All of the above were differences between all of the rest of the colonies and Georgia.

4. The main staple of the Carolinas' economy by the close of the seventeenth century was
   (A) cotton.
   (B) rice.
   (C) tobacco.
   (D) timber.
   (E) indigo.

5. The famous English philosopher
   _____ wrote the *Fundamental Constitutions of Carolina.*
   (A) Francis Bacon
   (B) Thomas Hobbes
   (C) Adam Smith
   (D) John Locke
   (E) Sir John Colleton

6. The founder of the Georgia colony was
   (A) William Penn.
   (B) Anthony Ashley Cooper.
   (C) James Oglethorpe.

(D) Roger Williams.

(E) John Mason.

7. The Plymouth Colony was ultimately absorbed by which colony?
   (A) Maryland
   (B) Pennsylvania
   (C) Virginia
   (D) Massachusetts
   (E) Delaware

8. In Massachusetts Bay, "freeman status" was granted to adult males who
   (A) were church members.
   (B) were no longer indentured servants.
   (C) owned land.
   (D) agreed to abide by the colony's legal codes.
   (E) were married.

9. Anne Hutchinson's skillful self-defense at her trial before the Bay's magistrates was ruined by
   (A) her affinity for the dictum of works.
   (B) her claim of personal revelation.
   (C) her reliance on the Scriptures.
   (D) her rejection of free grace.
   (E) the fact that she was female.

10. Penn published brochures to market aggressively his new colony. All of the following were countries in which the brochures were published except
    (A) Italy.
    (B) England.
    (C) Denmark.
    (D) Ireland.
    (E) Germany.

Free-Response Question

Compare and contrast the English colonies of the Chesapeake with their counterparts at Massachusetts Bay. What were their similarities and their differences?

ANSWERS AND EXPLANATIONS

Multiple-Choice Questions

▌ **1. (E) is correct.** Choices A through D were reasons that stimulated immigration to the New World. There were few incentives for the poor to move except as punishment in lieu of debtor's prison or as an indentured servant.

▌ **2. (D) is correct.** The Catholics who wanted to flee the Church of England migrated to the colony of Maryland. This was possible only after Sir George Calvert (Lord Baltimore) secured sponsorship for a settlement free of religious persecution or preference.

▌ **3. (C) is correct.** Georgia became a royal colony after its founding. Choice A is not correct because the question asks about the time the colony was founded. When Georgia was founded, it was feared that the Spanish would attack South Carolina. Carolinians took hold of Spanish lands to build that buffer.

▌ **4. (B) is correct.** The geography of South Carolina was conducive for rice production. However, it did not develop into a staple until after 1690.

▌ **5. (D) is correct.** John Locke was an Enlightened Despot. He was directly responsible for many of the political theories used in the creation of American government. He outlined many of his theories in his Second Treatise.

■ **6. (C) is correct.** James Oglethorpe received a royal decree to settle the newly conquered land below South Carolina. He established the first city near modern-day Savannah.

■ **7. (D) is correct.** The Plymouth Colony was absorbed into the Massachusetts colony as a result of King Philip's War. In 1685, King James II sent officials to New England to restructure the colonial governments. The colonial charters were revoked and Plymouth Colony became part of the United Colonies of New England, along with Massachusetts Bay, Connecticut, Rhode Island, New York, and New Jersey.

■ **8. (A) is correct.** Church membership was the key to "freeman status." This decision greatly expanded the franchise of the colony.

■ **9. (B) is correct.** This revelation was tantamount to heresy as obedience to God was the cornerstone to the Massachusetts Bay region. Her views could have been viewed as civil and religious anarchy.

■ **10. (A) is correct.** Penn promoted his colony to England, Ireland and Germany. He was hoping for quick sale on his investment. The response was overwhelming, leading to Pennsylvania becoming an eclectic mass of people.

Free-Response Essay Sample Response

Compare and contrast the English colonies of the Chesapeake with their counterparts at Massachusetts Bay. What were their similarities and their differences?

Massachusetts Bay colonies were established as refuges. The first colonies were refuges from religious persecution in England. Then ultimately, the other colonies were established as refuges from the Bay colonies.

The Chesapeake Colonies may have originally been refuges from religious persecution. These colonies established themselves as heterogeneous colonies that led to cultural diversity. This diversity affected the political, cultural and economic development of the colonies.

CHAPTER 3

Putting Down Roots: Opportunity and Oppression in Colonial Society

The character of the early English settlements varied because of regional factors. A common language and heritage helped pull English American settlers together, however, and by the 1690s, Parliament began to establish a uniform set of rules for an expanding American empire.

Sources of Stability: New England Colonies of the Seventeenth Century

Colonists in New England replicated a social order they had known in England.

- **The early settlers of New England** were grouped into families, providing a more stable basis for society. The population of New England grew rapidly because of an unprecedented increase in human longevity. Open spaces, pure drinking water, and a cool climate helped retard the spread of disease and promoted good health.

- **Both town and church** in New England were built upon a family foundation. The family was also the basis for educating children. As towns grew, they were required to open schools supported by local taxes.

- **Women's lives in Puritan New England** lacked the same economic, political, and legal rights afforded men, even though their contributions and labor were essential for a successful household. They worked on family farms alongside their husbands and managed the home.

- **New England colonials** gradually sorted themselves into new social and economic groups, such as **provincial gentry, yeomen, and indentured servants**. Most Northern colonists were yeomen farmers who worked their own land. There was some upward social and economic mobility.

The Challenge of the Chesapeake Environment

Society developed entirely differently in England's Chesapeake colonies.

- **Family life** was not as favorable for survival or longevity in the Chesapeake colonies because of contagious diseases and contaminated drinking water. Most colonists arrived alone rather than as members of a family, and there was an imbalance between the number of men and women. Family life was much more unstable, and childbearing was extremely dangerous.

- **The cultivation of tobacco** shaped Chesapeake society and perpetuated social inequality. Great planters dominated Chesapeake society by controlling large estates and the labor of **indentured servants** or slaves. **Freemen** (usually former indentured servants) formed the largest class. Because the tobacco-based economy was centered on plantations, cities and towns were slow to develop, and especially after the 1680s, newcomers discovered that upward social mobility was more difficult to attain than in the Northern colonies.

Race and Freedom in British America

Many of the first settlers in the Americas were not voluntary settlers, but were forced to migrate to colonies as slaves.

- **Black Africans** were considered by whites to be heathen and barbarous, and between the sixteenth and nineteenth centuries almost eleven million were brought to the Americas as slaves. There were few objections to enslaving Africans for life because economic considerations demanded cheap labor. As the black population expanded, lawmakers drew up ever-stricter **slave codes**.
- **Africans** developed their own unique **African-American culture** in terms of music, art, religion, and language. By the eighteenth century, **Creole** slaves (those born in America) multiplied in greater number than the slaves imported from Africa.

Rise of a Commercial Empire

After the restoration of the monarchy in 1660, a British policy of indifference toward the colonies was replaced by one of intervention.

- **England** developed a framework of regulatory policies, termed **mercantilism**, to increase exports, decrease imports, and grow richer at the expense of other European states.
- **Parliament** passed a series of **Navigation Acts** (beginning in 1660), which detailed commercial restrictions, and set up the **Board of Trade** to oversee colonial affairs and to limit competition. Some of the reforms included shipping guidelines and a list of **enumerated goods** that could only flow from the colonies directly to England.

Colonial Factions Spark Political Revolt, 1675–1691

In the second half of the seventeenth century, several of the colonies experienced instability as the local gentry split into competing political factions.

- **Bacon's Rebellion (1676)** stemmed from economic depression and political repression in the Virginia colony. **Nathaniel Bacon** capitalized on this rural unrest in leading an unsuccessful rebellion against the government of Lord Berkeley, ostensibly to protect western settlers against Indian raids, but probably because of the governor's monopoly of the fur trade.
- **King Philip's War (1675)** led England to annul the charter of the Massachusetts Bay Company and merge the colony of Massachusetts into the larger Dominion of New England with the tyrannical **Sir Edmund Andros** as governor. When James II was deposed during the Glorious Revolution in England, Americans in

New England overthrew Governor Andros, and the colony of Massachusetts received a new royal charter.

▌ **Witchcraft**, and its accompanying fear and reliance of the courts on **spectral evidence** resulted in the hanging of nineteen alleged "witches" in Salem, Massachusetts, in 1692. Religious discord and economic tension seem to have been the underlying causes.

▌ **The Glorious Revolution** sparked feuds among the colonial gentry in both New York and Maryland. In New York, **Jacob Leisler** led an abortive attempt to seize control of the colony from powerful Anglo-Dutch families. In Maryland, **John Coode** led an anti-Catholic group which successfully petitioned the Crown to transform Maryland into a royal colony, though the Baltimore family remained important.

Multiple-Choice Questions

1. In _____, charges of witchcraft caused considerable turmoil in the late seventeenth century.
   (A) Salem
   (B) London
   (C) Dedham
   (D) Boston
   (E) New York

2. Puritans viewed which of the following as essential to their New England commonwealth?
   (A) strict adherence to personal hygiene measures
   (B) a flexible form of colonial administration
   (C) a healthy family life
   (D) the rapid creation of an urban society in New England
   (E) honest public officials

3. The most important difference between the New England and Chesapeake colonies was
   (A) found in their different forms of agricultural production.
   (B) the Chesapeake's much higher mortality rate.
   (C) based on the differences between their respective proprietors.
   (D) the Chesapeake's much greater emphasis on the family.
   (E) their different religions.

4. In 1647, the Massachusetts legislature ordered all townships with fifteen or more families to _____ and support with local taxes.
   (A) provide police services
   (B) establish fire departments
   (C) hire a doctor
   (D) elect a mayor
   (E) open an elementary school

5. When historians refer to the "feminization of colonial religion," they are referring to
   (A) the influence of Catholic Church influences.
   (B) the effects of literacy on the female colonists.
   (C) women joining the church at a ratio greater than two-to-one.
   (D) both A & C
   (E) none of the above are reasons

6. Daily lives of New England residents revolved around all of the following EXCEPT
   (A) village meetings
   (B) business activities
   (C) militia training
   (D) church-related activities
   (E) neither A nor C were activities that revolved around colonial life

7. Of the estimated 11 million African slaves carried to America, the great majority were sent to
   (A) Brazil and the Caribbean.
   (B) British North America.
   (C) Chile.
   (D) Argentina.
   (E) Central America.

8. What percent of the eighteenth-century population of the lowlands of South Carolina was of African origin?
   (A) 30
   (B) 40
   (C) 50
   (D) 60
   (E) 70

9. British authorities based their colonial commercial policies on the theory of
   (A) feudalism.
   (B) monopolism.
   (C) federalism.
   (D) mercantilism.
   (E) republicanism.

10. During the Salem witchcraft hysteria, Increase Mather and other leading Congregational ministers
   (A) called for execution of the accused witches.
   (B) urged restraint and caution.
   (C) completely ignored the controversy.
   (D) called for colony-wide searches for accused witches.
   (E) questioned the validity of the testimony of minors.

Document-Based Question

Discuss the differences between the northern, middle, and southern English colonies. How do you account for the development of those differences? In your answer, draw on related information outside of the documents, as well as that contained within them.

DOCUMENT 1   Source: John Smith, "The Starving Time," 1624

It might well be thought, a Countrie so faire (as Virginia is) and a people so tractable, would long ere this have beene quietly possessed to the satisfaction of the adventurers, & the eternizing of the memory of those that effected it. But because all the world doe see a defailement; this following Treatise shall give satisfaction to all indifferent Readers, how the businesse hath bin carried; where no doubt they will easily understand and answer to their question, how it came to passe there was no better speed and successe in those proceedings....

DOCUMENT 2   Source: John Winthrop, "A Model of Christian Charity," 1630

The Lord will be our God and delight in all our ways, so that we shall see much more of His wisdom, power, goodness, and truth than formerly we have been acquainted with. We shall find that the God of Israel is among us, when ten of us shall be able to resist a thousand of our enemies, when He shall make us a praise and glory, that men shall say of succeeding plantations, the Lord make it like that of New England. For we must consider that we shall be as a city upon a hill, the eyes of all people are upon us. So that if we shall deal falsely with our God in this work we have undertaken and so cause Him to withdraw His present help from us, we shall be made a story and byword throughout the world, we shall open the mouths of enemies to speak evil of the ways of God and all professors for God's sake, we shall shame the faces of many of God's worthy servants, and cause their prayers to be turned into curses upon us till we be consumed out of the good land whither we are going.

DOCUMENT 3   Source: John Hammond, "Leah and Rachel, or the Two Fruitfull Sisters, Virginia and Mary-land," 1656

Those servants that will be industrious may in their time of service gain a competent estate before their Freedomes, which is usually done by many, and they gaine esteeme and assistance that appear so industrious: There is no Master almost but will allow his Servant a parcell of clear ground to plant some Tobacco in for himself, which he may husband at those many idle times he hath allowed him and not prejudice, but rejoyce his Master to see it, which in time of Shipping he may lay out for commodities, and in Summer sell them again with advantage, and get a Sow-Pig, or two, which anybody almost will give him, and his Master suffer him to keep them with his own, which will be no charge to his Master, and with one years increase of them may purchase a Cow Calf or two, and by that time he is for himself; he may have Cattle, Hogs, and Tobacco of his own, and come to live gallantly; but this must be gained (as I said) by industry and affability, not by sloth nor churlish behaviour.

And whereas it is rumoured that Servants have no lodging other then on boards, or by the Fire side, it is contrary to reason to believe it: First, as we are Christians; next as people living under a law, which compels as well the Master as the Servant to perform his duty; nor can true labour be either expected or exacted without sufficient cloathing, diet, and lodging; all which both their Indentures (which must inviolably be observed) and the Justice of the Country requires.

DOCUMENT 4   Source: William Penn, "Model of Government," 1681

Thirdly, I know what is said by the several admirers of monarchy, aristocracy, and democracy, which are the rule of one, a few, and many, and are the three common ideas of government when men discourse on that subject. But I choose to solve the controversy with this small distinction, and it belongs to all three: any government is free to the people under it (whatever to be the frame) where the laws rule, and the people are a party to those laws; and more than this is tyranny, oligarchy, and confusion.

DOCUMENT 5   Source: George Alsop, from *A Character of the Province of Maryland*, 1660

…The three main Commodities this Country affords for Trafique, are Tobacco, Furrs, and Flesh. Furrs and Skins, as Beavers, Otters, Musk-Rats, Rackoons, Wild-Cats, and Elke or Buffeloe, with divers others, which were first made vendible by the *Indians* of the Country, and sold to the Inhabitant, and by them to the Merchant, and so transported into *England* and other places where it becomes most commodious.

Tobacco is the only solid Staple Commodity of this Province: The use of it was first found out by the *Indians* many Ages agoe, and transferr'd into Christendom by that great Discoverer of *America Columbus.*

DOCUMENT 6 Source: James Oglethorpe "Some Account of the Designs of the Trustees for Establishing the Colony of Georgia," 1733

In America there are fertile lands sufficient to subsist all the useless Poor in *England,* and distressed Protestants in Europe; yet Thousands starve for want of mere sustenance. The distance makes it difficult to act thither. The same want that renders men useless here, prevents their paying their passage; and if others pay it for 'em, they become servants, or rather slaves for years to those who have defrayed the expense. Therefore, money for passage is necessary, but is not the only want; for if people were set down in America, and the land before them, they must cut down trees, build houses, fortify towns, dig and sow the land before they can get in a harvest; and till then, they must be provided with food, and kept together, that they may be assistant to each other for their natural support and protection.

The Romans esteemed the sending forth of Colonies, among their noblest works; they observed that Rome, as she increased in power and empire, drew together such a conflux of people from all parts that she found herself overburdened with their number, and the government brought under an incapacity to provide for them, or keep them in order. Necessity, the mother of invention, suggested to them an expedient, which at once gave ease to the capital, and increased the wealth and number of industrious citizens, by lessening the useless and unruly multitude; and by planting them in colonies on the frontiers of their empire, gave a new Strength to the whole; and *This* they looked upon to be so considerable a service to the commonwealth, that they created peculiar officers for the establishment of such colonies, and the expence was defrayed out of the public treasury.

DOCUMENT 7 Source: Tobacco Company Advertisement, 1659

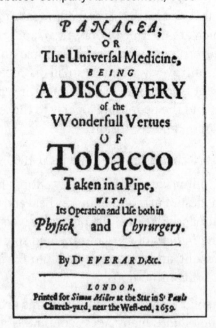

DOCUMENT 8   Source: English advertisement for Carolina, 1666

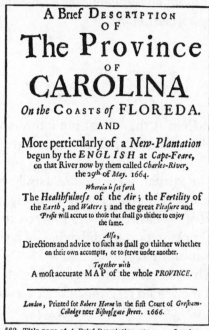

A Brief DESCRIPTION
OF
The Province
OF
CAROLINA
On the COASTS *of* FLOREDA.
AND
More perticularly of a *New-Plantation*
begun by the *ENGLISH* at *Cape-Feare*,
on that River now by them called *Charles-River*,
the 29th of *May*. 1664.

Wherein is set forth
The *Healthfulness* of the *Air* ; the *Fertility* of
the *Earth* , and *Waters* ; and the great *Pleasure* and
Profit will accrue to those that shall go thither to enjoy
the same.

Also,
Directions and advice to such as shall go thither whether
on their own accompts, or to serve under another.

Together with
A most accurate MAP of the whole *PROVINCE*.

London , Printed for *Robert Horne* in the first Court of *Gresham-
Colledge* next *Bishopsgate* street. 1666.

562 Title-page of *A Brief Description*, etc. . . . London,
1666, in the New York Public Library

DOCUMENT 9   Source: Ethnic distribution in the English colonies, circa 1763

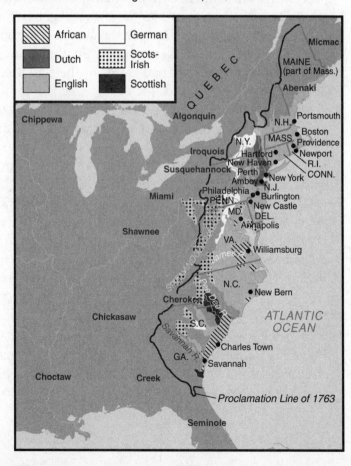

> Compare and contrast social and economic life in seventeenth-century New England with that of the Chesapeake colonies.

ANSWERS AND EXPLANATIONS

Multiple-Choice Questions

▌ **1. (A) is correct.** Salem is the site of the famous witchcraft paranoia. This paranoia was similar to the witchcraft crazes that had swept through Europe a century prior.

▌ **2. (C) is correct.** The Puritan society values family. In order to appreciate fully "God's Grace" a puritan must have a healthy family life.

▌ **3. (B) is correct.** All of the answers are plausibly correct. However, the key phrase in this question is "most important difference." The mortality rate retarded the growth of the Chesapeake Bay region.

▌ **4. (E) is correct.** The Massachusetts legislature felt that all citizens would be more productive if they could read the Bible. This was the main motivation for opening the first "public" schools in America.

▌ **5. (C) is correct.** Actually all of the choices are plausibly true; however, the best choice to answer the question that deals directly with feminization is choice C. Women were allowed to join as members of the church thus influencing the processes of the church. Offering plausible answers is a common tactic on AP exams; however, you must pick the answer that best fits the question.

▌ **6. (B) is correct.** Although there was business in the New England colonies, the majority of residents were yeomen. Choice E is incorrect because village life and militia training were two-thirds of the activities that residents centered life around.

▌ **7. (A) is correct.** These two regions were rich in sugar plantations. These plantations were labor intensive. The African slave was in high demand in these two regions.

▌ **8. (D) is correct.** It was estimated that two of every three inhabitants in the lowlands of South Carolina were of African ancestry.

▌ **9. (D) is correct.** Current British economic theory was based on the theory of mercantilism. Therefore, the colonies were simply an extension of the theory.

▌ **10. (B) is correct.** When one thinks of the witchcraft hysteria, the idea is that everyone was involved in the hunting and persecution of witches. However, there were many leaders, clergy and laity, who urged restraint and caution.

Document-Based Question Sample Response

> Discuss the differences between the northern, middle, and southern English colonies. How do you account for the development of those differences? In your answer, draw on related information outside of the documents, as well as that contained within them.

The northern, middle, and southern English colonies had many distinctive differences. The north had a more religious base, whereas the middle and southern colonies were more based on agriculture. The geographies of the regions differed, so by extension the economies would have to differ as well. There were differences in the workforce and social structure as well.

The Pilgrims and Puritans came for religious reasons. **(DOCUMENT 2)** Many in England felt that the Anglican Church had drifted too far from the proper path, and wanted a place where they could practice their religion as they saw fit. The New England economy tended to be trade, manufacturing, shipping, and small farming. As such, it was less suitable for slavery than the southern colonies. Most of the inhabitants of the region were of English background. **(DOCUMENT 9)**

The middle and southern colonies developed differently from the north. The Virginia colony was set up as a business and almost failed. **(DOCUMENT 1)** The main cash crop of the southern colonies was tobacco, although other agriculture was done as well. **(DOCUMENTS 7 AND 8)** The remaining colonies were settled for a variety of reasons. Georgia started as a penal reform for England and a place to put much of its excess prison population. **(DOCUMENT 6)** Pennsylvania was in many ways the most democratic of the colonies. **(DOCUMENT 4)** Other factors came into play as well. After Bacon's Rebellion, the southern labor force shifted away from indentured servitude **(DOCUMENT 3)** and towards African slavery. Maryland and the Chesapeake region specialized in tobacco, furs, and other commodities. **(DOCUMENT 5)** The colonies, north and south, were also a tremendous ethnic and linguistic mix, and that also accounts for much of the difference between them. **(DOCUMENT 9)**

Free-Response Essay Sample Response

Compare and contrast social and economic life in seventeenth-century New England with that of the Chesapeake colonies.

New England social and economic life centered around the concept of church first. Once the religious obligation goes away, the individual is safe. The resources in this region really affect this idea. These colonies also have difficulties because of the homogeneous nature. When someone objects the person becomes ostracized.

The heterogeneous nature of the Chesapeake colonies allow for worship as one sees fit. This then enhances a viable economy.

CHAPTER 4

Experience of Empire: Eighteenth-Century America

Eighteenth-century Americans, living in closer contact than their ancestors with the mother country, were in many ways torn between two cultures—one more sophisticated and traditional, the other more provincial and practical. Few societies in history have expanded in population as rapidly as colonial America of the eighteenth century.

Growth and Diversity

The English colonies experienced a remarkable annual population growth of 3 percent between 1700 and 1770. Voluntary newcomers to America increasingly moved to **the backcountry**, where living conditions were demanding and often violent.

▌ **The Scotch-Irish** arrived in great numbers throughout the eighteenth century. Many who came were more interested in improving their material lives than in finding religious freedom.

▌ **Germans** comprised the second largest group of non-English settlers, arriving from the upper Rhine Valley. They first came for religious toleration, but soon came for the potential gains in their material lives. They most often settled in the **Middle Colonies**, especially Pennsylvania.

▌ **Convicts** comprised a large group of immigrants to the New World. Between 1715 and 1775, some 50,000 convicts were shipped to America from Britain to be employed as **indentured servants**.

▌ **Native Americans** migrated to the western backcountry and joined existing confederacies of Indian tribes. Rather than isolating themselves from European colonials, the Indians interacted, traded, and compromised with Europeans as much as possible.

Spanish Borderlands of the Eighteenth Century

From the time the Spanish established settlements in North America until the early nineteenth century, they tenuously held onto their northern frontier.

▌ **International rivalries** and the lure of gold and silver attracted Spanish settlers to North America. Spanish enthusiasm waned significantly by the eighteenth century. California played little role in Spanish settlement until much later.

▌ **Spanish outposts** in North America grew very slowly. Spanish colonials exploited and enslaved Native Americans, and their settlements lacked the resources for sustained growth.

The Impact of European Ideas on American Culture

An urban cosmopolitan culture developed among the more established Atlantic colonies.

▌ **Urban populations** remained small in colonial America, but were growing quickly. Most **American cities** were intermediary trading ports where the latest in European ideas and styles were successfully integrated.

▌ **Americans** accepted and followed many of the ideals of the European **Enlightenment**, especially the search for useful knowledge and ideas.

▌ **Benjamin Franklin** was the true eighteenth-century American representative of the cosmopolitan, materialistic Atlantic culture. He became the symbol of material progress through human ingenuity.

▌ **Economic Transformation.** Despite the growth of the population, living standards kept pace, and actually improved. Growing trade with the **West Indies**, coupled with the ability to purchase cheap manufactured products on **credit** from England, enriched living standards. England remained the most important trading partner for the colonies.

▌ **American indebtedness** increased dramatically after 1690 as Americans imported far more commodities than before. This influx of British manufactured goods helped to "Anglicize" American culture.

Religious Revivals in Provincial Societies

The Great Awakening had a profound impact in colonial America and caused colonists to rethink their basic assumptions about church and state institutions.

▌ **The Great Awakening** brought with it a profound infusion of evangelical exhortations and revival spirit.

▌ **Preachers** like **George Whitefield and Jonathan Edwards** vividly depicted the horrors of hell to captivated audiences in an effort to restore religious vitality. The movement swept the colonies through the work of **itinerant preachers**, brought Americans closer together, gave them an awareness of a larger religious community, and enhanced their optimism.

Clash of Political Cultures

Political theorists often revered the British form of government and its "unwritten" constitution.

▌ **The English Constitution's makeup** divided political power among the monarch and his council of advisors, the two-chamber Parliament, and various local governments. Each group provided a check on the ambitions of the others.

▌ **The Reality of British Politics** was a system vulnerable to corruption and idleness. Some protesters, such as the **Commonwealthmen**, observed that many of England's rulers were corrupt and that the institutions of the "mixed" constitution were no longer in balance.

▌ **Government in America** was decidedly different, although colonial leaders attempted in many ways to recreate British-style institutions. **Legislative assemblies**, which helped to offset the ineptitude of royal governors appointed by the Board of Trade in England to oversee colonial affairs, rose to prominence in the colonies.

- **Colonial Assemblies** were often aggressive in asserting power, as they fought to protect the rights of the American colonists.

Century of Imperial War

A number of wars, the results of the imperial ambitions of Britain and France, developed for mastery of North America.

- **King William's and Queen Anne's Wars** resulted in little change in territorial control, as both sides realized the enormous stakes in their rivalry for control in North America.
- **King George's War** revealed the capability of American colonial forces in waging war against the French, as well as the colonial desire to gain complete control of the West. The struggle spread to the Ohio Valley by the 1750s.
- **Benjamin Franklin** proposed a most ambitious **Albany Plan** for common colonial defense and western expansion. The British general, **Edward Braddock**, led an unorganized and failed attempt to seize control of the Ohio Valley by attempting to take Fort Duquesne from the French.
- **The Seven Years' War**—the showdown for North American supremacy—began between 1756 and 1760. The British were overwhelmingly triumphant over the French, largely owing to the efforts of **William Pitt** in London and their strength of numbers in America. The war left Britain with an empire that expanded around the globe.

Multiple-Choice Questions

1. The population of the late colonial era was characterized as fairly young. It is estimated that one half of the population was under the age of _____.
   (A) 17
   (B) 12
   (C) 20
   (D) 15
   (E) 16

2. The largest group of white, non-English immigrants to the colonies were
   (A) the Dutch.
   (B) the Germans.
   (C) the Swedish.
   (D) the Scotch-Irish.
   (E) the French.

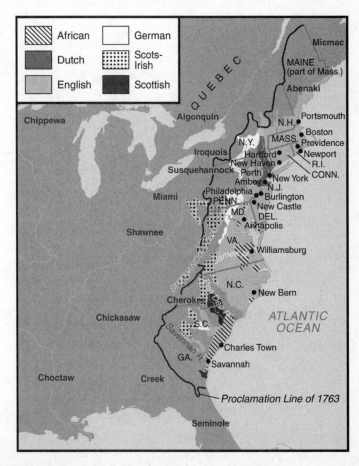

3. What was responsible for most of the growth in the American colonies between 1700 and 1770?
   (A) natural reproduction of colonial families
   (B) a great wave of immigration during that period
   (C) a program of forced migration instituted by the monarchy
   (D) a dramatic upsurge in the importation of slaves
   (E) increasing intermarriage between settlers and Native Americans

4. The first large group of German immigrants moved to America seeking
   (A) free land.
   (B) religious tolerance.
   (C) an opportunity to become wealthy farmers.
   (D) markets for their craft products.
   (E) work.

5. _____ was the most important embodiment of the Enlightenment in America.
   (A) Jonathan Edwards
   (B) Benjamin Franklin
   (C) John Locke
   (D) Isaac Newton
   (E) Thomas Jefferson

6. Which of the following was NOT a consequence of the Seven Years' War?
   (A) It made colonists more aware of their land.
   (B) It led to the creation of a new colony.
   (C) It trained a corps of American officers.
   (D) It revealed British discontent with America's contribution to its own defense.
   (E) It forced the colonists to cooperate on an unprecedented scale.

7. Which of the following wars between England and France had the greatest political and economic impact on colonial America?
   (A) King William's War
   (B) Queen Anne's War
   (C) King George's War
   (D) the Seven Years' War (also called the "French and Indian War")
   (E) the War of the League of Augsburg

8. Colonial legislators saw their primary function as
   (A) improving the lives of their constituents.
   (B) preventing encroachments on the people's rights.
   (C) implementing the governor's policies.
   (D) mediating between the royal governor and the people.
   (E) ingratiating themselves to the governor in hopes of attaining patronage appointments.

9. What did the Great Awakening, intercolonial trade, and the rise of the colonial assemblies have in common?
   (A) They created disdain for England.
   (B) They created a rebellious spirit in America.
   (C) They exacerbated the problems of an already divided citizenry.
   (D) They helped create imperial rivalry between England and France.
   (E) They all contributed to a growing sense of shared identity among the colonists.

10. _____ was responsible for authoring the Albany Plan.
    (A) Benjamin Franklin
    (B) Jonathan Edwards
    (C) John Locke
    (D) Isaac Newton
    (E) Thomas Jefferson

Free-Response Question

> Discuss the ways that the Anglo-American economic relationship changed during the Eighteenth Century. Further, discuss what impact those changes had upon the colonial economy.

ANSWERS AND EXPLANATIONS

Multiple-Choice Questions

1. **(E) is correct.** The population in the late colonial period was finally starting to have children. Although a good number of Europeans were migrating, the colonist children were able to account for one-half of the population being under the age of 16.

2. **(D) is correct.** The map shows clearly that the Scotch-Irish had the largest percentage of immigrants. The Scotch-Irish immigrated because of potato famines and persecution by the Church of England. Most Scotch-Irish started in Philadelphia, eventually pushing west into Pennsylvania.

3. **(A) is correct.** The colonial growth was due to natural reproduction. There was a need, especially in frontier areas, for large families to help work the land. This factor helped accelerate the growth.

4. **(B) is correct.** About 100,000 people from the upper Rhine Valley moved to America. They were in search of freedom from religious persecution. They were a small pietistic protestant sect, similar to the Quakers, known as Mennonites.

5. **(B) is correct.** Franklin is the embodiment of a philosophe. He was scientifically curious with a practical knowledge of the world. He appealed to all classes of citizens throughout the colonies.

6. **(D) is correct.** Although it is true Americans participated in the fighting during the Seven Years' War, Britain did not expect them to protect themselves. In the British Colonial system, the British military protected the colony. This was an unnecessary tax on the British Exchequer. The remaining answers are true and offered valuable experience for the American Revolution.

7. **(C) is correct.** The previous wars were primarily fought in Europe. This trend would have continued had it not been for King George II's minister, William Pitt. Pitt believed the best way to attack France was to expel it from North America. Thus, the French and Indian War was fought on North American soil. This war had an unprecedented impact on American soil because colonists were forced to cooperate. It also drew them closer to Britain.

8. **(C) is correct.** The majority of colonial legislatures felt it was their job to implement policies of the colonial governor. This may be due to the fact the governor had some hand in selecting legislatures.

9. **(E) is correct.** These factors combined with the French and Indian War were responsible for a growing sense of commonality.

10. **(A) is correct.** Franklin saw a need for intercolonial cooperation. The Albany plan was a bold proposal for a Grand Council to oversee matters of defense, expansion and Indian affairs. This plan included a taxation proposal.

> *Discuss the ways that the Anglo-American economic relationship changed during the Eighteenth Century. Further, discuss what impact those changes had upon the colonial economy.*

During the Eighteenth Century, the economic relationship between England and America changed while staying the same. As far as changing, the American colonial needs and tastes changed. What had once been dependent was now rising to be semi-sufficient. The British were trying to legislate status quo.

The two tried to maintain some aspects of their relationship. The Americans continued to enjoy free royal protection. The British tried to maintain the trade imbalance they had enjoyed throughout the relationship.

CHAPTER 5

The American Revolution: From Elite Protest to Popular Revolt, 1763–1783

Between 1763 and 1783, Americans increasingly rebelled against English rule, declared independence, and finally won the military struggle against the British.

Structure of Colonial Society

At the end of the **Seven Years' War**, American society, on the whole, was young, optimistic and prosperous, and looked to the future with considerable political and economic expectation. However, Britain was left with a large debt to pay, and their attention turned to the colonies as a new source of revenue.

▌ **King George III**, his ministers, and Parliament throughout the mounting conflict until 1776, based their views on the colonies on inaccurate information while Parliament stubbornly defended their own "sovereign supreme power over every part of the dominions of state."

▌ **"No Taxation Without Representation"** became the American view on the power of colonial assemblies, representative government, and freedom from England's revenue taxation.

▌ **The American ideology** also contained a heavy emphasis on religious and moral components based on various sources from the **Great Awakening** and **John Locke** to the **Commonwealthmen**.

▌ **The Americans** found **power** dangerous unless contained by **virtue**; to believers political error resulted from corruption and sin.

Eroding the Bonds of Empire

After the war with the French, the British maintained a large military presence in the colonies, which Americans opposed for two reasons: British troops failed to protect the thousands of Americans who died during uprisings by the Native Americans of the backcountry; and after the **Proclamation of 1763** was issued, British troops obstructed western settlement.

▌ **George Grenville** insisted that Americans help pay for British troops with new taxes and restrictions on trade. Well-to-do American merchants quickly protested a scheme they saw as depriving the American colonies' right to assess their own taxes.

▌ **The popular protests** of gentlemen grew to a mass movement with opposition to Britain's **Stamp Act**. Americans resisted in colonial assemblies, in a "congress" in the streets, and in a boycott effected by the **Sons of Liberty** and by newly mobilized colonial women.

- **A new English government** repealed the law while maintaining the principle of **parliamentary supremacy**, including the right to levy taxation, but the crisis had reduced American respect and loyalty for Britain's imperial officeholders.
- **Charles Townshend's** new ministry tried new taxes on American imports and new enforcement mechanisms including customs commissioners supported by **admiralty courts**. Americans resisted with a boycott, "rituals of non-consumption," and a **circular letter** suggesting ways to thwart the acts.
- **A British transfer of troops** to Boston heightened tensions even more, and patriots again resisted. One confrontation with British troops resulted in the **Boston Massacre**. Parliament, now led by **Lord North**, dropped all of the **Townshend Duties** except that on tea, a symbol of Parliament's sovereignty.
- **Calm and apparent reconciliation followed**. But the actions of corrupt imperial officials and the continued agitation of radicals led by **Sam Adams** brought about a renewal of tensions.
- **The Boston Tea Party**, a colonial response to new English regulations, led to the **Coercive Acts** and American rebellion.

Steps Toward Independence

With the fighting begun, fifty-five American delegates from twelve of the colonies met in a **Continental Congress**, which Adams soon led into a radical stance of boycotts and **nonimportation**.
- **"The Shot Heard 'Round the World"**: Before the Continental Congress reconvened, the first blows of the American Revolution fell at **Lexington and Concord**.
- **A Second Continental Congress (1775)** slowly took control of the American war effort but only debated independence until British aggressions and **Thomas Paine's** *Common Sense* pushed it to an open declaration of revolution and war.

Fighting for Independence

English military and economic power might have prevailed had it not been for Britain's logistical problems and the American commitment to independence. The Americans maintained a regular army to symbolize the new country's independence and to attract foreign support. Meanwhile, **colonial militia** controlled large areas of the country and demanded support for the patriots' war effort. Thousands more took up arms for the British, hoping in either case to gain "unalienable rights."
- On July 2, 1776, Congress voted for independence, and two days later accepted Thomas Jefferson's **Declaration of Independence**.
- **George Washington's army** suffered several serious defeats in New York and New Jersey and was in retreat by late 1776.
- **"The Times That Try Men's Souls"**: In 1777 the Americans captured Burgoyne's army at **Saratoga**, but then lost a series of battles in an unsuccessful attempt to prevent Howe from reaching Philadelphia, lost again at Germantown, then dug in at **Valley Forge**.
- **The American victory at Saratoga** persuaded the French to offer an alliance, founded on their desire for revenge against the British and Franklin's brilliant

diplomacy—an alliance that turned the American rebellion into a global war.

▌**The British southern strategy** let loose a fury. Americans, more determined than ever, dug in and won a final victory at **Yorktown**.

The Loyalist Dilemma

Many Americans remained loyal to the Crown, often because they feared independence would bring social disorder, which would threaten the very liberties for which their American patriot opponents fought. American hatred and British distrust forced almost one hundred thousand loyalists into bitter flight from their homeland.

Winning the Peace

A highly talented American peace delegation, Benjamin Franklin, John Adams and John Jay, negotiated a very successful treaty with the British, gaining not only independence but also very favorable boundaries and important fishing rights.

Multiple-Choice Questions

1. American colonists, in the years just after the conclusion of the Seven Years' War, could be characterized best as
   (A) hostile toward the British.
   (B) optimistic about the future.
   (C) apathetic about relations with Great Britain.
   (D) eager for independence from Great Britain.
   (E) trying to rebuild.

2. Although it is impossible to know exactly how many people fled America because they felt a loyalty to the British Crown, all of the following are true EXCEPT
   (A) over 100,000 left
   (B) they all were upper class wealthy merchants
   (C) they were spread throughout the colonies
   (D) many remained silent throughout the war
   (E) those that fled went to several countries including Canada, England and the West Indies.

3. England passed the Coercive Acts in response to
   (A) the colonial boycott of the Stamp Act.
   (B) the American victory at Saratoga.
   (C) the Boston Tea Party.

   (D) the Declaratory Act.
   (E) the Tea Act.

4. The boycott movement against the Stamp Act
   (A) was championed by the colonial press.
   (B) had little effect on Great Britain.
   (C) ultimately hurt American businessmen more than British.
   (D) was opposed by New England businessmen.
   (E) was badly organized.

5.

This picture is of a painting of the conditions of a British prison ship. Based on this picture the conditions could be best described as

(A) gentlemanly.

(B) humane.

(C) clean.

(D) spacious.

(E) squalid.

6. The tensions leading to the Boston Massacre were caused by

(A) widespread British murders of American leaders.

(B) Parliament's repeal of the Stamp Act.

(C) the Boston Tea Party.

(D) the presence of several thousand British soldiers in Boston.

(E) anger at Charles Townshend.

7. The pamphlet, _____, presented justification to Americans for their break with Great Britain.

(A) *Common Sense*

(B) *The Prince*

(C) *The Declaration of the Rights of Man*

(D) *Treatise on Government*

(E) *American Crisis*

8. The American victory that brought about the French alliance occurred at

(A) Trenton.

(B) Yorktown.

(C) Breed's Hill.

(D) Philadelphia.

(E) Saratoga.

9. General Howe was replaced by

(A) General Gage.

(B) General Cornwallis.

(C) General Clinton.

(D) General Paine.

(E) General Johnston.

10. The radical American group which first emerged during the Stamp Act crisis was known as

(A) the Loyalists.

(B) the Federalists.

(C) the Democratic Republicans.

(D) the Sons of Liberty.

(E) Oliver's Raiders.

Free-Response Question

Discuss the relationship between England's internal political problems and the loss of its colonial empire in America.

ANSWERS AND EXPLANATIONS

Multiple-Choice Questions

▌ **1. (B) is correct.** Immediately following the Seven Years' War there was a wave of optimism that swept throughout the colonies. This was due to the British-American victory over the French and Indians. This provided a temporary peace that helped to promote this feeling. Unfortunately, this peace left the British treasury empty and caused the actions that led to the American Revolution.

▌ **2. (B) is correct.** All of the answers are true except for the issue of social classes. Loyalty to the crown crossed economic barriers.

▌ **3. (C) is correct.** The Coercive Acts were known as the Intolerable Acts in America. The Act mandated (1) the port of Boston be closed until the East India Tea Company was compensated for the tea, (2) the restructure of the

Massachusetts government, (3) that the royal governor was allowed to transfer British officials arrested for offenses committed in the line of duty to England, and (4) authorization of quartering troops wherever and whenever needed.

■ **4. (A) is correct.** One of the most powerful responses to the Stamp Act came out of the Virginia Assembly in the form of the Virginia Resolves by Patrick Henry. His proposals were controversial but were picked up and ran in most large papers throughout the colonies.

■ **5. (E) is correct.** The conditions in war for prisoners are almost always questionable. During the Revolutionary War this was true. The British often kept prisoners on ships floating in harbors for months and sometimes years.

■ **6. (D) is correct.** The tensions had grown in Boston as the British army was consolidated in Boston. Both sides caused the tensions. However, on March 5, 1770, young boys and street thugs were throwing rocks and taunting a patrol of redcoats outside the custom commissioner's office. As dusk fell, the soldiers panicked and opened fire leaving five dead Americans.

■ **7. (A) is correct.** Thomas Payne's *Common Sense* became the American revolutionary's guide. His editorials were used as justification for the revolution.

■ **8. (E) is correct.** The French had secretly been supporting the colonies throughout the war. The support was not because the French monarchy believed in independence, quite the opposite. The success of the American Revolution can be attributed to the French Revolution. Instead, the French Monarchy wanted to help embarrass the British monarchy. The French had been encouraged to recognize American independence. They advised patience and once the Battle of Saratoga was won, the French officially declared support, believing the Americans had the resolve to win.

■ **9. (C) is correct.** General Howe quickly resigned after his defeat at the Battle of Saratoga and was replaced by General Henry Clinton.

■ **10. (D) is correct.** The "Sons of Liberty" were located in Boston. They burned effigies of stamp distributors. This group scared the upper class and fueled the lower classes.

Free-Response Essay Sample Response

Discuss the relationship between England's internal political problems, and the loss of its colonial empire in America.

The "main" internal political problem in England was the fact the exchequer was empty. This fact meant that there were several proposals between the King, his ministers and the parliament. All of the solutions really saw the American colonies as the monetary solution to the crisis. The problem was in the execution of the adopted plan.

Instead of forcing the taxes, what should have happened was a better explanation of the situation to the colonial governors and legislatures. It could be best explained like this: either the colonies can pay a small tax to protect them or they can pay for all their expenses. This is in essence what happened.

CHAPTER 6

The Republican Experiment

After the Revolution, Americans tried to construct practicing governments based on republican principles.

Defining Republican Culture

In the 1780s, many Americans feared their Revolution could still fail if not grounded in a virtuous government steeped in **republicanism**, but ordinary folk, influenced by evangelism, expected God-given progress founded on "goodness and not wealth."

Living in the Shadow of Revolution

Although less wrenching than the great social upheavals of modern times, the Revolution caused Americans to consider the role of equality in their society.

Social and Political Reform

▪ **Republicans**, fearful of privilege, insisted on the appearance of equality and some social and political reforms. They abolished remnants of aristocratic privilege, changed electoral patterns in part by **lowering property requirements**, and moved toward **separation of church and state**.

▪ **A contradiction** was noted by some republicans between their ideals of virtue and the evils of slavery, and many **African Americans** issued claims for equality based on that glaring inconsistency and the achievements of their people, including, for example, **Benjamin Banneker** and **Phillis Wheatley**. Northerners attacked and abolished the institution, but refused to accept freedmen as their equals; many southerners questioned the morality of slavery; few defended it as a "positive good."

▪ **Women** began to demand more of their husbands and society by the 1770s, and to claim special responsibility for nurturing in their children the virtues essential to republican government.

▪ **Republicans** of the era made few concrete achievements of equality, but established ideals and assumptions that would influence later generations.

The States: Experiments in Republicanism

After 1776, Americans wrote new provisional, sometimes experimental, state constitutions that reflected their social and regional differences.

▪ **New state constitutions** resulted from political change that reflected the American distrust of power that followed the revolution against the British government.

- **Natural Rights** The new state constitutions tended to emphasize fundamental freedoms, especially those of religion, speech, and press, and to grant great power to legislatures…little to governors.
- **Massachusetts** set an important precedent by drafting its constitution in a special convention called for that purpose. In all states, more of "the People's men" appeared in government. Its words were echoed in the later federal constitution.

Stumbling Toward a New National Government

During the military crisis of the Revolution, the Second Continental Congress assumed national authority, but independence would result in the creation of greater central authority.

- **The Articles of Confederation** created a weak national **Congress** because Americans trusted state power more than central power, but most felt only apathy for their new government—a government that they saw as powerless.
- **The major point of dispute** for the new government was the ownership of **western lands** claimed by some of the new states—territory that other states felt should be shared by all with ownership granted to the new confederation government.
- **The Northwest Ordinance (1787)** and other legislation did acquire these western lands, and provided for their orderly survey, sale, and governance, which prevented the chaotic conditions of earlier settlement in the southwest of the new country. In addition, the act outlawed slavery.

Strengthening Federal Authority

Complaints about the Articles of Confederation abounded, most of them reflecting economic frustrations.

- **The nationalist critique of the Articles** said the national government lacked the power to do much about some important national problems. The economy floundered, but Congress could not regulate trade; the government owed money but could not tax—leading a group of **nationalists** to call for major constitutional reforms. This debate was led by **Alexander Hamilton** and **James Madison**, and centered at first on whether or not the new country could pay its debts.
- **In foreign affairs**, Congress claimed lands occupied by the Spanish and the English, but did not have the power to challenge the Europeans for control of the land. Internal affairs were not much better, and the control of Congress was suspect.

"Have We Fought For This?"

Most Americans still feared centralized power, but many prosperous Republicans had come to fear that ordinary citizens lacked republican virtue and threatened order and that the weakness of the Confederation threatened commercial prosperity. Only a strong central government, they argued, could solve both problems.

- **James Madison** provided these anxious federalists with a theory to sustain their hope for a large republic with a strong government.
- **The Constitutional Reform movement** grew stronger because of fears aroused by **Shays' Rebellion** and culminated in the **constitutional convention**.
- **In Philadelphia**, the fifty-five men who were to write the constitution were mostly young, practical, and prominent nationalists.

- *Madison's Virginia Plan* called for a strong central government "consisting of a supreme Legislature, Executive, and Judiciary." The opposing **New Jersey Plan** gave each state one vote in the federal government and thus favored small states.
- **The delegates compromised**, especially on the issues of representation and of counting slaves as population, but retained the essentials of the Virginia Plan.
- **The slavery issue** threatened to disrupt the convention, but the delegates compromised repeatedly in order to complete what most of them saw as the most important responsibility, the establishment of a strong national government. This issue foreshadowed the conflicts that would arise over this issue in the next century.
- **The Last Details** of the delegates' work consisted of creating a stronger executive, a president independent of Congress, and selected by an **electoral college**.
- **Approval** was required from special state conventions, with the Constitution going into effect when approved by nine states.

Whose Constitution? The Struggle for Ratification

The delegates sent their handiwork to the **Confederation Congress**, which submitted it to the states to consider for ratification. No one predicted an easy battle for ratification.

- **Federalists** were better organized, financed, and led than their opponents, but **Anti-federalist** views, especially their aversion to centralized power, had wide appeal. The Federalists won the struggle for ratification—agreeing to add the Bill of Rights, the first ten amendments to the Constitution—but Anti-federalist views would remain influential throughout American history.

Multiple-Choice Questions

1. The _____ proposed a new form for government that was acceptable to the smaller states.
   - (A) Virginia Plan
   - (B) "three-fifths rule"
   - (C) Connecticut Plan
   - (D) Franklin Compromise
   - (E) New Jersey Plan

2. Most new state constitutions after the American Revolution
   - (A) strengthened the power of the governors.
   - (B) weakened the power of the legislature.
   - (C) avoided the creation of a written constitution.
   - (D) included Declarations of Rights.
   - (E) affirmed the freedom of speech and press but not of religion.

3. Compared with the revolutions in France, Russia, and China, the American Revolution could be characterized as

   - (A) much more radical and violent.
   - (B) about the same in terms of the degree of change.
   - (C) less defined in terms of the needs of the people.
   - (D) more tame and less wrenching.
   - (E) happening much more quickly.

4. An important procedural decision approved at the opening of the Constitutional Convention involved
   - (A) the decision to keep deliberations as secret as possible.
   - (B) refusing to allow the small states to present their plans for constitutional revisions.
   - (C) publicizing the convention's meetings and debates.
   - (D) the election of James Madison as chairman.
   - (E) the requirement of a plurality rather than

a simple majority to implement changes.

5. The Newburgh Conspiracy involved
   (A) discontented officers of the Continental Army.
   (B) supporters of the Articles of Confederation.
   (C) those who believed the Articles gave too much power to the national government.
   (D) individuals dissatisfied with the military leadership of George Washington.
   (E) French soldiers who had not been paid.

6. Which of the following was NOT a criticism of American government under the Articles of Confederation?
   (A) It failed to deal with the nation's economic problems.
   (B) It gave too much power to a central government.
   (C) It failed to adequately confront threats from Britain and Spain along American borders.
   (D) It was unable to deal with the country's fiscal instability.
   (E) Its single legislative body gave some states an unfair advantage.

7. The most obvious contradiction to the principles expressed in the founding of the American republic was
   (A) the way women were treated.
   (B) the failure to allow businessmen a say in planning the nation's future.
   (C) the continued existence of slavery in much of the nation.

(D) the fact that some states continued to require property as a prerequisite for voting.
(E) the failure to address matters of religion.

8. He was considered the most important political figure of the Confederation Period.
   (A) James Madison
   (B) Robert Morris
   (C) Alexander Hamilton
   (D) Benjamin Franklin
   (E) John Hancock

9. A major fear of the Antifederalists was that
   (A) voters would be too distanced from their representatives.
   (B) voters would have too much direct contact and thus influence on their representatives.
   (C) voters would corrupt their national representatives.
   (D) national representatives would rely too consistently on local voters for their ideas and decisions.
   (E) the average voter was not educated enough to make good decisions.

10. How many states did not have to draft new constitutions, since they already had republican governments as part of their colonial charters?
    (A) none
    (B) one
    (C) two
    (D) three
    (E) four

Free-Response Question

Compare the strengths and weaknesses of the Confederation and Constitutional governments.

ANSWERS AND EXPLANATIONS

Multiple-Choice Questions

▌ **1. (E) is correct.** The New Jersey Plan called for a scheme that remained the unicameral legislature with each state having one vote. The plan also gave Congress broader powers over trade and taxation. This plan was flatly defeated at the Constitutional Convention.

▌ **2. (D) is correct.** Eight state constitutions contained a specific Declaration of Rights. Although they may have varied on the specifics, all eight had three basic rights. The freedoms were religion, speech and press.

▌ **3. (D) is correct.** There was little radical transformation of government because of the American Revolutions. The pattern of revolution exists and is consistent through all four revolutions. The American Revolution did not end with the execution of a monarch, but only with the severing of ties.

▌ **4. (A) is correct.** As soon as the convention started, it was decided that nothing neither spoken nor written would be communicated outside of the hall. The downside to this is that modern jurists have difficulty in determining the "framer's intent."

▌ **5. (A) is correct.** No one knows all of the details of the Newburgh Conspiracy. What is known is that officers of the Continental Army worried that Congress would disband without funding their pensions. They threatened a takeover of the new country. George Washington in an act of vulnerability single-handedly stopped the rebellion.

▌ **6. (B) is correct.** The Articles of Confederation by its definition was a loose coupling of states. This would indicate there was very little central government. Even the institutions that were consolidated were weak and often ignored by the states.

▌ **7. (C) is correct.** Quaker leader John Woolman probably did more than any white man of the era did. Woolman was an outspoken critic of the "dark gloominess of slavery." He and others felt the issue of slavery was the great unanswered question of the revolution.

▌ **8. (B) is correct.** Robert Morris, a Philadelphia merchant, was appointed the first superintendent of finance under the Articles of Confederation. He commingled public and private funds; this action was legal for this time.

▌ **9. (E) is correct.** The term was a misleading term. The rhetoric of the Antifederalist had broad public appeal. However, the press seldom printed their ideals. The Antifederalists were highly suspicious of a strong central government.

▌ **10. (C) is correct.** The two states that had republican forms of government were Rhode Island and Connecticut. Their constitutions provided for both an elected governor and legislature.

Free-Response Essay Sample Response

Compare the strengths and weaknesses of the Confederation and Constitutional governments.

[Use ideas from the chart on page 177.] The Articles offered very little central government. There was no court system to decide disputes. States taxed citizens; the national unicameral congress would request money from the states as needed. The Articles had no executive. There was a weak regulation of trade. All changes require confirmation by all states.

The Constitution offered many corrections. The first correction was ratification by three-fourths of states. A bicameral legislature was created. Separate executive branch. Separate judicial branch with a Supreme Court and inferior courts to enforce federal law. The Constitution granted powers of taxation and regulation of trade.

CHAPTER 7

Democracy in Distress: The Violence of Party Politics, 1788–1800

A debate in the first **United States Senate** in 1789 over what title to use when addressing George Washington as president revealed the range of political questions to be considered by early politicians, and perhaps foreshadowed later attitudes adopted by rival groups over the proper roles and powers of the new government.

Principle and Pragmatism: Establishing a New Government

▌ **George Washington** began his career as president in 1789, an office he managed successfully and with popular approval. Congress refined the machinery of government with the creation of **executive departments** and a **federal court system** and provided revenue with passage of a **tariff act**.

Conflicting Visions: Jefferson and Hamilton

In spite of Washington's disdain for political squabbling, Americans began to divide into two camps: the **Federalists**, led by Secretary of the Treasury **Alexander Hamilton**, and the **Republicans**, led by Secretary of State **Thomas Jefferson**. The factions developed differing conceptions about the nature of government and society, economic policy, foreign affiliations, and interpretation of the Constitution.

Hamilton's Plan for Prosperity and Security

Hamilton argued for a **strong national government** and central economic planning in the hands of the moneyed elite to ensure order in political and economic affairs. **Jefferson** feared such a government would become oppressive, threatening states' rights and infringing upon individual liberty. Hamilton wished to transform the United States into a self-sufficient industrial power, while Jefferson hoped the nation would remain one of small, independent farmers.

▌ **Hamilton** argued that the national government must **fund (repay) the national debt** as well as assume any outstanding state debts. Critics argued that the scheme enriched current money speculators at the expense of original investors.

▌ **Hamilton** urged creation of a **Bank of the United States**, owned primarily by private stockholders, to administer the country's finances and supervise its currency. While opponents complained that such a bank was unconstitutional,

Hamilton argued that the Constitution should be loosely interpreted to expand the powers of the national government whenever "necessary and proper."

▌**Congress** had passed Hamilton's earlier financial plans, but Madison and Jefferson rallied opponents with a variety of political and moral objections to defeat Hamilton's call for governmental promotion of manufacturing.

Charges of Treason: The Battle Over Foreign Affairs

Jefferson admired the French and hoped that the outbreak of the **French Revolution (1789)** indicated a worldwide republican assault on absolute monarchy and aristocratic privilege. Hamilton cautioned against the anarchic results of excessive democracy and urged closer American ties to Britain.

▌**Warfare between Britain and France (1793)** complicated American politics. Britain continued to maintain forts in the **Northwest Territory** while seizing American ships and **impressing** American sailors on the high seas. The efforts of French minister **Edmond Genet** to solicit private American aid for the French cause spurred an official **Proclamation of Neutrality** from President Washington.

▌**Chief Justice John Jay** was sent to London to negotiate a settlement of America's grievances. Secretly forewarned by Hamilton that the Americans would compromise on most issues, the British remained firm. While the resultant **Jay's Treaty** maintained peace, Republican critics denounced it as a "sellout" of American rights.

▌**The Federalists** regained some popularity with other treaties that extracted major concessions in the West. **Indian resistance** in the Northwest Territory was crushed and Spain agreed to favorable American terms in **Pinckney's Treaty**.

Popular Political Culture

The ratification of Jay's Treaty sparked and encouraged factionalism in the American political spectrum. Neither the Federalists nor the Republicans saw it in their best interest to compromise, and each saw the demise of any opposition as the only solution.

▌**Newspapers and political clubs** emerged to champion both the Republican and Federalist causes. The journals were fiercely partisan, presenting rumor or opinion as fact, while the purpose of the clubs was clearly political indoctrination. Political debates were bitter as each faction became convinced of its choices and increasingly suspicious of the other's wisdom and motives.

▌**The Whiskey Rebellion** was branded as civil unrest and Republican agitation by the Federalists. Jefferson felt the Federalists used the episode as an excuse to create an army for the purpose of intimidating Republicans.

▌**Washington's Farewell Address (1796)** warned Americans to avoid political factions and entangling foreign alliances. Written largely by Hamilton, the address sought to serve the Federalist cause in the forthcoming election.

The Adams Presidency

Hamilton's attempt to manipulate the election of 1796 backfired, angering newly elected president John Adams and heightening tensions within the Federalist party.

▪ **Adams's presidency** saw the relations between the United States and France steadily deteriorated. This period of increasing hostility became known as the **Quasi-War**. An American commission sent by Adams to pursue a peaceful settlement was met by French officials who arrogantly demanded a bribe as the price for negotiations. This so-called **XYZ Affair (1798)** humiliated and infuriated Americans.

▪ **The Federalists** used the outpouring of anti-French sentiment in America as an excuse to increase the nation's military defenses, a move intended to stifle internal political opposition, as well as thwart French aggression.

▪ **The Alien and Sedition Acts** were Federalist measures designed to harass Republican spokespersons by disallowing criticism of the government. These blatantly political attempts to silence opposition ultimately proved counterproductive.

▪ **The Virginia and Kentucky Resolutions** (Jefferson and Madison) asserted that the individual states had the right to interpret federal law, while labeling the Alien and Sedition Acts as unconstitutional.

▪ **Adams** pursued peaceful negotiations with France. **The Treaty of Mortefontaine** ended the **Quasi-War** and restored good relations between France and the United States.

The Peaceful Revolution: The Election of 1800

The Federalists lost office in 1800 partly as a result of internal party disputes, but more importantly, as a result of losing touch with public opinion.

Multiple-Choice Questions

1. Which of the following did Hamilton and Jefferson have in common?
   (A) faith in a republican society
   (B) belief that the national government should be strong
   (C) faith in the common man
   (D) fears of the effect of the French Revolution on American society
   (E) great respect for the purity of the British constitution

2. Why did Spain agree to the terms of the Pinckney Treaty?
   (A) It feared the terms of Jay's Treaty.
   (B) It needed the additional sources of revenue.
   (C) It needed protection on its southwest borders.
   (D) The United States threatened direct military action.
   (E) It thought there was a secret agreement between the United States and France to take their North American possessions.

3. Which of the following individuals is incorrectly matched with his position in George Washington's first Cabinet?
   (A) Alexander Hamilton: Secretary of the Treasury
   (B) Thomas Jefferson: Secretary of State
   (C) Henry Knox: Secretary of War
   (D) James Madison: Secretary of Commerce
   (E) Edmund Randolph: Attorney General

4. Which of the following would Alexander Hamilton have proposed?
   (A) strong diplomatic ties with France
   (B) the purchase of western lands
   (C) giving the common man the vote
   (D) providing government subsidies to manufacturers
   (E) establish the banking system on the German model

5. During Washington's second term in office,
   (A) the European war unified American officials in support of France.
   (B) relations with Great Britain and France improved dramatically.
   (C) Hamilton and Jefferson resolved their differences over domestic policy.
   (D) Hamilton ceased to be a force in American politics.
   (E) foreign affairs became a much more important focus.

6. The Genet affair involved
   (A) American interference in French-British relations.
   (B) American assistance offered to the French during their revolution.
   (C) France's use of American ships in violation of U.S. pledges of neutrality.
   (D) America's refusal to repay debts incurred as a result of the French-American alliance.
   (E) a secret arms agreement with the French foreign minister.

7. The emergence of political parties in the 1790s
   (A) created a harmonious atmosphere for political debate.
   (B) had both good and bad consequences for the nation at the time.

(C) led to closer relations between the factions that had appeared during Washington's administration.
   (D) was a very negative experience in the history of the time.
   (E) meant one of George Washington's goals for the new government was realized.

8. Washington's Farewell Address
   (A) warned against creating a strong military.
   (B) attempted to bring harmony to the political system.
   (C) supported the political ideology of Jefferson and Madison.
   (D) wholeheartedly endorsed the two-party system.
   (E) advised against permanent alliances with nations that were not interested in promoting American security.

9. The election of 1796 was complicated by
   (A) changes in the nation's voting laws.
   (B) interference from British diplomats.
   (C) behind-the-scenes manipulations by Alexander Hamilton.
   (D) Washington's refusal to stay out of politics.
   (E) confusion over the differences between Federalists and Republicans.

10. As a result of the actions taken by John Adams while president,
    (A) he was overwhelmingly reelected in 1800.
    (B) the United States had harmony with France.
    (C) the Federalist Party remained the major party.
    (D) France compensated the United States for ships taken.
    (E) the French added even more restrictions on U.S. commerce.

Document-Based Question

How do you account for the development of political parties in the United States during the period 1787–1800? In your answer, draw on your knowledge of the time period in question as well as the documents below.

DOCUMENT 1 Source: Patrick Henry speaks against the ratification of the Constitution, 1788

This proposal of altering our federal government is of a most alarming nature! Make the best of this new government—say it is composed by any thing but inspiration—you ought to be extremely cautious, watchful, jealous of your liberty; for, instead of securing your rights, you may lose them forever. If a wrong step be now made, the republic may be lost forever. If this new government will not come up to the expectation of the people, and they shall be disappointed, their liberty will be lost, and tyranny must and will arise. I repeat it again, and I beg gentlemen to consider, that a wrong step, made now, will plunge us into misery, and our republic will be lost....What right had they to say, *We, the people?* My political curiosity, exclusive of my anxious solicitude for the public welfare, leads me to ask, Who authorized them to speak the language of, *We, the people,* instead of, *We, the states?* States are the characteristics and the soul of a confederation. If the states be not the agents of this compact, it must be one great, consolidated, national government, of the people of all the states....It is not mere curiosity that actuates me: I wish to hear the real, actual, existing danger, which should lead us to take those steps, so dangerous in my conception. Disorders have arisen in other parts of America; but here, sir, no dangers, no insurrection or tumult have happened; every thing has been calm and tranquil.

DOCUMENT 2 Source: James Madison defends the Constitution, 1788

He informs us that the people of the country are at perfect repose,—that is, every man enjoys the fruits of his labor peaceably and securely, and that every thing is in perfect tranquillity and safety. I wish sincerely, sir, this were true. If this be their happy situation, why has every state acknowledged the contrary? Why were deputies from all the states sent to the general Convention? Why have complaints of national and individual distresses been echoed and reechoed throughout the continent? Why has our general government been so shamefully disgraced, and our Constitution violated? Wherefore have laws been made to authorize a change, and wherefore are we now assembled here?

DOCUMENT 3 Source: Preamble to the Constitution of the United States, 1787

We the People of the United States, in Order to form a more perfect Union, establish Justice, insure domestic Tranquility, provide for the common defense, promote the general Welfare, and secure the Blessings of Liberty to ourselves and our Posterity, do ordain and establish this Constitution for the United States of America.

DOCUMENT 4   Source: The Bill of Rights, 1789

Amendment IX

The enumeration in the Constitution, of certain rights, shall not be construed to deny or disparage others retained by the people.

Amendment X

The powers not delegated to the United States by the Constitution, nor prohibited by it to the States, are reserved to the States respectively, or to the people.

DOCUMENT 5   Source: Proclamation of Neutrality, 1793

April 22, 1793

BY THE PRESIDENT OF THE UNITED STATES
A PROCLAMATION

Whereas it appears that a state of war exists between Austria, Prussia, Sardinia, Great Britain, and the United Netherlands, of the one part, and France on the other; and the duty and interest of the United States require, that they should with sincerity and good faith adopt and pursue a conduct friendly and impartial toward the belligerant Powers;

I have therefore thought fit by these presents to declare the disposition of the United States to observe the conduct aforesaid towards those Powers respectfully; and to exhort and warn the citizens of the United States carefully to avoid all acts and proceedings whatsoever, which may in any manner tend to contravene such disposition.

And I do hereby also make known, that whatsoever of the citizens of the United States shall render himself liable to punishment or forfeiture under the law of nations, by committing, aiding, or abetting hostilities against any of the said Powers, or by carrying to any of them those articles which are deemed contraband by the modern usage of nations, will not receive the protection of the United States, against such punishment or forfeiture; and further, that I have given instructions to those officers, to whom it belongs, to cause prosecutions to be instituted against all persons, who shall, within the cognizance of the courts of the United States, violate the law of nations, with respect to the Powers at war, or any of them.

In testimony whereof, I have caused the seal of the United States of America to be affixed to these presents, and signed the same with my hand. Done at the city of Philadelphia, the twenty-second day of April, one thousand seven hundred and ninety-three, and of the Independence of the United States of America the seventeenth.

DOCUMENT 6   Source: Portrait of Alexander Hamilton

DOCUMENT 7   Source: Informal drawing of Thomas Jefferson

DOCUMENT 8   Source: The Alien and Sedition Acts, 1798

Be it enacted by the Senate and House of Representatives of the United States of America, in Congress assembled, That whenever there shall be a declared war between the United States and any foreign nation or government, or any invasion or predatory incursion shall be perpetrated, attempted, or threatened against the territory of the United States, by any foreign nation or government, and the President of the United States shall make public proclamation of the event, all natives, citizens, denizens, or subjects of the hostile nation or government, being males of the age of fourteen years and upwards, who shall be within the United States, and not actually naturalized, shall be liable to be apprehended, restrained, secured and removed, as alien enemies.

Be it enacted by the Senate and House of Representatives of the United States of America, in Congress assembled, That if any persons shall unlawfully combine or conspire together, with intent to oppose any measure or measures of the government of the United States…he or they shall be deemed guilty of a high misdemeanor, and on conviction, before any court of the United States having jurisdiction thereof, shall be punished by a fine not exceeding five thousand dollars, and by imprisonment during a term not less than six months nor exceeding five years.

And be it further enacted, That if any person shall write, print, utter or publish, or shall cause or procure to be written, printed, uttered or published, or shall knowingly and willingly assist or aid in writing, printing, uttering or publishing any false, scandalous and malicious writing or writings against the government of the United States, or either house of the Congress of the United States, or the President of the United States…then such person, being thereof convicted before any court of the United States having jurisdiction thereof, shall be punished by a fine not exceeding two thousand dollars, and by imprisonment not exceeding two years.

DOCUMENT 9   Source: The Virginia and Kentucky Resolutions, 1798, 1799

That this Assembly doth explicitly and peremptorily declare, that it views the powers of the federal government, as resulting from the compact, to which the states are parties; as limited by the plain sense and intention of the instrument constituting the compact; as no further valid that they are authorized by the grants enumerated in that compact; and that in case of a deliberate, palpable, and dangerous exercise of other powers, not granted by the said compact, the states who are parties thereto, have the right, and are in duty bound, to interpose for arresting the progress of the evil, and for maintaining within their respective limits, the authorities, rights and liberties appertaining to them.

That the General Assembly doth particularly protest against the palpable and alarming infractions of the Constitution, in the two late cases of the "Alien and Sedition Acts" passed at the last session of Congress; the first of which exercises a power no where delegated to the federal government, and which by uniting legislative and judicial powers to those of executive, subverts the general principles of free government; as well as the particular organization, and positive provisions of the federal constitution; and the other of which acts, exercises in like manner, a power not delegated by the constitution, but on the contrary, expressly and positively forbidden by one of the amendments thereto.…

That the several states who formed (the Constitution), being sovereign and independent, have the unquestionable right to judge of its infraction; and that a nullification, by those sovereignties, of all unauthorized acts done under colour of that instrument, is the rightful remedy…

During the contest of opinion through which we have passed the animation of discussions and of exertions has sometimes worn an aspect which might impose on strangers unused to think freely and to speak and to write what they think…

Let us, then, fellow-citizens, unite with one heart and one mind. Let us restore to social intercourse that harmony and affection without which liberty and even life itself are but dreary things. And let us reflect that, having banished from our land that religious intolerance under which mankind so long bled and suffered, we have yet gained little if we countenance a political intolerance as despotic, as wicked, and capable of as bitter and bloody persecutions…

We are all Republicans, we are all Federalists. If there be any among us who would wish to dissolve this Union or to change its republican form, let them stand undisturbed as monuments of the safety with which error of opinion may be tolerated where reason is left free to combat it. I know, indeed, that some honest men fear that a republican government can not be strong, that this Government is not strong enough; but would the honest patriot, in the full tide of successful experiment, abandon a government which has so far kept us free and firm on the theoretic and visionary fear that this Government, the world's best hope, may by possibility want energy to preserve itself?

Free-Response Question

Compare the foreign policies of Washington and Adams.

ANSWERS AND EXPLANATIONS

Multiple-Choice Questions

▌ **1. (A) is correct.** Although Jefferson and Hamilton disagreed on how the republic should conduct its affairs, there is no dispute they both had faith in the republican society.

▌ **2. (A) is correct.** Spanish officials, fearful that Jay's Treaty was actually a secret alliance between England and the United States, capitulated extraordinary concessions. These concessions included use of the Mississippi, access to New Orleans, and a secure southern boundary at the 31st parallel.

▌ **3. (D) is correct.** There was no Department of Commerce in Washington's cabinet. Additionally, Madison was in the Senate leading the charge for a strong executive.

▌ **4. (D) is correct.** Hamilton thought in terms of broad and social commercial development. This would reduce dependence on foreign trade. Thus, he would have been in favor of subsidies to manufacturers.

▌ **5. (E) is correct.** During Washington's second term, he had to deal with numerous domestic situations. Among the issues were pushing Native Americans aside, party politics, and the Whiskey Rebellion.

▌ **6. (C) is correct.** Genet was an incompetent French Minister to the United States. He declared that the United States would seize British vessels in the name of

France. This embarrassed Thomas Jefferson. The action forced Washington to issue a Proclamation of Neutrality.

▌ **7. (B) is correct.** The creation of political parties led to both pros and cons. One thing that was never in dispute was both parties were in search of what was good for the republic.

▌ **8. (E) is correct.** Washington's single greatest fear as he left office was that political parties would destroy the fabric of the republic.

▌ **9. (C) is correct.** Alexander Hamilton manipulated the Electoral College voters to drop John Adams and pick only the Vice Presidential candidate Thomas Pickney. This angered northern voters who dropped Pickney. The net result was a Federalist President, Adams, and a Republican Vice President, Jefferson.

▌ **10. (B) is correct.** President Adams conducted an end run around Alexander Hamilton by appointing a Minister to France. The new negotiation team got an agreement from Napoleon's government that all but eliminated Hamilton's grip on the government.

Document-Based Question Sample Response

How do you account for the development of political parties in the United States during the period 1787–1800?

Many factors contributed to the early development of political parties in this time period. Among them are the ratification of the Constitution, the interpretation of the Constitution, views on American foreign policy, and the continuing debate on the proper role of government.

By 1787, it was obvious that the Articles of Confederation needed revising. Many, however, did not agree with the extent of the revision that was done at Philadelphia. **(DOCUMENT 1)** Much of the difference in opinion was geographically based, with the agricultural south favoring a more limited role for government, and the industrial north wanting a more powerful central government. Many felt that the proposed federal government would be too powerful, but James Madison and others used the Federalist Papers and other outlets to convince enough people that this was the appropriate governing document for the United States and that they need not be concerned. **(DOCUMENT 2)** The Constitution itself reflects these tensions. The Preamble stresses a "more perfect union," and the document sets up a government much stronger than that under the Articles of Confederation. However, in order to get it ratified, a Bill of Rights had to be added, and the Bill of Rights tends to stress individual rights and limitations on the Federal government. **(DOCUMENTS 3 AND 4)** These are essentially the roots of the two main American political parties, with one tending to favor strong central governments and the other state governments and individual rights.

Foreign policy was also a factor in the development of political parties. As Europe was thrown into the throes of the French Revolution and the Napoleonic Wars, President George Washington officially kept the US neutral. **(DOCUMENT 5)** However, many Americans did not agree with that. The southern anti-Federalists tended to side with the French; the Northern Federalists tended to side with the British. Economic policy also played a role. The question of chartering a national bank was debated. The Federalists, headed by Alexander Hamilton, felt the bank was constitutional and necessary; the anti-Federalists, headed by Thomas Jefferson, did not. **(DOCUMENTS 6 AND 7)** The Alien and Sedition Acts, and the Virginia and Kentucky Resolutions, were the main legal embodiments of these two conflicting ideologies of government. **(DOCUMENTS 8 AND 9)** The election of 1800 was one of the nastiest in American history. In his inaugural address, Thomas Jefferson makes a plea for the now firmly-established parties to unite for the greater good of the country and to remember the commonalities that they shared.

Free-Response Essay Sample Response

Compare the foreign policies of Washington and Adams.

Washington had to deal with Great Britain and the fact that Britain treated the United States with arrogance. Washington also had to blaze the trail by establishing the first U.S. Foreign Policy. During Washington's administration, there were threats from Britain, Spain and France.

Adams had to deal with France as its threat. Additionally, Adams had to deal with warring factions within his own party that wanted war. Adams had the XYZ Affair that almost railroaded U.S. foreign policy.

CHAPTER 8

Republican Ascendancy: The Jeffersonian Vision

In theory, advocates of Jeffersonian democracy declared their passion for liberty and equality. In practice, however, they lived in a society whose members accepted slavery and sought to remove Native Americans from the path of the White man's progress. In theory, Jeffersonians had insisted upon a strict interpretation of the constitution, peaceful foreign relations, and reduction of the size and powers of the federal government. As president, however, Jefferson interpreted the Constitution broadly to accommodate the Louisiana Purchase, increased federal power to enforce the embargo of 1807, and led the country to the brink of war.

Regional Identities in a New Republic

Substantial **population growth**, improved **transportation** links within the various sections, and attacks on the institution of **slavery** contributed to a growing sense of **regionalism** in the new nation. Powerful sectional loyalties had already begun to undermine national unity.

▍ **The trans-Appalachian West**—with its rich soil and developing system of water transportation—experienced substantial growth after 1790. Rather than the earlier settlers who were mostly men, these new settlers often traveled as families.

▍ **Native Americans** offered some resistance efforts, especially by Tenskawatawa and his brother Tecumseh. Their efforts were overwhelmed by the onrushing settlers.

▍ **Economic growth** in the United States before 1820 was built on agriculture and commerce. The success of the **carrying trade** diverted investment from more risky manufacturing ventures—although some innovations, especially in the **textile** industry, did appear. American workers reacted to new machines with ambivalence, fearful of reduced wages and loss of independence and status.

▍ **American cities** were small, and only about 7 percent of the population lived in the cities. They served primarily as depots for international trade.

Jefferson as President

Although a shy and introspective man, **Thomas Jefferson** proved to be a capable and pragmatic president. The Federalists would fail to recapture power because of their reluctance to adopt popular campaigning techniques, their resistance to territorial expansion, and their opposition to the **War of 1812**.

- **Jefferson** accomplished most of his early goals of reduction of the federal bureaucracy, taxes, and military spending. He regarded a large federal deficit as dangerous to republican institutions and a large military presence as liable to provoke hostilities.
- **With the Louisiana Purchase (1803)** Jefferson managed to double the territory of the United States for only $15 million. Although initially concerned that such an action might be unconstitutional, Jefferson recognized a good deal and quickly presented the treaty for Senate ratification.
- **The Lewis and Clark expedition (1804–1806)** for western exploration was authorized by Jefferson in the midst of the Louisiana controversy.
- **Jefferson dispatched** an American fleet to battle the **Barbary Pirates**, rather than submit to their demands for tribute. Concluding his first term on a wave of popularity, Jefferson enjoyed an overwhelming reelection in 1804.

Jefferson's Critics

Jefferson's reform efforts, while successful on some fronts, did anger his critics, and contributed to disunity among the Republicans.

- **Angered by the Judiciary Act of 1801**, the Republicans repealed the law and then proceeded with their own attempts to remove jurists and prevent other Federalist judges from obtaining office. While proclaiming victory in *Marbury* v. *Madison* **(1803)**, few Republicans realized that the **Supreme Court's** decision established the precedent of **judicial review** of federal statutes.
- **Vice-President Aaron Burr** schemed with dissident Federalists, quarreled with and **shot Alexander Hamilton** in a duel, and launched a potentially treasonous expedition against the United States. During Burr's subsequent trial, **Chief Justice John Marshall's** disallowance of circumstantial evidence helped earn Burr an acquittal and ensure that in the future, treason could not be charged lightly or for purely political purposes.
- **Congress** considered and passed a bill **prohibiting the importation of slaves beginning in 1808**. Lax American enforcement, however, especially in the South, resulted in continued illegal operations of slave smugglers.

Embarrassments Overseas

During Jefferson's second term, a military stalemate in the resumed warfare between Britain and France forced the belligerents into an economic struggle. Owing to its naval superiority, Britain was more successful at this, not only seizing American ships, but also **impressing** American sailors. The British attack on the American warship *Chesapeake* in 1807 for its refusal to submit to a British search infuriated Americans.

- **An embargo of American goods in 1807 (The Embargo Act)** failed to win foreign respect for American neutrality. Jefferson's policy of "peaceable coercion" succeeded only in depressing the economy and angering northern merchants, and was repealed in 1809.
- **Newly-elected James Madison** won the **election of 1808**, but proved to be an ineffective president. Poorly designed Republican policies failed to keep America

out of war. **General William Henry Harrison** defeated an Indian army at **Tippecanoe**, but drove the Indian leader Tecumseh into the arms of the British.

- **Aggressive War Hawks in the United States** were convinced that war against Britain would restore national honor, remove British aid to western Indians, and open Canada to American expansion.

The Strange War of 1812

In spite of early optimism, American war efforts were marred by poor preparation, ineffective leadership, and an ill-designed strategy. Although momentarily preoccupied with Napoleon, Britain appeared no better in executing offensive operations once its full attention could be directed at the United States.

- **In late 1814**, disgruntled Federalists gathered at **Hartford** to protest the war and recommend constitutional changes designed to protect the minority interests of New England. The demands, presented in Washington just as news broke concerning what seemed a successful conclusion to war, made the Federalists appear foolish if not treacherous, hastening their demise as a political force.

- **The Treaty of Ghent**, signed on **Christmas Eve 1814**, ended the deadlock of war with no major concessions granted by either side. A belated American victory, with **Andrew Jackson** routing the British at the **Battle of New Orleans** led to a widespread conception that the United States had won the War of 1812.

Multiple-Choice Questions

1. The Barbary States were located in
   (A) North Africa.
   (B) South America.
   (C) the Caribbean.
   (D) South Africa.
   (E) Mexico.

2. As the chief negotiator with France, who engineered the Louisiana Purchase?
   (A) James Madison
   (B) John Quincy Adams
   (C) John Marshall
   (D) James Monroe
   (E) Thomas Jefferson

3. Jefferson's foreign policy
   (A) allowed Madison to return to domestic concerns.
   (B) had seriously damaged the British economy.
   (C) brought an alliance with France.
   (D) created more harm than good for the United States.
   (E) strengthened relations with Europe, despite the war.

4. Under Jeffersonian Republicanism,
   (A) Americans believed opportunities were available to them.
   (B) few Americans were able to advance in society.
   (C) the social structure of society was well defined.
   (D) blacks were provided opportunities in society.
   (E) servants "knew their place."

5. By 1810, one-fifth of the American population was made up of
   (A) Native Americans.
   (B) immigrants.
   (C) African Americans.
   (D) women.
   (E) Catholics.

6. Thomas Jefferson's attitude toward Native Americans showed that he
   (A) considered them to be expendable.
   (B) believed their way of life worth protecting and preserving.

(C) found them to be savages unworthy of serious concern.

(D) wanted to try to assimilate them into the nascent American culture.

(E) respected them as people, but was not impressed by their culture.

7. What difficulty did Jefferson face in purchasing the Louisiana Territory?
   (A) possible confrontation with Great Britain
   (B) lack of support from the American people
   (C) the constitutionality of his actions
   (D) whether to accept foreign citizens on the land
   (E) finding $15 million in the federal budget

8. After 1800, Federalists retained control of
   (A) the presidency.
   (B) the judiciary.
   (C) Congress.
   (D) the military.
   (E) the Supreme Court.

9. The decision in *Marbury v. Madison* was the first time the Supreme Court
   (A) ruled on the constitutionality of federal laws.
   (B) compelled federal officials.
   (C) discussed the powers of the judiciary.
   (D) had a unanimous ruling.
   (E) asserted its right to judge the constitutionality of congressional acts.

10. Samuel Chase's impeachment trial
    (A) destroyed the authority of the courts.
    (B) maintained the independence of the judiciary.
    (C) forced Marshall to resign.
    (D) showed Jefferson to be a conciliatory leader.
    (E) was a rather dull affair.

Free-Response Question

Compare and contrast the differences in American society of 1776 and 1812.

ANSWERS AND EXPLANATIONS

Multiple-Choice Questions

▌ **1. (A) is correct.** The Barbary States consisted of the states of Algiers, Tangier, Tripoli and Tunis. They were famous for their Barbary Pirates who would extort bounty from nations. Jefferson refused to pay when they wanted to up the amount. All of these actions led to unimpressive combat and the capture of a United States frigate. Yet the United States is credited by Europe for taking care of the Barbary States.

▌ **2. (D) is correct.** James Monroe was the chief negotiator. He was instructed to negotiate use of New Orleans and the Mississippi. When he arrived, he found Napoleon had lost his quest for an American empire and offered the entire Louisiana Purchase for $15 million.

▌ **3. (D) is correct.** Jefferson's foreign policy at the beginning of his second term was one of startling offense. At the end of his tenure in office, an embargo had been put in place against Britain. This embargo crippled the U.S. economy.

▌ **4. (A) is correct.** The idea of Jeffersonian Republican ideals was one of equality of the masses and of good possibilities.

▌ **5. (C) is correct.** Jefferson signed a law to outlaw the importation of slaves into the United States in 1808. The problem was the wording of the law that allowed slaves to pour into Southern ports for years to come.

■ **6. (E) is correct.** Jefferson did not view the culture as anything particularly impressive. He viewed them as expendable in the face of expansion.

■ **7. (C) is correct.** Jefferson anguished over the constitutionality of the purchase of the Louisiana territory. What prodded him to change his mind was Napoleon's impatience.

■ **8. (B) is correct.** With Jefferson's election and Republican control of Congress, the Federalist Party only controlled the judiciary because judges were appointed for life terms.

■ **9. (E) is correct.** *Marbury v. Madison* sets up the precedent for judicial review of laws.

■ **10. (B) is correct.** While the impeachment of Samuel Chase was politically motivated, the result demonstrated that the Judicial Branch was an independent partner in the government.

Free-Response Essay Sample Response

Compare and contrast the differences in American society of 1776 and 1812.

In 1776, you had a society that was reeling in its independence. The nation as a whole was European, especially British. Politically the distinction was revolutionary or loyalist.

In 1812, there was a great division in political circles and great fear of foreign invasion. The War of 1812 was underway. The United States experienced major victories but major setbacks as well. The nation was economically depressed due to embargo.

CHAPTER 9

Nation Building and Nationalism

A great surge of westward expansion and economic development, accompanied by soaring nationalist fervor, characterized the United States after the War of 1812.

Expansion and Migration

Before the abundant potential wealth of the **Mississippi Valley** could be realized, a dramatic westward surge of settlers had to be encouraged.

■ **John Quincy Adams** hammered out the **Transcontinental Treaty of 1819** with Spain, confirming the belief of most Americans in a continental destiny. Interest in the West grew as **John Jacob Astor** carried the fur trade to the Pacific Northwest, and the legends of **mountain men** were popularized.

■ **Settlers**, pushing the Indian tribes before them, surged westward into the trans-Appalachian West. Although tribes, such as the Cherokee and Seminole, tried to assimilate or resist by force, the federal government's policy of **Indian Removal** and a series of treaties with the Indians resulted in the Indians being stripped of their lands east of the Mississippi River. Most of the land originally passed through the hands of speculators, who purchased it at a feverish rate, to squatters who could eventually gain title through **preemption rights**. Many local marketing centers rapidly became cities.

■ **Family units** were the typical settler groups, and they carried the elements of their "civilized" eastern existence with them. Communal cooperation eventually accomplished most of the work that had previously required self-reliance. Attracted by more land to the west, many settlers pulled up stakes after only a few years.

■ **Political leaders** realized the importance of linking these distant citizens with the rest of the nation through a **viable transportation network**.

A Revolution in Transportation

The **National (or Cumberland) Road** was the first of the overland toll roads. Chartered by the states, these **turnpikes** failed to meet the need for cheap transportation over great distances.

■ **America's river network** proved to be the best system, and the Ohio-Mississippi system beckoned first the flatboat trade and, after **Robert Fulton's** invention in 1807, the **steamboat**.

■ **A system of canals** was needed to link the Great Lakes, the Ohio, and the Mississippi with the coastal states. **In 1825, the Erie Canal was finished**, signaling the birth of the "canal boom," which lasted until the late 1830s.

Emergence of a Market Economy

Increasing farm productivity promoted the transition from low-profit diversification farming to **high-profit staple farming in regional concentrations**. The availability of good farmland, increasing demand for cotton, the invention of the **cotton gin**, and **slave labor** made the South the world's greatest cotton producer.

▮ **The extension of credit** by local merchants and manufacturers was crucial—it insured profits, the expansion of capital, and the need for banking. This demand for money after the War of 1812 caused the number of state and private banks to proliferate.

▮ **The surge of a market economy** encouraged new industrial development. **The factory system** was first applied to textile manufacturing in New England. The development of **infant industries** before the 1840s, however, was less dramatic here than in some parts of Europe, and as late as 1840 only 8.8 percent of the nation's population was employed in factories.

The Politics of Nation Building After the War of 1812

Awakening nationalism provided the dominant theme (**the Era of Good Feelings**) for public policies after the War of 1812.

▮ **Henry Clay** called for an **American System** of protective tariffs and financed internal improvements. **A second Bank of the United States (1816)** was chartered to promote the nation's financial stability.

▮ **James Monroe** projected the image of a high-principled, disinterested statesman. Congress responded weakly to the **economic crisis of 1819**, and Monroe had no program of his own. He insisted that he was not responsible for the drastic economic downturn. He prized national harmony over economic prosperity.

▮ **A national calamity** was narrowly averted with the **Missouri Compromise (1820)**, which temporarily settled the question of slavery status in the newly created states of the West. Although Jefferson called the decision "a fire bell in the night," it seemed that for the moment, nationalism was triumphant.

▮ **The Supreme Court** made great contributions to nationalism and the expansive powers of the federal government. In such decisions as *McCulloch* v. *Maryland* and *Gibbons* v. *Ogden,* the Supreme Court supported economic nationalism at the expense of certain state powers. Under Marshall, the Court played a powerful role in supporting the growth of a prosperous nationwide, capitalist economy.

▮ **Recognizing the threat of a European Grand Alliance**, and concerned with the **collapsing Spanish empire** in Latin America, and with the possibility of **European re-colonization** in the Western Hemisphere, President Monroe and Secretary of State John Quincy Adams issued **the Monroe Doctrine (1823)**, which was delivered as a warning to European powers that the United States opposed further colonization and political interference in the Americas.

▮ **John Quincy Adams** was the supreme spokesman for nonpartisan and scientific achievement, but his leadership could not survive the growing sectional and economic divisions in the nation.

Multiple-Choice Questions

1. The Adams-Onis Treaty
   (A) excluded Spain from the North American continent.
   (B) reduced British influence in Florida.
   (C) granted the Northwest Territory to the United States.
   (D) weakened the Spanish position in Latin America.
   (E) made Florida a U.S. territory.

2. Between 1815 and 1824, the United States
   (A) grew rapidly in size and population.
   (B) was threatened by foreign invasion.
   (C) revised its form of government.
   (D) was unable to expand its economy.
   (E) invaded and occupied Canada.

3. The first great federal transportation project was the
   (A) building of the National Roads.
   (B) Lancaster Turnpike.
   (C) Erie Canal.
   (D) transcontinental railroad.
   (E) Union and Pacific Railroad.

4. The great canal building boom of the 1820s and 1830s ended
   (A) because of the limited useful lifespan of canals.
   (B) when canals proved to be an unprofitable means for transportation.
   (C) as a result of natural barriers to canals.
   (D) because of the lack of popular support for canals.
   (E) when environmentalists won legislation to stop canal projects.

5. The most important decision of the Marshall Court was
   (A) *Gibbons v. Ogden.*
   (B) *Dartmouth College v. Woodward.*
   (C) *McCullough v. Maryland.*
   (D) *Fletcher v. Peck.*
   (E) *Bakke v. California.*

6. The main diplomatic challenge facing James Monroe in 1820 was
   (A) the continuing threat of English intervention in the United States.
   (B) the development of trading rights with Latin America.
   (C) establishing friendly relations with France.
   (D) responding to the revolt of Spain's Latin American colonies.
   (E) the "Indian problem."

7. The Monroe Doctrine
   (A) was immediately accepted by European powers.
   (B) had little significance for the United States in 1823.
   (C) opposed the independence of Spain's Latin American colonies.
   (D) required too much money to enact.
   (E) made little impression on the European powers.

8. The development of profitable commercial farming resulted from
   (A) dramatic advances in agricultural technology.
   (B) an available supply of cheap labor.
   (C) the availability of good land and the revolution in marketing.
   (D) major increases in the prices paid for staple crops.
   (E) the population boom on the east coast, which created increased demand.

9. John Quincy Adams was the handpicked selection for President by President Monroe. What office did he hold in the Monroe Administration?
   (A) Vice President
   (B) Ambassador to France
   (C) Secretary of War
   (D) Secretary of State
   (E) Secretary of Treasury

10. The _____ were the Native
American tribe that attempted to assimilate
into American Society.
   (A) Cherokee   (D) Iroquois
   (B) Seminole   (E) Huron
   (C) Creek

Free-Response Question

> *Describe the evolution of American policies and actions toward Native Americans*
> *between 1816 and 1830.*

ANSWERS AND EXPLANATIONS

Multiple-Choice Questions

1. (E) is correct. The Adams-Onis Treaty formally granted Florida to the United States from Spain. In return, the United States would assume $5 million worth of claims of U.S. citizens against Spain.

2. (A) is correct. The population grew rapidly during this period because of natural birth rates due to better living conditions and the stability of the nation. However, the national population grew primarily because of the expansion of the national boundaries. In other words, adding new states and territories added population.

3. (A) is correct. The National Road system was the first true federal transportation project. It connected Cumberland, Maryland and Wheeling, Virginia. This in essence connected the Potomac and Ohio Rivers.

4. (B) is correct. The building of canals ended because of economic depression and dwindling state budgets. This showed that canals did not prove feasible for all areas.

5. (C) is correct. The decision of *McCulloch v. Maryland* on the surface was about taxes. However, this decision was important for two large Constitutional reasons. First, the decision was unanimous. The Supreme Court set forth the idea of "implied powers." The decision therefore upheld that a national bank was constitutional, and taxing a federal entity by a state was not.

6. (D) is correct. During the Napoleonic Rule of Spain, much of its Latin American holdings were largely ignored by Spain. This started uprisings that lead to revolt. Monroe therefore had to deal with whether or not to recognize them as an independent republic. Officially, Monroe's administration was neutral.

7. (E) is correct. The Monroe Doctrine was a very brazen move by a fledgling democracy. The more established European powers were unimpressed. In fact, had it not been for England agreeing to abide by it the doctrine would have been ignored by the rest of Europe.

8. (C) is correct. The rise of commercial agriculture in this country was due to the ever-expansive country and the abundant amount of land. Additionally, technological advances caused the boom in commercial agriculture.

9. (D) is correct. John Q. Adams was the Secretary of State. In this capacity, Adams was uniquely poised to learn the office. He helped to formulate foreign policy. He was also responsible for the push to have standard weights and measures.

10. (A) is correct. The Cherokee adopted white institutions such as a republican type of government, agriculture and slavery, and a written language. The primary motivation behind this was to try and prevent encroachment on and removal from their lands.

Free-Response Essay Sample Response

Describe the evolution of American policies and actions toward Native Americans between 1816 and 1830.

The Native American tribes were forced through broken promises, broken treaties and by force to leave their native land. As the era 1816 to 1830 progressed the Americans became more violent towards Native Americans. The idea was to push the Natives to reservations far away.

Native Americans were often forced out at the discovery by white settlers of something valuable on their land. This is especially true in the South. Even though the tribes were "civilized," they were considered a nuisance to the states.

CHAPTER 10

The Triumph of White Men's Democracy

The 1820s and 1830s witnessed the rise of popular democracy and a swelling of national political involvement. European visitors were amazed at the equalizing tendencies that were exposed in everything from hotels to the legal and clerical professions.

Democracy in Theory and Practice

The nation's founders had believed that "democracy" contained dangerous impulses, but by the 1820s and '30s the term had become more acceptable and applicable to American institutions. **Alexis de Tocqueville** noticed the decline of deference and the elevation of popular sovereignty in America. "Self-made" men could now rise in stature.

- **Social equality** became the dominant principle of the age. Special privilege and family connections could no longer be counted on to guarantee success. **Industrialization**, however, perpetuated inequality, not in the traditional sense of birth or privilege, but rather in terms of wealth and attainment.

- **Romanticism in American literature** often appealed to the feelings and intuitions of ordinary people. A mass reading audience developed, and poets, writers, and artists directed their work to a democratic populace. **American artists** (although striving to elevate popular tastes) were encouraged to contribute to the general welfare by supporting virtue and middle-class sentiments.

- **Property requirements** for **manhood suffrage** had been eliminated by 1820, and as public political involvement swelled, **a permanent two-party system** became a forum for political ideas. It became understood that a **loyal opposition** was essential to democratic government.

- Loans extended freely by the Bank of the United States were recalled suddenly, which played a role in the **Panic of 1819**.

- **Economic questions** (prompted by the Panic of 1819) and the role of the federal government were major concerns that assisted a great swelling of popular political interest.

- **Workingmen's parties and trade unions** emerged as workers became convinced that the government should protect the rights of labor as well as those of the producers.

- **Abolitionists** sought an end to slavery and supported the civil rights of free African Americans and women.

Jackson and the Politics of Democracy

Andrew Jackson symbolized the triumph of democracy and egalitarianism from the 1820s to the 1840s.

- **Popular hero Andrew Jackson**, a "common man," rose to prominence as a result of "popular sovereignty." **Despite winning a plurality of popular votes**, Jackson was denied the presidency in **1824** by the House of Representatives, in favor of Adams. Rumors of a **corrupt bargain** between Adams and Henry Clay and controversy over tariff policy (**the tariff of abominations**) damaged Adams' administration.

- **Supported by the new Democratic party**, Jackson returned to defeat Adams convincingly in **1828** in an election that featured a massive popular turnout. Possessed of indomitable will, Jackson became one of the most forceful presidents in history. He endorsed the **spoils system** as a way to provide himself with loyal advisors.

- **Beginning in 1830**, Jackson ordered the swift and forceful **removal of all Indian tribes** to reservations located west of the Mississippi River. Jackson ignored humanitarian and practical protests. In 1832, he joined Georgia's defiance of the Supreme Court's decision in *Worcester* v. *Georgia* that denied the right of a state to extend its jurisdiction over tribal lands. By **1838**, the last of the southeastern tribes, **the Cherokee**, were forced to abandon ancestral grounds and embark on the **"Trail of Tears."**

- **Jackson** regarded **nullification (the right of a state to set aside federal laws)** as a major threat to federal authority. After **South Carolina nullified the Tariff Acts of 1828 and 1832** in defiance of federal authority, Jackson threatened forceful intervention to bring the nullification crisis to an end. Appeased by the protests of lower tariffs, South Carolina suspended its nullification ordinance in **1833**.

The Bank War and the Second Party System

Jackson's successful attack on the **Bank of the United States** aroused great controversy and called into question the president's power over the nation's finances.

- **Nicholas Biddle**, president of the Bank of the United States, sought rechartering in **1832**, and Jackson promptly declared war on this "monster" corporation, which he was convinced violated the fundamental principles of a democratic society.

- **Jackson's response** to an early recharter bill through Congress included **vetoing** the bill and calling on the people for support. Jackson's overwhelming victory in the **1832 election** was considered to be a mandate for the Bank's destruction.

- **Jackson** ordered that federal deposits in the Bank be removed and deposited in selected **"pet banks."** Strong opposition to Jackson's fiscal policy developed in Congress as fear spread that the destruction of the Bank would be disastrous for the nation's economy.

- **The Whigs** emerged in Jackson's second term. Led by **Henry Clay and Daniel Webster**, the Whigs **opposed the growth of presidential power** and prerogative under "King Andrew." When over-speculation and currency devaluation staggered the country's economy, Jackson ordered the **specie circular**, as economic depression set in.

■ **Martin Van Buren**, with Jackson's endorsement, gained the presidency in **1836**. Van Buren attempted to improve the faltering economy with his creation of an **independent sub-treasury**, but the persistent depression was beyond the control of governmental policies. The state of the economy cost Van Buren reelection in **1840** to the Whig candidate **William Henry Harrison**.

Heyday of the Second Party System

Promoting the idea of the **"positive liberal state,"** the Whigs challenged the Democrats on equal terms in the 1840s. The Whigs called for a government that was active and responsive in economic affairs. Although they supported a market economy, the Whigs wanted to restrain disorder and selfish individualism by calling on the government to enforce high moral standards and community values. The Democrats appealed to small farmers, workers, rising capitalists, immigrants, and Catholics with their support for individualism and personal liberty.

Multiple-Choice Questions

1. The nullification controversy occurred in the state of
   (A) Pennsylvania.
   (B) Georgia.
   (C) New York.
   (D) South Carolina.
   (E) New Jersey.

2. _____ came to symbolize the triumph of democracy.
   (A) Henry Clay
   (B) John C. Calhoun
   (C) Daniel Webster
   (D) Martin Van Buren
   (E) Andrew Jackson

3. _____ denied states the right to take Native American tribal lands.
   (A) *McCulloch v. Maryland*
   (B) Southern legislatures
   (C) *Worcester v. Georgia*
   (D) *Fletcher v. Peck*
   (E) *Wallace v. Tennessee*

4. Andrew Jackson killed the national bank
   (A) by withdrawing federal deposits from it.
   (B) through further legislation.
   (C) through the actions of the Supreme Court.
   (D) by letting it expire in 1836.

   (E) by accusing Nicholas Biddle of treasonous acts.

5. From Jackson's response to the nullification crisis, one can conclude that he
   (A) was a strong supporter of states' rights.
   (B) believed in the limited use of federal power but also that states were not truly sovereign.
   (C) supported the unlimited use of federal power.
   (D) supported higher tariffs.
   (E) supported lower tariffs.

6. Andrew Jackson's attitude toward Native Americans was that
   (A) they should be removed to areas beyond white expansion.
   (B) they should be allowed to remain on their tribal lands.
   (C) they should be assimilated into white society.
   (D) they should be treated as equals to the white man.
   (E) they should be exterminated.

7. John Quincy Adams' victory in 1824 was aided by
   (A) Martin Van Buren.
   (B) John C. Calhoun.

(C) Henry Clay.

(D) William Crawford.

(E) Nicholas Biddle.

8. The most obvious indicator of the supremacy of democracy in the United States was
   (A) the high percentages of people who voted.
   (B) the widespread use of the "spoils system."
   (C) the absence of any kind of social or economic classes.
   (D) the development of universal manhood suffrage.
   (E) the increase in the number of appointed officials.

9. The "Trail of Tears" refers to
   (A) the destruction of the national bank.
   (B) the forced relocation of the Cherokees to Oklahoma.
   (C) passage of the tariff of abominations.
   (D) the nullification controversy.
   (E) the Oregon Trail and westward expansion.

10. Between 1824 and 1840, voter participation in elections
    (A) changed little.
    (B) increased dramatically.
    (C) increased slightly.
    (D) declined somewhat.
    (E) declined precipitously.

Free-Response Question

> *Illustrate why the 1830s should be referred to as "the Age of Democracy."*

ANSWERS AND EXPLANATIONS

Multiple-Choice Questions

▌ **1. (D) is correct.** The nullification crisis was pushed by Vice President Calhoun. The idea of nullification was that any state could nullify any federal act or law that it disagreed with.

▌ **2. (E) is correct.** Andrew Jackson's election was viewed as the success of democracy. Jackson's election started with his loss in 1824 to Adams. Jackson started a "grassroots" campaign. He had a committee in every county and city of significance in every state by the time of the election of 1828.

▌ **3. (C) is correct.** *Worchester* was a hollow victory. Although it was a victory for the Native Americans, it was largely ignored by the states. This behavior was encouraged by President Jackson himself.

▌ **4. (A) is correct.** Jackson vowed that the bank had nearly killed him. He would in turn kill the bank by withholding deposits.

▌ **5. (B) is correct.** Jackson did not want to have full federal sovereignty nor did he believe the states were above the federal government.

▌ **6. (A) is correct.** Jacksonian policies were clear. He successfully pushed the Natives beyond the boundaries onto the reservations beyond the majority of settlements.

▌ **7. (C) is correct.** The Election of 1824 was thrown into the House of Representatives. Adams was elected after one of his competitors in the General Election, Henry Clay, threw his support behind Adams. There was controversy over this action as Adams then appointed Clay as his Secretary of State.

■ **8. (D) is correct.** As the democracy that is the United States has developed, so too has the development of universal manhood suffrage. The longer this idea has developed the more participatory the democracy has become.

■ **9. (B) is correct.** The "Trail of Tears" was the forced movement from the areas of Georgia and Tennessee to the reservation in Oklahoma. This push was accelerated after gold was discovered on the Cherokee's lands.

■ **10. (B) is correct.** The population grew during this period. The idea of Universal Manhood Suffrage changed to include more of the middle and eventually lower classes. Once the voting privileges were earned, they were used.

Free-Response Essay Sample Response

Illustrate why the 1830s should be referred to as "the Age of Democracy."

The 1830s was the era of Jacksonian Democracy. The people's choice had been elected to the Presidency in Andrew Jackson. He had not been born of an aristocratic family, nor had he been a Washington insider.

The decade also brought more voting rights to more citizens. This in turn meant more people voting in elections. Many historians believe that this is what the Founding Fathers intended for the Republic.

CHAPTER 11

Slaves and Masters

In the South in the first half of the nineteenth century, an elite group of whites dominated the society and made profits on the labor of slaves of African origin, who nonetheless were able to develop a rich culture of their own.

The Divided Society of the Old South

The Old South was a deeply divided society; a society divided by race and economic class. It was held together by a common economy and culture.

The World of Southern Blacks

Slaves, struggling against tremendous odds, managed to create a full, rich culture.

▍ **Slaves' lives** varied according to the region in which they lived and the type of plantation on which they worked. They constituted over half of the human population in the **Cotton Belt** of the lower South. Many were used in agricultural production, but a smaller minority performed a wide range of domestic chores.

▍ **Strong and complicated family ties** supported the individual slaves, as well as their children, when facing an essentially hostile white culture. Families were not always based on blood relations. Circumstance helped form kinship groups.

▍ **Distinctive religions** were formed by the slaves, which became a foundation of their unique culture. The **African Methodist Episcopal Church** was very successful and was a cornerstone of the free Black community.

▍ **Although slave resistance** in the form of violence (**Vesey Conspiracy, 1822**) and escape (**the Underground Railroad**) were not often successful strategies, African-American slaves **resisted passively** or by **sabotage**, and thus maintained their self-respect.

▍ **Free blacks** numbered more than 500,000 in the North and the South combined, more than ten percent of the black population. They faced many **legal restrictions**, and generally sympathized with the slaves.

White Society in the Antebellum South

Plantation culture was clearly dominated by an elite class of slave-holding planters.

▍ **Despite popular portrayals** of the South filled with majestic plantations, most southern families owned no slaves, and only a very small minority owned more than fifty slaves. Few **planters** were men of leisure.

▍ **Hardworking businesspeople**, the planters treated their slaves in a **paternalistic** manner consistent with a desire to maximize profits. The basis for white authority was the use of fear. Below this elite, several classes of whites scratched out a living, some with but most without the aid of slaves. Often isolation and the lack of transportation limited economic opportunity.

- **Small slaveholders** (twenty or fewer slaves) constituted 88 percent of all slaveholders in the 1860s.
- **Yeoman farmers** owned the land that they worked themselves and were often ambitious young men seeking the capital to become large-scale landowners.
- As tobacco farming became less important, the states of Virginia, Maryland, and Kentucky raised other crops and began infant industries.
- **The elites**, threatened by the slightest challenge to slavery, increasingly used any means to end discussion or debate on the subject. Numerous arguments were used to justify the institution of slavery.

Slavery and the Southern Economy

The staple crop **cotton** and the labor of slaves dominated the economy of the **lower South** prior to the Civil War. During this time, however, the **upper South** sold slaves and diversified their agriculture. As tobacco farming became less important, the states of **Virginia, Maryland, and Kentucky** raised other crops and began infant industries.

- **The invention of the cotton gin** and the introduction of **"short-staple" cotton** to the lower South made cotton the single most important export and the most profitable business in the United States. The amount of cotton that was grown in the Deep South grew dramatically between 1817 and 1860.
- **Although many Southerners** considered methods to diversify and industrialize their region, most investment dollars went into cotton. The **dependence on slavery and cotton** impeded industrialization in the South.
- **The cotton/slavery system** profited the planter directly, but it probably limited the South's development.

Multiple-Choice Questions

1. Slavery's hold on the South was strengthened by the increasing importance of
   - (A) rice.
   - (B) indigo.
   - (C) long-staple cotton.
   - (D) sugar cane.
   - (E) short-staple cotton.

2. During the nineteenth century, the center of cotton production
   - (A) remained in the Southeast.
   - (B) moved northward.
   - (C) stabilized in Alabama and Mississippi.
   - (D) shifted rapidly westward.
   - (E) was in Georgia.

3. A leading advocate of the need for southern self-sufficiency was
   - (A) Stephen Douglas.
   - (B) Daniel Webster.
   - (C) Robert Fogel.
   - (D) J. D. B. DeBow.
   - (E) William Gregg.

4. At the time of the Civil War,
   - (A) one quarter of white southerners owned slaves.
   - (B) almost all southerners owned at least one slave.
   - (C) only the upper class were slave owners.
   - (D) the percentage of whites owning slaves was increasing.
   - (E) 30 percent of white southerners owned slaves.

5. The yeoman farmer of the South was
   (A) a slave owner.
   (B) shiftless.
   (C) proud and self-reliant.
   (D) much different from his northern counterpart.
   (E) a squatter on unproductive land.

6. Southern proslavery arguments did NOT include the belief that slavery was
   (A) the natural status for blacks.
   (B) sanctioned by the Bible.
   (C) mandated by the United States Constitution.
   (D) consistent with the humanitarian spirit.
   (E) eventually going to become unnecessary.

7. Southern apologists claimed the master-slave relationship was more humane than employer-worker relationships because
   (A) it offered more opportunities for job training.
   (B) it afforded greater long-term security.
   (C) slaves were not exploited as badly as free laborers.
   (D) it was actually a freer relationship.
   (E) it included women in the work force.

8. The conspiracy for slave rebellion uncovered in South Carolina in 1822 was led by
   (A) Denmark Vesey.
   (B) Nat Turner.
   (C) Gabriel Prosser.
   (D) Frederick Douglass.
   (E) George Fitzhugh.

9. The foundation of the African American culture was
   (A) a shared language.
   (B) political activity.
   (C) art.
   (D) music.
   (E) religion.

10. Free African Americans in the South were
    (A) unsympathetic to the plight of slaves.
    (B) actively involved in helping fugitive slaves.
    (C) prohibited from helping slaves.
    (D) passive to the plight of slaves.
    (E) often persuaded to preserve the status quo.

Free-Response Question

How did the South's reliance on a slave labor system restrict its ability to diversify its economy?

ANSWERS AND EXPLANATIONS

Multiple-Choice Questions

▌ **1. (E) is correct.** The demand for cotton and the fact that cotton production was a year-round crop strengthened the stranglehold on the dependence of slave labor.

▌ **2. (D) is correct.** The growing of short-staple cotton required more space and more frost-free days, which were available in the West.

▌ **3. (D) is correct.** De Bow, in his review, called for the South to develop its own industry, commerce and shipping. De Bow believed the South needed slavery to accomplish this. He was pro-slavery.

▌ **4. (A) is correct.** Even in the Cotton Belt, 40 percent of whites were slave owners. Twenty percent of Southern whites owned more than twenty slaves.

▌ **5. (C) is correct.** The yeoman farmers were just below the small slaveholder in the hierarchy of the South. They were proud and self-reliant. They often lived in the "back-country" of each state.

- **6. (C) is correct.** Answers A, B, D and E are correct. There was never a discussion in the South that the U.S. Constitution mandated it. More often they understood the delicate balance of writing the Constitution and avoiding the issue altogether.
- **7. (B) is correct.** The idea of security was proposed by George Fitzhugh. He claimed that slaves actually have more security against unemployment and poverty. Additionally, they do not have to worry about care in old age, class conflicts, or ample necessities of life.
- **8. (A) is correct.** Denmark Vessey was a freed black in Charleston, South Carolina. He planned to seize local armories, then arm local slaves and seize the city.
- **9. (E) is correct.** Much of the religion for African Americans in the South was an extension of the African culture. It manifested itself through songs, sermons and scriptures.
- **10. (B) is correct.** Although they were always suspect and under observation by southern whites, free African Americans in the South were involved in the movement to help fugitive slaves.

Free-Response Essay Sample Response

How did the South's reliance on a slave labor system restrict its ability to diversify its economy?

The South's reliance on slavery actually restricted the economy. The economy never developed an effective reason to grow under the slavery system. Although De Bow may have favored slavery, his rationale for developing industry, shipping and commerce would have grown the economy. Unfortunately, his ideas fell on the deaf years of successful plantation owners.

CHAPTER 12

The Pursuit of Perfection

Social and economic upheaval in the early nineteenth century resulted in religious fervor, moral reform, and sometimes confusion.

The Rise of Evangelicalism

During the early nineteenth century, turmoil was common for American Protestantism. **Revivals** were effective tools to increase membership and extend religious values.

- **Beginning on the southern frontier**, a revival movement known as the **Second Great Awakening** provided an emotional outlet, a right of passage, and social cohesion. Camp meetings became a regular feature of religious life in the South and the lower Midwest.
- **Baptists** licensed uneducated farmers to preach to their neighbors.
- **Methodists** sent out circuit riders to preach the gospels.
- **In both New England and upstate New York**, other evangelical revivals (usually Congregationalists or Presbyterians) spread doctrines emphasizing free choice and free will.
- **The evangelical revivals of the North** often spawned middle-class reform movements, such as the **temperance movement**, which emphasized self-improvement, and the **Unitarians** who took religious rationalism to the point of denying the possibility of the Holy Trinity.

Domesticity and Changes in the American Family

Increasingly, reformers celebrated the family, and especially the mother, as important to society.

- **Love** became important in choosing a marital partner.
- **Women** also gained some measure of power, especially in their sphere, the home **(the cult of domesticity)**. This glorification of the role of the wife/mother was referred to as the **"cult of true womanhood."** Middleclass women in particular gained from this concept.
- **Lower birthrates and smaller families** led parents to place more emphasis on affectionate child rearing rather than just treating children as "small adults." Corporal punishment declined.
- **Birth control** began to be widely practiced.

Institutional Reform

Responsibility for the reform of the individual eventually spread from the family to the larger community and society's important institutions.

- **Public education** developed, especially in the North, under the leadership of reformers such as **Horace Mann.** Tax money was used to finance new schools under newly appointed boards of education, supplementing the informal education that was common in most towns and cities.
- **The classical three R's of education** (reading, 'riting, and 'rithmetic) was augmented by the teaching of the **Protestant ethics** of industry, punctuality, sobriety, and frugality.
- **Reformers worked for rehabilitation** of those who were judged insane, criminal, or hopelessly impoverished by placing them in **asylums**, hospitals, penitentiaries, or poorhouses to isolate them from the larger community. **Dorothea Dix** worked to raise the level of care for these inmates of society.

Reform Turns Radical

Some of the reformers insisted on reforms so extreme that many considered them radical, such as **William Lloyd Garrison** and his publication, *The Liberator*.

- **Arguments** between the adherents of moderate reform and those supporting quicker change split many organizations, especially in the antislavery (abolition) movement.
- **The abolitionist movement**, growing out of the evangelical reform movement, succeeded—especially in the small- and medium-sized towns in the North. It faced considerable opposition, especially near and below the Mason-Dixon Line, and there was widespread disagreement within the abolitionist movement itself.
- **Black abolitionists** from the North were crucial for the movement's success. **Fredrick Douglass, Charles Remond, William Wells Brown, Robert Purvis, Sojourner Truth and Frances Harper** all played significant roles.
- **Women**, such as Elizabeth Caty Stanton, served in the abolitionist movement and consequently began to work for their own liberation, and organized the first gathering for women's rights in the United States at **Seneca Falls in 1848**.
- **Some Americans** in the early to mid-nineteenth century sought a **perfect social order** and formed **utopian socialist communities** such as those promoted by **Robert Owen** and **Charles Fourier**, or within the **Oneida** community. **Transcendentalism** was promoted by others such as **Ralph Waldo Emerson**.

Multiple-Choice Questions

1. The approach viewed by many American religious leaders as the best way to extend religious values was called
   - (A) orthodoxy.
   - (B) secularism.
   - (C) revivalism.
   - (D) spiritualism.
   - (E) "spreading the Gospel."

2. The Second Great Awakening began
   - (A) in the Congregationalist churches of New England.
   - (B) along the Ohio River.
   - (C) among dissenters in the cities.
   - (D) as a result of the activities of English missionaries.
   - (E) on the southern frontier.

3. The reform movement in New England began as
   - (A) an effort to defend Calvinism against Enlightenment ideas.
   - (B) an attempt to maintain the status quo in religion.

(C) a result of the actions of social radicals in religion.

(D) an outgrowth of Deism.

(E) a rejection of Catholicism.

4. The reform movement did NOT inspire
   (A) the establishment of missionary societies.
   (B) the publication of religious tracts.
   (C) dramatic changes in Protestant theology.
   (D) the founding of moral reform societies.
   (E) aid for the redemption of "abandoned women."

5. As a reform effort, the temperance movement
   (A) was only moderately successful.
   (B) was directed at a serious social problem.
   (C) had little impact outside religious circles.
   (D) emphasized religion more than social concerns.
   (E) was enormously popular.

6. An important change in the American family in the nineteenth century was
   (A) the growing significance of mutual affection in marriage.
   (B) the increase in the size of the family.
   (C) the decreased importance of the extended family.
   (D) the loss of some legal rights by men.
   (E) the emergence of women as heads of households.

7. Which one of the following individuals was NOT a prominent preacher of the Second

Great Awakening?
   (A) Charles Finney
   (B) Theodore Dwight
   (C) Lyman Beecher
   (D) Henry David Thoreau
   (E) Nathaniel Taylor

8. In practice, working-class families viewed the new public school
   (A) as a welcomed learning opportunity for themselves and their children.
   (B) as essential to the improvement of their economic situation.
   (C) indifferently.
   (D) as an indication of the helpful concern of the upper classes.
   (E) as depriving them of needed wage earners.

9. In theory, prisons and asylums
   (A) were intended for rehabilitation.
   (B) were to substitute for the family.
   (C) were simply to confine the disorderly.
   (D) should focus on "breaking down the ego."
   (E) were designed for punishment.

10. Abolitionism received its greatest support in the
   (A) border states.
   (B) frontier territories.
   (C) large cities.
   (D) small- to medium-sized towns of the upper North.
   (E) northern state legislatures.

Free-Response Question

Discuss how the American social reform movement evolved out of the Second Great Awakening.

ANSWERS AND EXPLANATIONS

Multiple-Choice Questions

■ **1. (C) is correct.** Revivalism is credited for bringing about the Second Great Awakening. The revivalists used the same ideas to push up the number of followers.

■ **2. (E) is correct.** The Second Great Awakening began in Kentucky in 1801.

▌ **3. (A) is correct.** Reverend Timothy Dwight, President of Yale College, was disturbed by youth followings of the Deist ideals. He started several campus revivals to combat the tide.

▌ **4. (C) is correct.** The idea of original sin and predestination were counter to the appeal presented by the republic with its freedom and progress.

▌ **5. (B) is correct.** Due to the fact that in many areas alcohol was more readily available and cheaper than milk, and safer than water, many evangelicals formed the Temperance League. They viewed drink as a great societal problem because males were seen as losing self-control.

▌ **6. (A) is correct.** Mid-nineteenth century parents had less control over children's marriage plans. Romantic novels had started to popularize the idea of love in marriage.

▌ **7. (D) is correct.** Thoreau was a novelist of the era. The others were all preachers in the Second Great Awakening.

▌ **8. (E) is correct.** Initially, working-class families did see education as a deprivation of wage earners. As time went on that attitude changed, and many saw it as a way to improve conditions.

▌ **9. (B) is correct.** The institutions were viewed as a substitute for the family. Custodians were meant to act as parents, providing moral advice and training.

▌ **10. (D) is correct.** The small- to medium-sized cities of the North were probably most open to the abolition movement because of the citizens and their heritage. They typically came from cultures that did drink so it was easy for the women to be interested in the movement.

Free-Response Essay Sample Response

Discuss how the American social reform movement evolved out of the Second Great Awakening.

The Great Second Awakening led itself to other social reforms in the area of education, health care, mental health and prisons. The Awakening provided the fuel for average middle-class citizens to help control the destiny of the nation.

CHAPTER 13

An Age of Expansionism

A popular mood known as **"Young America"** emerged in the 1840s. Its adherents brashly promoted **territorial and economic expansion** and development of the United States, but displayed little concern or awareness of the practical consequences of such actions.

Movement to the Far West

In the 1830s and 1840s, Americans moved to the **Far West** all the way to the Pacific Ocean. Some went for economic reasons, while others went for the adventure or to avoid religious persecution.

▍ **Beginning in the 1820s**, American traders and settlers were lured west of the American borders, attracted by adventure, the prospect of financial gain and, for the **Mormons**, religious freedom. A potential American thrust toward Canada was diverted with the settlement of Anglo-American differences in the **Webster-Ashburton Treaty of 1842**.

▍ **An influx of Americans** into Mexican-owned **Texas** during the 1820s produced cultural, economic, and political conflict, resulting in Mexican restrictions on Anglo immigration and slaveholding. A revolution by the Texans followed in 1835–1836.

▍ **Remembering defeats** inflicted by the Mexicans at the **Alamo and Goliad**, Texans rallied for a major victory at **San Jacinto**, capturing **Santa Anna** and forcing his recognition of Texas independence. **General Sam Houston** became the first president of the **"Lone Star Republic,"** a separate nation until 1845.

▍ **Opened in 1821, the Santa Fe Trail** introduced Americans to the riches **of New Mexico**. In the 1840s, more than five thousand Americans traveled the famous **Oregon Trail** to that territory in the Northwest. Quickly outnumbering British residents, Americans demanded an end to the joint occupation of **Oregon** with Britain that had first been arranged in 1818 and indefinitely extended in 1827.

▍ **The Mormons**, seeking relief from public hostility to their unorthodox beliefs and practices, moved from New York to Ohio to Missouri to Illinois, where leader and founder **Joseph Smith** was attacked and killed by an angry mob. Smith's successor, **Brigham Young**, led a group of Mormons into Mexican-owned **Utah** in 1847, establishing an effective community based on discipline and cooperation.

Manifest Destiny and the Mexican War

Many in the United States thought that God had ordained that they occupy as much territory as they could, causing conflicts with the states to the north and south of the young country.

- **Tyler and Texas...** Hoping for a popular issue to revive his sagging political fortunes, **President John Tyler** promoted **the annexation of Texas** by treaty in 1844. The Senate rejected the document, however, when **Secretary of State John Calhoun** linked Texas too closely to the interests of the South and slavery.

- **The Triumph of Polk and Annexation...** In 1844, Americans had the rare opportunity to draw a rather clear-cut distinction between the platforms of presidential candidates. In contrast to the **anti-expansionist Whig candidate Henry Clay**, Democrats in **1844** nominated dark horse **James K. Polk**, an aggressive spokesman for the annexation of Texas and sole American occupation of Oregon. Ironically, the antislavery **Liberty party** candidate drew just enough votes away from Clay to throw the election to Polk. The "mandate" for expansion resulted in a joint resolution by Congress annexing Texas.

- **Journalist John L. O'Sullivan** coined the phrase **"manifest destiny"** to signify the growing feeling among Americans in the **1840s** that God intended them to extend their ideals of republican government and economic opportunities to the unsettled as well as "under-settled" portions of the continent.

- **British rejection** of an American proposal to divide Oregon provoked cries of **"Fifty-four forty or fight"** among Americans who demanded all of the territory. Cooler heads prevailed, however, and Polk negotiated **a treaty with Britain in 1846 dividing Oregon** along the 49th parallel, giving the valuable **Puget Sound** to the United States, while allowing Britain to retain **Vancouver Island**.

- **Mexico's refusal** to accept Texan (and American) claims to a **Rio Grande boundary** as well as refusal to sell additional lands led the United States to declare **war in May 1846**. American forces scored a succession of military victories under **Zachary Taylor** in northern Mexico, **Stephen Kearney** in New Mexico, **John C. Frémont** in California, and **Winfield Scott** in the decisive campaign to capture the capital of **Mexico City**.

- **Eschewing annexation of all Mexico**, American diplomat **Nicholas P. Trist** negotiated a successful end to the **Mexican War** with the **Treaty of Guadalupe Hidalgo (February 1848)**. The treaty provided for the Mexican **cession of New Mexico and California** to the United States for $15 million, recognition of the Rio Grande border, and the assumption by the United States government of American claims against Mexico.

Internal Expansionism

New technologies, such as the **telegraph and the railroad**, aided internal expansion.

- **The Triumph of the Railroad...** In the 1840s and the 1850s, **railroads replaced canals** as the means for hauling America's freight traffic. Expansion of the railroads stimulated the domestic iron industry and encouraged modern methods for financing business enterprise.

- **Technological advances**, especially the development of sophisticated **machine tools**, helped bring about mass production techniques in American industry and agriculture. The **factory mode** of production, first used in the **textile** industry, expanded to industries producing iron, shoes, firearms, clocks, and sewing machines.

■ **Immigration…** The growth of industrial work opportunities in the United States, combined with economic hardships in many parts of Europe, sparked a period of mass immigration, especially from **Ireland and Germany**. The Irish, mostly Catholic, poor, and unskilled, crowded into urban slums and accepted low-paying factory jobs, evoking scorn from those Americans whose descendants had earlier established themselves in the country.

■ **Considering wage labor a temporary condition**, most workers resisted appeals for organization along class lines or workers' strikes. The new **working class** "protested" long hours and low pay, however, in more subtle and indirect ways—by tardiness, absenteeism, and drunkenness. An age of expansionism had extracted a price. **External (territorial) expansion** generated sectional conflict and **internal (economic) expansion** fueled class and ethnic rivalries.

Multiple-Choice Questions

1. Which of the following was NOT a characteristic of the Young America movement?
   (A) a weak foreign policy
   (B) territorial policy
   (C) economic expansion and growth
   (D) technological progress
   (E) a celebration of American virtue

2. The American population moved westward in the 1830s and 1840s for all of the following reasons EXCEPT
   (A) fertile land
   (B) economic opportunity
   (C) religious freedom
   (D) loyalty to Mexico and Great Britain
   (E) a sense of adventure

3. The most plausible reason for the Texas Revolution was
   (A) the harsh oppression of the Catholic Church.
   (B) the discovery of fertile cottonlands in east Texas.
   (C) the unwillingness of Anglo-Americans to accept Mexican rule.
   (D) the Texans' desire to create an independent nation.
   (E) the inability of Texans to settle their land disputes.

4. Manifest Destiny was based, in part, on
   (A) the belief that God was on the side of American expansionism.
   (B) the political needs of the Democratic party.
   (C) the desire for new territory for slavery.
   (D) the desire to drive Spain out of North America.
   (E) simple greed.

5. The Treaty of Guadalupe Hidalgo
   (A) provided the United States with all the territory conquered from Mexico.
   (B) led to political harmony between the Whigs and the Democrats.
   (C) allowed the United States access to trade with Asian nations.
   (D) provided the opportunity for additional expansion by the United States.
   (E) was never ratified.

6. For the American economy, railroads
   (A) had little effect.
   (B) affected only those segments related to transportation.
   (C) had an enormous effect.
   (D) were a boom only for agricultural interests.
   (E) took a few years to become an important component.

7. Between the 1830s and 1840s, most of the immigrants to the United States came from
   (A) the Far East.
   (B) Western Europe.
   (C) Eastern Europe.

(D) Latin America.

(E) China.

8. In _____, Herman Melville produced a novel, original in form and conception, to fulfill the demand of Young Americans for a New Literature.

(A) *Tristram Shandy*

(B) *Ulysses*

(C) *The Scarlet Letter*

(D) *Uncle Tom's Cabin*

(E) *Moby Dick*

9. The inventor of the mechanical reaper was

(A) John Deere.

(B) Robert Lowell.

(C) Charles Goodyear.

(D) Henry Bessemer.

(E) Cyrus McCormick.

10. The leader of the Mormon trek to Utah was

(A) Moses Austin.

(B) Brigham Young.

(C) Joseph Smith.

(D) John C. Fremont.

(E) Josiah Deseret.

Free-Response Question

Compare the United States' foreign policy toward Mexico and Great Britain in the 1830s and 1840s. To what do you account the similarities and differences in America's actions toward these countries?

ANSWERS AND EXPLANATIONS

Multiple-Choice Questions

▌ **1. (A) is correct.** Young Americans were for a strong everything. This movement was in favor of pushing the nation forward in the 1850s.

▌ **2. (D) is correct.** Answers A, B, C and E are all reasons for moving westward. Loyalty to Mexico and Great Britain prevented westward expansion. These ideas were central in the idea of Manifest Destiny.

▌ **3. (C) is correct.** Issues involved conversion to Catholicism, slavery and Mexican citizenship. In the end it boiled down to Anglo-Americans being ruled by Mexicans.

▌ **4. (A) is correct.** The idea of Manifest Destiny tied several movements together including Young America. However, at its heart was the idea America was blessed and would expand to all of North America.

▌ **5. (D) is correct.** The United States gained 500,000 square miles of territory because of the Treaty of Guadalupe Hidago. It also formalized the Mexican-American border along the Rio Grande River.

▌ **6. (C) is correct.** The railroads had an enormous effect on the economy as a whole. It spurred the creation of the domestic iron industry and also was responsible for closing the canal industry.

▌ **7. (B) is correct.** In this period, most immigrants came from the British Isles and Germany. It is estimated that 700,000 people immigrated.

▌ **8. (E) is correct.** Melville wrote a piece of literature to fulfill those demands. Melville was, however, a deep thinker and his characters were deeper than just what appeared on the surface.

■ **9. (E) is correct.** McCormick's invention mechanized the harvesting of grain. The reaper was a tremendous labor saver.

■ **10. (B) is correct.** Brigham Young succeeded Joseph Smith after Smith was killed. Young sent an exploration party to study the possibility of moving to the Great Salt Lake. Then he led a group of twelve thousand west towards the Great Salt Lake.

Free-Response Essay Sample Response

Compare the United States' foreign policy toward Mexico and Great Britain in the 1830s and 1840s. To what do you account the similarities and differences in America's actions toward these countries?

The Young America movement coupled with the idea of Manifest Destiny shaped U.S. Foreign Policy. These ideas pit both English and Mexican holdings in North America at odds with American policy.

The similarities and differences were really a matter of timing. The United States was at a maturation point in the nation's development. America wanted territory from both England and Mexico. They were treated differently because they were of different ancestry.

CHAPTER 14

The Sectional Crisis

After giving a fiery speech condemning the South over slavery, **Senator Charles Sumner of Massachusetts** was severely beaten with a cane by **Representative Preston Brooks of South Carolina.** This incidence demonstrated the growing sectional conflict of the 1850s and foreshadowed the violence on the battlefield between armies of the North and the South.

The Compromise of 1850

Conflict over slavery escalated in the 1840s, and by the end of the decade, it was at a crisis point. Compromise was still possible, though fragile coalitions held the country together.

▍ **The Constitution** gave the federal government the right to abolish the international slave trade, but no power to regulate or destroy the institution of slavery where it already existed. Nonetheless, Congress had prevented the extension of slavery to certain territories in the **Missouri Compromise of 1820.** So long as both the free North and the slave South had some opportunities for expansion, compromise had been possible.

▍ **The Wilmot Proviso of 1846** proposed to ban African Americans, whether slave or free, from any territory acquired from the Mexican War. This blend of racist and antislavery sentiments appealed to many Northerners anxious to preserve new lands for free Whites. Congress ultimately rejected the proviso as well as the extreme alternative of allowing slavery in all of the Mexican cession.

▍ **Rejecting an extension of the Missouri Compromise line** as too beneficial to southern interests, many Northerners supported the idea of **"squatter"** or **"popular sovereignty,"** leaving the question of slavery in a territory to the actual settlers. In **the election of 1848**, **Whig Zachary Taylor**, avoiding a stand but promising no executive interference with congressional legislation, defeated two challengers: **Democrat Lewis Cass** who urged "popular sovereignty," and **Free-Soiler Martin Van Buren** who favored the Wilmot Proviso.

Taylor Takes Charge

President Taylor proposed admitting California and New Mexico directly as states, bypassing **territorial status** and the arguments over slavery. The possibility, however, that only free states would emerge from the Mexican cession provoked southern resistance and talk of secession.

▍ **Although Taylor resisted compromise until his death**, his successor **Millard Fillmore** supported a series of resolutions known as the **Compromise of 1850.** Voting on the measures separately, members of Congress agreed to **admit**

California as a free state, organize the territories of **New Mexico and Utah** on the basis of popular sovereignty, retract the borders of **Texas** in return for assumption of the state's debt, and abolish the slave trade in **the District of Columbia**. The most controversial provision created a strong **Fugitive Slave Law**, denying suspected runaways any rights of self-defense, and requiring northerners to enforce slavery.

Political Upheaval, 1852–1856

The Compromise of 1850 may have weakened the second-party system as people sought alternatives to the dominant parties.

- **The Compromise of 1850** robbed the political parties of distinctive appeals and contributed to voter apathy and disenchantment. Although a colorless candidate, **Democrat Franklin Pierce** won the election of 1852 over **Winfield Scott**, the candidate of a Whig party that was on the verge of collapse from internal divisions.
- **In 1854, Democratic Senator Stephen Douglas**, anxious to expand American settlement and commerce across the northern plains while promoting his own presidential ambitions, pushed an act through Congress organizing the territories of **Kansas and Nebraska** on the basis of popular sovereignty. This repeal of the long-standing Missouri Compromise, along with publication of the **"Ostend Manifesto"** urging the United States acquisition of **Cuba**, convinced an increasing number of Northerners that Pierce's Democratic administration was dominated by pro-southern sympathizers, if not conspirators.
- **The American, or Know-Nothing party** appealed to the **anti-immigrant sentiments** of American citizens who feared and resented the heavy influx of European immigrants. Although enjoying temporary success, the Know-Nothing party soon lost influence and numbers because of inexperienced leaders, a lack of cohesion, and a failure to address the nation's major problems.
- **The Republican party** adopted a firm position opposing any further extension of slavery. Election fraud and violence in Kansas discredited the principle of popular sovereignty and strengthened Republican appeal in the North.
- **In 1856, Democrat James Buchanan** won the presidency over Republican John C. Frémont and Know-Nothing candidate Millard Fillmore.

The House Divided, 1857–1860

Sectionalism deepened during Buchanan's term as president, and a series of incidents led to the actual division of the country.

- **Cultural Sectionalism...** Before the actual political division of the nation occurred, American religious and literary leaders split into opposing camps. Southern intellectuals reacted defensively to outside criticism and rallied to the idea of **southern nationalism**.
- **In a controversial case**, the Supreme Court ruled that **Dred Scott** was a slave and that **African Americans (whether slave or free) had no rights as citizens**. Further, the Court declared the Missouri Compromise unconstitutional, denying that Congress had any power to prohibit slavery in the territories. Rather than resolve disputes over the slavery question, the decision intensified sectional discord.

- **Proslavery forces in Kansas** resorted to electoral fraud to secure a convention to draft a slave state constitution. When finally submitted to a fair vote by the residents of Kansas in 1858, **the Lecompton Constitution** was overwhelmingly rejected.
- **In the 1858 Illinois Senate race**, Republican **Abraham Lincoln** asked Democrat **Stephen Douglas** how he could reconcile the idea of popular sovereignty with the Dred Scott decision. Douglas offered the **"Freeport Doctrine,"** a suggestion that territories could dissuade slaveholders from moving in by providing no supportive legislation for slavery. Coupled with his stand against the Lecompton Constitution, Douglas's Freeport Doctrine guaranteed loss of southern support for his presidential bid.
- **Two events of 1859–1860** intensified southern fears of Republican intentions: northern expressions of sympathy at the execution of **crazed abolitionist John Brown**; and public endorsement by a prominent Republican politician of **Hinton Rowan Helper's** *Impending Crisis of the South*. The objective of John Brown's raid on the federal arsenal at **Harpers Ferry, Virginia**, had been to equip a slave army and **Helper's book condemned slavery on economic grounds**, urging lower-class whites of the South to unite against planter domination and abolish slavery.
- **The Election of 1860…** Unable to agree on a platform or candidate, the Democrats split: a northern wing nominated **Stephen Douglas** and endorsed popular sovereignty, and a southern wing nominated **John C. Breckinridge** and demanded federal protection of slavery in the territories. Border state conservatives formed the Constitutional Union party and nominated **John Bell** of Tennessee. Republicans nominated **Abraham Lincoln** on a Free-Soil position and a broad economic platform. Although he won only 40 percent of the popular vote, **Lincoln swept the North** for a majority of the electoral votes and election as president. Political leaders of the lower **South immediately launched the movement for secession**.

Multiple-Choice Questions

1. The Compromise of 1850
   - (A) abolished the slave trade in the District of Columbia.
   - (B) served as the basis for lasting sectional peace.
   - (C) prohibited slavery in the New Mexico territory.
   - (D) drove the South to a new extremist position.
   - (E) was revised in 1851.

2. The Wilmot Proviso sought to
   - (A) limit territorial expansionism.
   - (B) prevent the Mexican War.
   - (C) guarantee the right of slavery in the territories.
   - (D) ban slavery in the territory acquired from Mexico.
   - (E) simplify the Kansas-Nebraska Act.

3. According to the principle of popular sovereignty,
   - (A) Congress would determine whether a territory would have slavery.
   - (B) territorial legislatures would determine whether a territory would have slavery.
   - (C) settlers would determine whether a territory would have slavery.
   - (D) the Supreme Court would determine whether a territory would have slavery.
   - (E) the House of Representatives would determine whether a territory would have slavery.

4. In the Kansas-Nebraska Act, Stephen Douglas attempted to set up territorial government based on
   (A) the Compromise of 1850.
   (B) Free Soil ideology.
   (C) congressional approval or disapproval of slavery.
   (D) presidential approval or disapproval of slavery.
   (E) popular sovereignty.

5. Why did the Know-Nothings become popular?
   (A) They reflected the growing differences between the sections.
   (B) They developed a national platform that appealed to a broad cross section of Americans.
   (C) They appealed to German and Irish immigrants.
   (D) They nominated well-known political figures to run for office.
   (E) They were unpretentious and not considered dishonest like most politicians.

6. The Republican Party
   (A) received broad-based support throughout the nation.
   (B) was primarily a sectional party.
   (C) was a party of farmers and laborers.
   (D) was the party of northern industrialists.
   (E) struggled in its first years of existence.

7. In the 1850s, the most important example of literary abolitionism was
   (A) *Walden.*
   (B) *Moby Dick.*
   (C) *Uncle Tom's Cabin.*
   (D) *The Raven.*
   (E) *Incidents in the Life of a Slave Girl.*

8. In the *Dred Scott* case, the Supreme Court decision was largely the work of
   (A) John Marshall.
   (B) Roger Taney.
   (C) Stephen Douglas.
   (D) William Marbury.
   (E) Thurgood Marshall.

9. The Republican Party platform in 1860
   (A) dealt exclusively with slavery.
   (B) ignored the issue of slavery.
   (C) presented a moderate position on slavery.
   (D) attempted to broaden the party's appeal in the South.
   (E) attempted to broaden the party's appeal in the North.

10. Individuals who opposed the expansion of slavery into the territories because they feared its effect on the labor system were known as
    (A) political nativists.
    (B) Know-Nothings.
    (C) Democrats.
    (D) Free Soilers.
    (E) Republicans.

Document-Based Question

What issues arose in the period 1848–1860, ultimately leading to the outbreak of civil war in 1861? In your response, draw on your knowledge of the time period in question, as well as the information in the documents.

DOCUMENT 1   Source: Mexican-American War map, 1846–1848

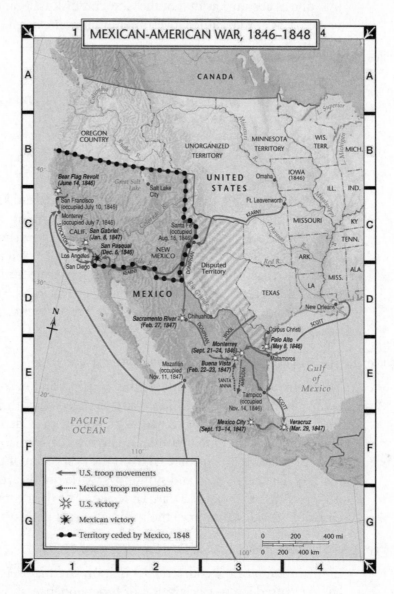

MEXICAN-AMERICAN WAR, 1846–1848

DOCUMENT 2   Source: John C. Calhoun, *Proposal to Preserve the Union*, 1850

…The first question, then, presented for consideration, in the investigation I propose to make, in order to obtain such knowledge, is: What is it that has endangered the Union?

One of the causes is, undoubtedly, to be traced to the long-continued agitation of the slave question on the part of the North, and the many aggressions which they have made on the rights of the South during the time.…

There is another, lying back of it, with which this is intimately connected, that may be regarded as the great and primary cause. That is to be found in the fact that the equilibrium between the two sections in the Government, as it stood when the Constitution was ratified and the Government put in action has been destroyed.…

What was once a constitutional federal republic is now converted, in reality, into one as absolute as that of the Autocrat of Russia, and as despotic in its tendency as any absolute Government that ever existed.

DOCUMENT 3 Source: Harriet Beecher Stowe, *Uncle Tom's Cabin*, 1852

And now," said Legree, "come here, you Tom. You see, I told ye I didn't buy ye jest for the common work. I mean to promote ye, and make a driver of ye; and tonight ye may jest as well begin to get ye hand in. Now, ye jest take this yer gal and flog her; ye've seen enough on't [of it] to know how." "I beg Mas'r' pardon," said Tom; "hopes Mas'r won't set me at that. It's what I an't used to–never did–and can't do, no way possible."

"Ye'll larn a pretty smart chance of things ye never did know, before I've done with ye!" said Legree, taking up a cowhide and striking Tom a heavy blow across the cheek, and following up the infliction by a shower of blows. "There!" he said, as he stopped to rest; "now, will ye tell me ye can't do it?" "Yes, Mas'r," said Tom, putting up his hand, to wipe the blood that trickled down his face. "I'm willin' to work, night and day, and work while there's life and breath in me. But this yer thing I can't feel it right to do; and, Mas'r, I never shall do it—never!"

DOCUMENT 4 Source: George Fitzhugh, *Cannibals All! Or Slaves Without Masters*, 1857

The negro slaves of the South are the happiest, and in some sense, the freest people in the world. The children and the aged and infirm work not at all, and yet have all the comforts and necessaries of life provided for them. They enjoy liberty, because they are oppressed neither by care or labor. The women do little hard work, and are protected from the despotism of their husbands by their masters. The negro men and stout boys work, on the average, in good weather, no more than nine hours a day. The balance of their time is spent in perfect abandon. Besides, they have their Sabbaths and holidays.

DOCUMENT 5 Source: Opinion of the Supreme Court in *Dred Scott v Sanford*, 1857

In the opinion of the court, the legislation and histories of the times, and the language used in the Declaration of Independence, show, that neither the class of persons who had been imported as slaves, nor their descendants, whether they had become free or not, were then acknowledged as a part of the people, nor intended to be included in the general words used in that memorable instrument....

They had for more than a century before been regarded as beings of an inferior order, and altogether unfit to associate with the white race, either in social or political relations, and so far inferior, that they had no rights which the white man was bound to respect; and that the negro might justly and lawfully be reduced to slavery for his benefit....

...there are two clauses in the constitution which point directly and specifically to the negro race as a separate class of persons, and show clearly that they were not regarded as a portion of the people or citizens of the government then formed.

…upon full and careful consideration of the subject, the court is of opinion, that, upon the facts stated,…Dred Scott was not a citizen of Missouri within the meaning of the constitution of the United States and not entitled as such to sue in its courts.…

DOCUMENT 6   Source: Abraham Lincoln, A House Divided speech, 1858

If we could first know where we are, and whither we are tending, we could better judge what to do and how to do it. We are now far into the fifth year since a policy was initiated with the avowed object, and confident promise, of putting an end to slavery agitation. Under the operation of that policy, that agitation has not only not ceased but has constantly augmented. In my opinion, it will not cease until a crisis shall have been reached and passed. "A house divided against itself cannot stand." I believe this government cannot endure permanently half-slave and half-free. I do not expect the Union to be dissolved—I do not expect the house to fall—but I do expect it will cease to be divided. It will become all one thing or all the other. Either the opponents of slavery will arrest the further spread of it and place it where the public mind shall rest in the belief that it is in the course of ultimate extinction or its advocates will push it forward, till it shall become alike lawful in all the states, old as well as new—North as well as South.

DOCUMENT 7   Source: Abraham Lincoln, First Inaugural Address, 1861

Again, if the United States be not a government proper, but an association of States in the nature of contract merely, can it, as a contract, be peaceably unmade, by less than all the parties who made it? One party to a contract may violate it—break it, so to speak; but does it not require all to lawfully rescind it?

One section of our country believes slavery is right, and ought to be extended, while the other believes it is wrong, and ought not to be extended. This is the only substantial dispute.

In your hands, my dissatisfied fellow countrymen, and not in mine, is the momentous issue of civil war. The government will not assail you. You can have no conflict, without being yourselves the aggressors. You have no oath registered in Heaven to destroy the government, while I shall have the most solemn one to "preserve, protect and defend" it.

I am loath to close. We are not enemies, but friends. We must not be enemies. Though passion may have strained, it must not break our bonds of affection. The mystic chords of memory, stretching from every battle-field, and patriot grave, to every living heart and hearthstone, all over this broad land, will yet swell the chorus of the Union, when again touched, as surely they will be, by the better angels of our nature

DOCUMENT 8 Source: 1860 Election cartoon

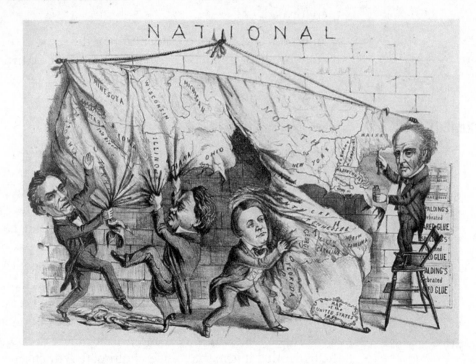

DOCUMENT 9 Source: The Kansas-Nebraska Act, 1854

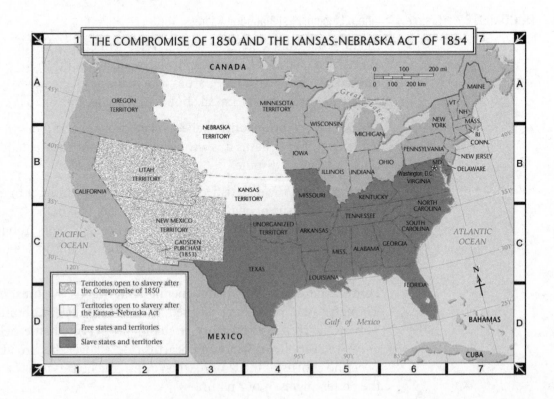

Free-Response Question

> *Was the conflict over the settlement of Kansas a rehearsal for the Civil War? In what ways did popular sovereignty stir up sectional tensions in the 1850s?*

ANSWERS AND EXPLANATIONS

Multiple-Choice Questions

▌ **1. (A) is correct.** Originally an Omnibus Bill, the logjam was broken with the death of President Taylor. A compromise was created. The main components were choice for New Mexico and Utah and the ending of slave sales in the District of Columbia.

▌ **2. (D) is correct.** The Wilmot Proviso was an attempt by Northern congressmen to prevent slavery in the areas conquered during the Mexican War. This bill was first attached to the appropriations bill for the war. It was ultimately defeated but led to continued debate.

▌ **3. (C) is correct.** This was one of the compromises to avoid a vote where congressmen would be on record for voting for or against slavery.

▌ **4. (E) is correct.** Douglas disregarded the compromise line in an attempt to maintain harmony between free and slave states and members of the Democratic Party.

▌ **5. (A) is correct.** The platform of the Know Nothing Party was to keep the new Irish and German immigrants from yielding much political power. Despite all the tensions over slavery, the ideas of the Know Nothing Party were popular throughout the country.

6. (B) is correct. The Republican Party was primarily a Northern party. The party grew out of the Free-Soil Party.

7. (C) is correct. *Uncle Tom's Cabin* was meant to be a rally call against slavery. It was highly effective in rallying Northern calls for reform.

8. (B) is correct. Taney's brief struck not only a blow to Scott by claiming he could not sue or gain his citizenship. Further, Taney's brief ruled the Missouri Compromise unconstitutional.

9. (E) is correct. Although ending slavery was at the heart of the Republican platform, the party broadened its ideas by making the economy the main issue in the election of 1860.

10. (D) is correct. The Free-Soilers were the precursor to the Republican Party.

Document-Based Question Sample Response

What issues arose in the period 1848–1860, ultimately leading to the outbreak of civil war in 1861? In your response, draw on your knowledge of the time period in question, as well as the information in the documents.

The over-riding issue of this time period was the issue of slavery and its expansion. Many things happened which forced that issue to the forefront and ultimately caused the United States to break out in civil war in 1861.

Since the Compromise of 1820, the country had been able to "paper over" the issue of the growth of slavery. However, the Mexican War added a tremendous amount of territory to the United States and re-opened the issue of whether the territories would be free or slave, and the delicate political balance between free and slave states was again threatened. **(DOCUMENT 1)** The Compromise of 1850 was an attempt the re-balance the country and avoid civil war over the issue. **(DOCUMENT 2)** However, instead of quieting the issue, it brought it to the forefront. The main mechanism of this was the fugitive slave law that was part of the Compromise. Before that, the north was never directly faced with slavery. The law required them to look at it directly, and many northerners reacted against it. That reaction was shown in many ways, one of which was the publication of *Uncle Tom's Cabin*, an anti-slavery novel. **(DOCUMENT 3)** Other issues brought slavery to the fore as well. The Kansas-Nebraska Act allowed the people of the territories to decide on slavery. **(DOCUMENT 9)** Instead of settling the issue, it inflamed it. The attacks of abolitionist John Brown at Pottawatomie Creek and Harper's Ferry terrified the south. When he was executed, many northerners decried the loss of what they considered to be a hero. **(DOCUMENT 10)**

In many ways this increased the antagonism that many southerners felt towards the north. Many southerners felt that slavery was a "positive good" that was the best way for the races to relate, and the Dred Scott decision stated clearly that slaves were property and that Congress could not legislate away your property rights. **(DOCUMENTS 4 AND 5)** By the end of the 1850s the tensions between the sections were rising rapidly. The debates between Lincoln and Douglas in the race for the Illinois Senate seat were all over the issue of slavery and secession; and Lincoln's First Inaugural Address is a plea for unity. **(DOCUMENTS 6**

AND 7) The 1860 election was splintered between 4 regional candidates, and to the south, the election of Abe Lincoln, who did not want slavery to spread, was intolerable. **(DOCUMENT 8)**

Free-Response Essay Sample Response

Was the conflict over the settlement of Kansas a rehearsal for the Civil War? In what ways did popular sovereignty stir up sectional tensions in the 1850s?

The settlement was a precursor to the Civil War. One should argue that the settlement offered no concrete answers. The lack of answers only festered and fueled the flames of the Civil War. Popular sovereignty was responsible for tensions. This is because there were no answers available to the region.

CHAPTER 15

Secession and the Civil War

Lincoln effectively guided the Union through the **Civil War** by inspiring northerners with his conviction that the struggle would be won. The war tested the American ideal of democracy. It was a defense of **political liberalism** at a time when much of Europe had rejected it.

The Storm Gathers

The war came after a compromise effort failed and the North resolved to fight to preserve the Union.

- **With the election of Lincoln**, the states of the Deep South followed South Carolina and seceded from the Union to better secure slavery. Those who advocated immediate secession by each state individually were opposed by the cooperationists, who believed in the South acting as a unit.
- When northern moderates attempted a reconciliation of the sections, Lincoln led the Republicans in rejecting the proposed compromise (**the Crittenden Compromise**) because it would have permitted the spread of slavery to the Southwest. Lincoln also believed that compromise would negate the platform that he had followed—and that a majority of Americans had voted for—in the election of 1860.
- **Lincoln then carefully avoided firing the first shot** by shifting the burden of decision to the **South Carolinians**, who fired on federal-held **Fort Sumter**. On **April 13, 1861**, the fort surrendered, marking the beginning of the Civil War.

Adjusting to Total War

The northern war aim, to force the South physically back into the Union, required a **"total war"** of societies and economies as well as armies. This formidable task required all of the North's demographic and economic advantages.

- **The South** chose to fight **"an offensive defense,"** while the North had two main goals: the Confederate capital in the East (eventually Richmond) and the Mississippi Valley in the West (**the anaconda policy**).
- **Both the North and the South** faced enormous difficulties in raising, equipping, and financing armies on such a large scale. The economy and society of both the Union and the Confederacy had to make massive adjustments for the war, adjustments that the North was better able to make.
- **Lincoln** exercised extraordinary powers to achieve his aims. **Jefferson Davis** took a more narrow—and less successful—view of his role as **Confederate President**.
- **The northern effort stalled in the East**, where **Confederate General Robert E. Lee** turned back successive attempts to capture Richmond, but in the West the Union took much of the **Mississippi Valley** and established its naval supremacy.

Some of the early battles of the war were the bloodiest ever fought, and pointed out that this would not be a brief war.

▪ **The South** failed in its attempt to **use its cotton supply** to attract the substantial European support necessary if she was to continue to hold out against the more powerful North. **France and England** feared a war against the North more than they needed cotton.

Fight to the Finish

In the final two and one-half years of the war, the North adopted increasingly extreme war measures to overcome determined southern resistance.

▪ **Lincoln moved slowly to emancipate the slaves**, and did so more from military, political, and diplomatic expediency than moral purpose. It was not until **early 1863** that a partial emancipation proclamation was issued by Lincoln.

▪ **Almost 200,000 African Americans** served in the Union armies and contributed significantly to a northern victory, though they faced discrimination and segregation.

▪ **The Southern armies, economy, diplomacy and society** could no longer resist the superior demographic and economic forces of the North. The North was slow to take advantage of these weaknesses and the North, too, was increasingly war weary.

▪ **The Northern victory** achieved the Union's several military objectives, including the **capture of Richmond**, and turned back a Northern peace movement, **assuring Lincoln's reelection** and the successful conclusion of the war.

▪ **Four years of struggle** had changed the status of women, African Americans, and working people. Most clearly, the war had **broadened federal powers**, channeling them into a new corporate, industrial economy. The war effort also encouraged a shift away from traditional individualism toward **social discipline and collective action** and cemented the idea that **the federal government was supreme over the states**. It also cost **the lives of more than 600,000 soldiers**.

Multiple-Choice Questions

1. Which one of the following does NOT apply to Lincoln's initial policy toward the Confederacy?
   (A) a cautious and limited use of force
   (B) a strategy of inactivity to buy time to resolve the conflict
   (C) a strategy designed to make the Confederacy look like the aggressor if war occurred
   (D) a strategy designed to avoid any "hostile" action toward the South by the North
   (E) the deployment of troops along the "border states" to demonstrate a Union resolve to fight

2. Which of the following was NOT a provision of the Confederate Constitution?
   (A) prohibition of protective tariffs
   (B) guarantee of slavery
   (C) protection of slavery in the territories
   (D) a strong central government
   (E) restrictions on the finance of internal improvements

3. The chart labeled "Resources of the Union and the Confederacy, 1861" could suggest all of the follow statements as true EXCEPT

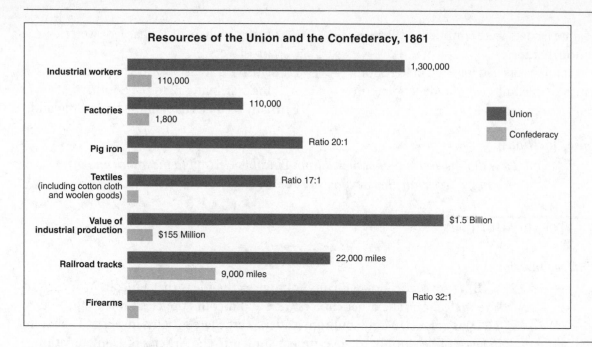

Resources of the Union and the Confederacy, 1861

	Union	Confederacy
Industrial workers	1,300,000	110,000
Factories	110,000	1,800
Pig iron	Ratio 20:1	
Textiles (including cotton cloth and woolen goods)	Ratio 17:1	
Value of industrial production	$1.5 Billion	$155 Million
Railroad tracks	22,000 miles	9,000 miles
Firearms	Ratio 32:1	

(A) The Union had an advantage in all resource areas.

(B) The Confederacy in order to be successful must form international alliances.

(C) The South was extremely industrialized due to the expansion of railroads.

(D) The Union held a 32:1 ratio in firearms.

(E) All of the above statements are true.

4. Which one of the following states was NOT part of the Confederacy?
   (A) Missouri
   (B) North Carolina
   (C) Texas
   (D) Tennessee
   (E) Florida

5. In the beginning, the Civil War was
   (A) a struggle to free the slaves.
   (B) a struggle to preserve the Union.
   (C) a contest of sectional supremacy.
   (D) a personal struggle between Abraham Lincoln and Jefferson Davis.
   (E) a struggle to preserve "King Cotton."

6. Which one of the following was NOT a Northern advantage throughout the war?
   (A) greater population
   (B) industrial superiority
   (C) familiar terrain and public support

(D) a superior railroad network

(E) greater access to natural resources

7. To secure the necessary troops for the war,
   (A) the South resorted to the draft.
   (B) the North resorted to the draft.
   (C) "press gangs," coercion and blackmail became the norm on both sides.
   (D) A and B
   (E) none of the above

8. Lincoln and Davis learned early in the war that
   (A) successful conduct of the war required active, executive leadership.
   (B) Congress should be allowed to conduct the war with minimal executive interference.
   (C) decentralization of power is most efficient in wartime.
   (D) the president is bound by the same constitutional restraints in war as in peace.
   (E) many of the decisions of the war were best left to popular vote.

9. The Emancipation Proclamation freed
   (A) all African Americans.
   (B) only slaves in the loyal border states.
   (C) all slaves.
   (D) only slaves in the military occupation zones of the Union army.
   (E) only slaves in the Confederacy.

10. Confederate leaders were confident of British recognition, because
    (A) British financiers had invested in the South.
    (B) British textile mills were so dependent on Southern cotton.
    (C) most members of Parliament were proslavery.
    (D) British capitalists stzood to profit by selling war material to the South.
    (E) many of them had family ties to England.

Free-Response Question

How did the events that occurred from Lincoln's election to the attack on Fort Sumter accelerate the inevitability of war?

ANSWERS AND EXPLANATIONS

Multiple-Choice Questions

■ **1. (E) is correct.** Choice E runs counter to the ideas that Lincoln proposed to save the Union. The other choices were all Lincoln's policies towards the South.

■ **2. (D) is correct.** Many southern leaders were State's Rights loyalists. They were in favor of decentralized government similar to the Articles of Confederation.

■ **3. (C) is correct.** One of the shortcomings of the Confederacy was a lack of an industrial base. Additionally, there was not a standardized railroad system throughout the Confederacy, which was a disadvantage throughout the war.

■ **4. (A) is correct.** Missouri, although a slave state, chose to remain in the Union.

■ **5. (B) is correct.** Lincoln's initial goal was to try to preserve the Union.

■ **6. (C) is correct.** Most of the war was fought in the South. This was one of the few disadvantages for Northern forces. It may have been the only advantage for the South.

■ **7. (D) is correct.** Both sides were forced to conscript recruits.

■ **8. (A) is correct.** Both Lincoln and Davis found that they must be involved in the planning and execution of the war plans. For both of them, this involvement took its toll both physically and emotionally.

■ **9. (E) is correct.** Because there were no slaves in the North, the Emancipation Proclamation freed only slaves in the South. Unfortunately the Emancipation Proclamation freed no slaves for two more years as the war raged on.

■ **10. (B) is correct.** Throughout the early stages of the war Confederate leaders were sure that Britain would recognize them because of their economic ties. In particular, the South thought the exchange of cotton would lead to recognition.

Free-Response Essay Sample Response

How did the events that occurred from Lincoln's election to the attack on Fort Sumter accelerate the inevitability of war?

The Deep South immediately thought the election of Lincoln was a negative thing. Before the actual hostilities could begin, there would be an attempt at reconciliation. The North had to commit to supporting military action for as long as necessary. When those hurdles were cleared the hostilities at Fort Sumter began.

CHAPTER 16

The Agony of Reconstruction

After the Civil War, the South faced a difficult period of rebuilding its government and economy and dealing with the newly freed African Americans.

The President Versus Congress

In the absence of constitutional guidelines, the president and Congress waged a bitter fight over how best to **reconstruct** the Union.

- **By 1863**, Lincoln and Congress had begun to debate two divisive issues: **the reconstruction of the southern states and the status of the freedmen**. In the months before his death, Lincoln proposed a moderate program to restore the southern states to the Union and showed some willingness to compromise with Congress (the Ten Percent Plan), which wanted more **radical reconstruction** legislation. But the **Reconstruction** issues remained unresolved.

- After the assassination of Lincoln, **Andrew Johnson's ascent to the presidency** led to a bitter clash with Congress. There was a uniform hope of breaking the power of the planter class, but Congress supported federal guarantees for black citizenship, and Johnson insisted that the South be permitted to reestablish statehood by encouraging the passing of the **Thirteenth Amendment**, repudiating the **Confederate debt**, and retroactively declaring the process of secession illegal.

- **Southern States** passed **Black Codes** that restricted the freed slaves' freedoms.

- **The Republican-led Congress**—determined to crush the old southern ruling class—extended the life of the Freedmen's Bureau and passed a civil rights bill to grant equal benefits and protection to the freedmen. Fearing that Johnson would not enforce the **civil rights act,** Congress passed the **Fourteenth Amendment** guaranteeing equal rights under the law to all Americans and defining national citizenship. After the southern states rejected the Fourteenth Amendment, and the president vetoed two Reconstruction bills.

- **The First Reconstruction Act of 1867 (part of the Radical Reconstruction)** temporarily placed the South under **military rule** and allowed for the re-admittance of southern states once **African American suffrage** was legitimized. Congress assumed that once freedmen could vote, they could protect themselves.

- **When the president obstructed the plan's implementation**, Congress retaliated with an attempt to remove him from office. Johnson narrowly avoided removal, preserving the office from congressional domination, but insuring also that Congress would have the upper hand in the reconstruction process.

Reconstructing Southern Society

The South was devastated and demoralized after the war, and was dominated by southern Whites who wanted to deny all rights to **freedmen**.

- **When Congress failed to enact a program of land redistribution,** southern landowners initiated a new labor system that forced freedmen into virtual peonage. Most of the ex-slaves had no alternative but to return to white-owned fields under a contract labor system.
- **While sharecropping** extended black servitude and economic dependence on the farm, segregation of the races was imposed in the towns with **Jim Crow laws** or by intimidation.
- **The Black Codes of 1865** attempted to require separation of the races in public places and facilities.
- **Reconstruction** established southern governments of Republican business people (**carpetbaggers**), poor whites, and the freedmen. Although often corrupt, these radical regimes initiated significant progressive reforms. They failed, however, to achieve interracial equality; community pressure established a social system based on segregation.
- The Freedman's Bureau made 40-acre grants to black settlers for three-year periods. After three years, the settlers had the option to buy the land at a low price ("forty acres and a mule").

Retreat from Reconstruction

In the South, **U.S. Grant's** administration failed to sustain black suffrage against violent groups bent on restoring white supremacy. Organizations like the **Ku Klux Klan** used terrorism, insurrection, and murder to intimidate southern Republican governments and prospective black voters. With the **Fifteenth Amendment** severely threatened, Congress passed the **"Force" Acts**, which allowed the president to use military force to quell insurrections.

- **What to do with the greenbacks** (paper money issued during the war) became a major problem by 1868.
- **Hard money advocates** clashed with **"green backers"** who wanted government-sponsored inflation.
- **The panic of 1873** intensified the argument, and the **Sherman Specie Resumption Act in 1874** failed to please either the inflationists or the hard-money advocates.
- **"Spoilsmen"** came to power determined to further their own private interests. The **Credit Mobilier** scandal, the **"Whiskey Ring,"** and the **impeachment of Secretary of War Belknap** for accepting bribes left liberal reform Republicans aghast and the Grant administration in shambles.

Reunion and the New South

The reconciliation of the sections came at the expense of southern Blacks and poor Whites.

- **Samuel Tilden**, the Democratic candidate, won the popular majority in the 1876 **presidential election**, as well as the uncontested electoral vote. But **disputed returns** in the three Republican-controlled southern states threw the election into turmoil.
- **The Compromise of 1877** ended military rule and insured that conservative **"home rule"** would be restored in the South. With southern Democratic acqui-

escence, Republican candidate **Rutherford Hayes** assumed the presidency, though under a cloud of suspicion.

- ■ **In the South**, upper-class **"Redeemers"** took power in the name of white supremacy and industrial development and then initiated a **"New South."**
- ■ **The economy** was dominated by northern capital and southern employers, landlords, and creditors. Economic and physical coercion, including hundreds of **lynchings**, effectively disenfranchised people of color.
- ■ **Some blacks**, justifiably bitter at the depth of white racism, supported black nationalism and emigration to Africa, but most chose to struggle within American society.

Multiple-Choice Questions

1. A minimal Reconstruction policy was favored by
   - (A) Republican senators.
   - (B) Congress.
   - (C) Northern states.
   - (D) the Supreme Court.
   - (E) President Lincoln.

2. Which of the following groups was disappointed by the Fifteenth Amendment?
   - (A) freedmen
   - (B) feminists
   - (C) scalawags
   - (D) Republicans
   - (E) Northerners

3. At their state constitutional conventions, Southerners were required to do all of the following EXCEPT
   - (A) guarantee the political and civil rights of the freedmen.
   - (B) ratify the Thirteenth Amendment.
   - (C) declare the ordinance of secession illegal.
   - (D) repudiate the Confederate debt.
   - (E) ratify the Fourteenth Amendment.

4. The legacy of Reconstruction for most African Americans was
   - (A) the benefits of freedom.
   - (B) poverty and discrimination.
   - (C) land ownership.
   - (D) skilled factory jobs.
   - (E) successful entry into the political arena.

5. The small number of African Americans elected to state or national office during Reconstruction demonstrated on the average
   - (A) a higher level of corruption than their white counterparts.
   - (B) a desire to implement radical social programs.
   - (C) more integrity and competence than their white counterparts.
   - (D) a strong desire for harsh revenge on former slaveholders.
   - (E) a lack of education that impeded their success.

6. Andrew Johnson was indicted by the House for his violation of the
   - (A) Civil Rights Act of 1866.
   - (B) Loyalty Act.
   - (C) Wade-Davis Bill.
   - (D) Fourteenth Amendment.
   - (E) Tenure of Office Act.

7. The South's refusal to ratify the Fourteenth Amendment
   - (A) forced the Republicans to abolish the existing Southern governments and give the vote to African Americans.
   - (B) caused Northern public opinion to support the Radicals' demands.
   - (C) led to a general land reform of the South.
   - (D) caused a thorough restructuring of Southern society.
   - (E) brought the Redeemers to power.

8. The organization that symbolized most vividly the "white backlash" of the Reconstruction era was
   (A) the Union League.
   (B) the Freedmen's Bureau.
   (C) the Redeemers.
   (D) the Ku Klux Klan.
   (E) the White Citizens Council.

9. Black Codes showed that
   (A) Southerners were willing to allow African Americans legal equality.
   (B) the freedmen would be allowed to vote and participate in the political process.
   (C) Southerners were interested in improving the education of the freedmen.
   (D) Southerners wanted African Americans to return to positions of servility.
   (E) the idea of "separate but equal" was already established.

10. Which of the following was NOT a scandal during the Grant administration?
    (A) Credit Mobilier
    (B) Whiskey Ring
    (C) Teapot Dome
    (D) Indian Trading Posts
    (E) Belknap "cover-up"

Free-Response Question

This cartoon is entitled: "Slavery Is Dead?" Describe this cartoon and its meaning and intended audience.

ANSWERS AND EXPLANATIONS

Multiple-Choice Questions

1. **(E) is correct.** Minimal Reconstruction meant quickly readmitting the South to the Union. The readmission would offer no guarantees beyond a ban on slavery. President Lincoln favored this as an attempt to move as quickly as possible beyond the war.

2. **(B) is correct.** Women felt neglected by the Fifteenth Amendment because it failed to offer voting privileges to women. Many feminists were so upset and bitter that they actual campaigned in opposition to the amendment.

3. **(A) is correct.** Many felt this action redundant as the Thirteenth and Fourteenth Amendments addressed these issues.

4. **(B) is correct.** Freedmen may have been emancipated but there was no concrete plan on what to do for them once they were free. Largely this was due to not wanting to widen further the rift between Southern landowners and the North.

5. **(C) is correct.** These representatives were Free Blacks who were educated. The most capable included Robert Smalls, Blanche K. Bruce, Robert Brown Elliot, and James T. Rapier.

6. **(E) is correct.** The Tenure Act was an attempt by Congress to limit the Constitutional power of the President by requiring him to seek Senate approval for the removal of all Senate confirmed officials. This was punishment for Johnson for disagreeing with the Congressional Reconstruction plan.

7. **(A) is correct.** Republicans forced the military to administer and establish reconstruction governments.

8. **(D) is correct.** The Ku Klux Klan and other white supremacy groups tried to intimidate and harass freedmen to keep them from exercising their Constitutional rights.

9. **(D) is correct.** The "Black Codes" were in essence attempts by whites to re-institutionalize slavery in the South.

10. **(C) is correct.** Many historians blame Grant for the scandals that ran wild in his administration. Grant could not be directly linked to most. The Teapot Dome Scandal came after his terms.

This cartoon is entitled: "Slavery Is Dead?" Describe this cartoon and its meaning and intended audience.

The cartoon demonstrates that little had changed after emancipation for southern freed slaves. The cartoon indicates that although the law had been changed, Lady Justice is blind and therefore incapable of changing the cultural mindset of the South.

The cartoon also implies that the North was "turning a blind eye" to the cultural bias that endured in the South. It indicates that the North had sold itself as the slaves had been sold in an attempt to rid itself of slavery.

CHAPTER 17

The West: Exploiting an Empire

After the Civil War, Americans—believing expansion was their **"manifest destiny"**—created a great colonial empire in the West, harnessed to eastern capital and tied increasingly to national and international markets. Its raw materials, sent east by wagon, train, and ship, helped fuel eastern factories. Western economies relied heavily on the federal government, which subsidized their railroads, distributed their land, and spent millions of dollars for the upkeep of soldiers and Indians.

Beyond the Frontier

Prior to the **Civil War**, the march of Anglo settlement was halted for various reasons at the border of the semiarid **Great Plains** (known to mapmakers as **The Great American Desert**), a temporary obstacle to further migration.

▮ The Great Plains extends from the Mississippi River to the Rocky Mountains.

Crushing the Native Americans

Because they were seen as an additional obstacle to further white migration, the **Native Americans** lost their lands and were forced to radically change their cultures by the end of the century.

▮ **After they acquired the Spanish horse**, the **Plains Indians** abandoned their former lifestyle in favor of a strong, nomadic, and warlike culture based upon the **buffalo**.

▮ **Plains Indians** divided themselves into a multiplicity of tribes, which in turn were divided into smaller bands.

▮ **The Great Plains** had been considered by the United States government as unusable for whites and was given to the **Native Americans**.

▮ **The discovery of gold** in the West prompted the federal government to begin a policy of **restricting tribes to reservations**. This new policy clearly led to conflicts with the Native Americans.

▮ **From 1867 to 1890**, the federal government fought a number of tribes in brutal campaigns, eliminating any semblance of resistance.

▮ **In 1887**, Congress began a policy to put an end to tribal life by turning the Native Americans into farmers.

▮ **Still another crushing blow** to the traditional tribal ways occurred when white hunters nearly exterminated the buffalo.

▮ **The Dawes Act of 1887 allowed 90 million acres of Indian lands to be sold** to white settlers, and by 1890, only **250,000** Native Americans counted in the census, down from nearly **five million** in 1492.

Settlement of the West

In the last three decades of the nineteenth century, Anglo farmers brought more land under the plow in America than ever before.

- **Settlers flocked to the West.** In the three decades after the **Gold Rush of 1849**, some one-half million individuals traveled the **Overland Trail** westward across half a continent in search of riches, adventure, and a healthier life.
- **Government policy provided free or cheap land** to individual settlers, land speculators, and private corporations, such as the railroads, all eager to build businesses to supply the needs of a growing nation. Often, unscrupulous speculators and companies took advantage of these government land programs.
- **The new territories of the West** were virtual colonies of the federal government.
- **The Spanish-Mexican heritage of the Southwest** gave a distinctive shape to that area's politics, language, society, and law.

The Bonanza West

Quests for quick profits led to a boom-bust cycle in the western economy.

- **Lured by mineral wealth** throughout the region, many settlers moved west, building hasty and often short-lived **placer mining** communities, which reflected primarily materialistic and exploitative interests.
- **Many of the miners** were foreign born, and faced hostility and discrimination.
- **Large profits** also were possible for the **cattle ranchers** who grazed the herds on the prairie grasses and drove them to the railheads.
- **Many of the cowboys** were black or Hispanic. By 1880, ranches with **barbed wire** and other new technology ended the great drives.
- **The sodbusters**, or the dirt farmers, who slowly moved out onto the Great Plains encountered enormous obstacles.
- **By 1900**, 30 percent of the population of the country lived west of the Mississippi River.
- **Several important inventions**, innovations, and adaptations made farming on the treeless, semiarid Plains possible. **Dry farming, new plants, and new machinery** were among these innovations.
- **Bad weather and low prices** stirred up the farmers' anger, leading some to form political lobbies, and others to adopt more scientific, businesslike methods.
- **The Grange** was one organization that lobbied for farmers and met important social and economic needs.
- **The Oklahoma land rush of 1889** symbolized the closing of the frontier and in many ways reflected the attitude of Anglo-Americans toward Native Americans and their land.

Multiple-Choice Questions

1. Which of the following best describe the Plains tribes?
   (A) sedentary and pacific
   (B) fishermen and farmers
   (C) builders of great cities
   (D) committed human sacrifice and built temples
   (E) nomadic and warlike

2. Which of the following was, perhaps, the greatest Native American victory over the United States Army?
   (A) Battle of Wounded Knee
   (B) Battle of Sand Creek
   (C) Custer's Last Stand
   (D) Fetterman Massacre
   (E) the "Trail of Tears"

3. Which of the following was NOT part of the national government's policy toward Native Americans in the 1870s and 1880s?
   (A) signing separate peace treaties with Indian tribes
   (B) trying Native Americans in federal courts
   (C) giving Native Americans individual parcels of land
   (D) assimilating Native Americans into urban life
   (E) establishing Native American schools

4. Which of the following was NOT done by the Dawes Act?
   (A) It greatly increased the power of tribal chiefs.
   (B) It turned most Native Americans into private property owners.
   (C) It established the criteria for citizenship for Native Americans.
   (D) It destroyed the remaining vestiges of Native American culture.
   (E) It increased revenues to Native American schools.

5. The _____ was established to help provide isolated farmers with social and cultural activities.
   (A) Knights of Labor
   (B) Populist movement
   (C) National Grange
   (D) Farmers Alliance
   (E) Ku Klux Klan

6. The Homestead Act of 1862 failed because
   (A) it charged too much for government land.
   (B) the land allotments were insufficient for farming arid land.
   (C) it did not adequately convert the Native Americans to farmers.
   (D) gold was discovered on land set aside for farming.
   (E) too few settlers were willing to migrate west.

7. Which of the following statements describes the journey for most settlers westward?
   (A) All members of the journey had tasks to fulfill on the trail.
   (B) Only men migrated westward.
   (C) Most settlers tried to make the journey as quickly as possible.
   (D) The journey was easier for men than women.
   (E) It was a disciplined and efficient enterprise.

8. In open range ranching, ranchers
   (A) often herded sheep and goats as much as cattle.
   (B) rounded up wild cattle roaming free on the range.
   (C) let their cattle roam freely within a fenced area.
   (D) slaughtered and butchered their cattle on the range.
   (E) were often arrested as thieves.

9. Frederick Jackson Turner was
   (A) founder of the National Grange.
   (B) discoverer of the Comstock Lode.
   (C) the most notorious of the western badmen.
   (D) the historian who first developed the "frontier thesis."
   (E) a famous wagon train boss.

10. The Plains tribes differed from the Eastern Woodland tribes because
    (A) Eastern Woodland tribes were stationary and had organized societies.
    (B) Plains tribes were dependent on buffalo and horses.
    (C) The Plains tribes were less hospitable to settlers in their territory.
    (D) B and C
    (E) All of the above

Free-Response Question

What impact did the frontier have on American attitudes, behavior, and institutions? Is the "frontier thesis" of Frederick Jackson Turner viable?

ANSWERS AND EXPLANATIONS

Multiple-Choice Questions

▌ **1. (E) is correct.** The Plains tribes believed they lived as the buffalo and the horse lived. Therefore, they were nomadic. They became warlike only after they were "hunted" by American policy.

▌ **2. (C) is correct.** All of the battles in A through D were important, but Custer's Last Stand showed that the American Army could be defeated by the Native Americans.

▌ **3. (D) is correct.** The main thrust of Native American policy was to get them on the reservations. The Native Americans argued that the reservations were a sea of poverty and despair.

▌ **4. (A) is correct.** The Dawes Act was trying to break the last of the tribal vestiges. Therefore, the act would definitely not strengthen the tribal chief.

▌ **5. (C) is correct.** The Grange offered social, cultural, and educational activities for its members. This was done because of the drabness of rural life.

▌ **6. (B) is correct.** Additionally, few farmers could afford to purchase the land or the equipment to farm the new homesteads. The land was too much to irrigate and not enough to dry farm.

▌ **7. (A) is correct.** Every member regardless of age or sex had specific duties on the trip west.

▌ **8. (B) is correct.** They then drove them to market. These cattle drives were, contrary to Hollywood, very orderly and with specific rules and a frontier code of ethics.

▌ **9. (D) is correct.** Turner was a Professor of History at the University of Wisconsin. He examined the importance of the West in a paper in 1893 entitled, "The Significance of the Frontier in American History."

▌ **10. (E) is correct.** The Eastern Woodland tribes were the first Americans to come into contact in North America with European settlers. These tribes tended to be the more "civilized" tribes, having governments and constitutions, while the

Plains tribes followed the buffalo and the horse. They were warlike and resented any infringement into their hunting and sacred grounds.

Free-Response Essay Sample Response

What impact did the frontier have on American attitudes, behavior, and institutions? Is the "frontier thesis" of Frederick Jackson Turner viable?

The frontier thesis of "Go West" fueled much speculation and opportunity to a society that was trying to heal divisive wounds. The frontier gave hope to many Americans who had endured war and its harshness. The theory is viable only if one believes it to be. The frontier offered many opportunities for wealth, adventure or both.

However, in recent years modern historians have started to reject Turner's thesis on the basis it is too simplistic and that it paints too naïve a perspective on the West.

CHAPTER 18

The Industrial Society

By their centennial of 1876, Americans were rapidly developing their own unique society.

Industrial Development

Several factors contributed to the rapid economic transformation of the era: **resources** for materials, **population** for labor and markets, **railroads** for transportation, **tariffs** for protection from competition, confident **investors** for capital, and **technology** for cutting-edge production. The government provided grants, stability, and freedom from regulation.

An Empire on Rails

Revolutionary changes in transportation and communication, especially the **railroads**, transformed American technology.

▍ **By ending rural isolation**, encouraging economic **specialization**, creating a **national market**, and capturing the nation's imagination, **the railroads** transformed production, distribution, and business practices.

▍ **By the end of the century**, Americans, with substantial aid and land grants from federal and state governments, had built almost **200,000 miles of track**.

▍ **Despite much waste and corruption**, the railroads probably did more good than harm; for example, they saved the federal government $1 billion from 1850–1945.

▍ **Before the Civil War**, railroad construction served local markets; after 1865 the railroads tied the nation together with a system of trunk lines.

▍ **The exception was the South**, where railroads were not consolidated and integrated into the national railroad system until the 1880s.

▍ **Congress** voted to allow two companies, the **Union Pacific**, working westward, and the **Central Pacific**, working eastward, to compete in the construction of the **first transcontinental railroad**. They completed the tracks in **May 1869** at Promontory Point, Utah.

▍ **By 1893**, four more railroad lines reached the West Coast.

▍ **Overbuilding** generated vigorous rate wars, but financiers like **J. P. Morgan** constructed regional monopolies to reduce or eliminate competition.

An Industrial Empire

The Bessemer process made possible an industrial empire and transportation system based on purified steel.

- **The process for manufacturing steel** required much capital, so new companies grew very large until **Morgan** combined a number of them, including **Carnegie's**, into the country's first billion-dollar corporation, **U.S. Steel**.
- **John D. Rockefeller** ordered the chaotic **oil business** into a third national economic giant; his **Standard Oil** trust of the 1880s, reorganized as a holding company in the 1890s, came to control over 90 percent of oil refining in America and typified the notion of **vertical integration** in economics.
- **The business of invention boomed**—from 2,000 patents per year to over 21,000 per year—and transformed the communication, food, and power industries.

The Sellers

Brand names, advertising, chain stores, and mail-order houses brought the new goods to households and initiated a new community of consumers. The increased output of the industrial age alone was not enough to ensure huge profits. The products still had to be sold, and that gave rise to a new science of **marketing**.

- **Women**, children, African Americans, Catholics, Jews, and immigrants carried the additional burden of discrimination within advertising and the fledgling media.

The Wage Earners

Although entrepreneurs were important, it was the labor of millions of men and women that built the new industrial society. In their individual stories, nearly all unrecorded, lay much of the achievement, drama, and pain of these years.

- **Workers** suffered grueling, dangerous jobs, although their lives improved in some respects because of new goods. Although immigrants were an important part of the work force, native-born workers were paid more on average. In 1882, Chinese workers were prohibited from immigrating for ten years by the **Chinese Exclusion Act**.
- **Before 1900**, most wage earners worked at least ten hours a day, six days a week.
- All found that the new **factory system** required difficult and often demeaning adaptations in age-old patterns of work. But most workers accepted the system because it offered substantial social mobility.
- **National unions** approached the problems in different ways: **The Knights of Labor**, for example, organized **like a fraternal order** and sought broad social reforms, while the **American Federation of Labor** organized craft unions of **skilled workers** and sought practical, immediate, and tangible improvements for its members.
- **Workers also organized** social and fraternal groups to offer members companionship, insurance, job listings, and even food for the sick.
- **Employees tried to humanize the factory** while employers tried to determine wages and conditions on the basis of supply and demand rather than the welfare of the workers.
- **The conflict of purposes** sometimes led to violent strikes such as the Haymarket Riot (1886) and the Homestead Strike.

Multiple-Choice Questions

1. The most important advances in industrialization
   (A) came in the last third of the nineteenth century.
   (B) were made during the Civil War.
   (C) had come to Western Europe by 1900.
   (D) had little effect on the American economy.
   (E) began with the dawn of the twentieth century.

2. Which of the following individuals is incorrectly associated with the industry he helped to found?
   (A) Andrew Carnegie: steel
   (B) J. P. Morgan: finance
   (C) Henry Bessemer: railroads
   (D) John D. Rockefeller: oil
   (E) William Kelly: steel

3. Which of the following companies was NOT a retail store marketing its products around the country in the late nineteenth century?
   (A) A & P
   (B) Woolworth's
   (C) Sears, Roebuck
   (D) Wal-Mart
   (E) Montgomery Ward

4. After 1870, the measure of a nation's industrial progress was determined by
   (A) the production of steel.
   (B) the production of iron.
   (C) the number of railroad lines.
   (D) agricultural output.
   (E) *per capita* exports.

5. As a result of the proliferation of patents in the late nineteenth century,
   (A) the country imported its technology.
   (B) the marketplace was oversaturated with goods.
   (C) American life radically changed.

   (D) few Americans participated in the economic changes.
   (E) Americans began to fear technology.

6. Which of the following was NOT a consequence of the advent of advertising?
   (A) Americans became consumers.
   (B) The demand for goods increased.
   (C) The national market was joined in all parts of the nation.
   (D) Most consumers felt threatened by the new industrial goods.
   (E) Americans became aware of needs they didn't know they had before.

7. In comparison to male workers, female workers
   (A) found equal pay for equal work.
   (B) were relegated to traditional, "feminine" jobs.
   (C) reaped the rewards of the industrial system.
   (D) were not considered important as income earners.
   (E) generally had female managers.

8. Why did the Knights of Labor fail?
   (A) It could not provide effective national leadership.
   (B) It was unable to organize the workers.
   (C) It had no successful strikes.
   (D) It was unable to develop a set of objectives.
   (E) Terence Powderly was imprisoned.

9. The Haymarket Square riot
   (A) brought public sympathy to the plight of the workers.
   (B) strengthened the national labor movement.
   (C) weakened the national labor movement.
   (D) forced government regulation of unions.
   (E) took place in New York City.

10. The two transcontinental railroad lines (map below) met at
(A) Sacramento, California.
(B) Reno, Nevada.
(C) Promontory, Utah.
(D) Santa Fe, New Mexico.
(E) Salt Lake City, Utah.

Railroads, 1870 and 1890

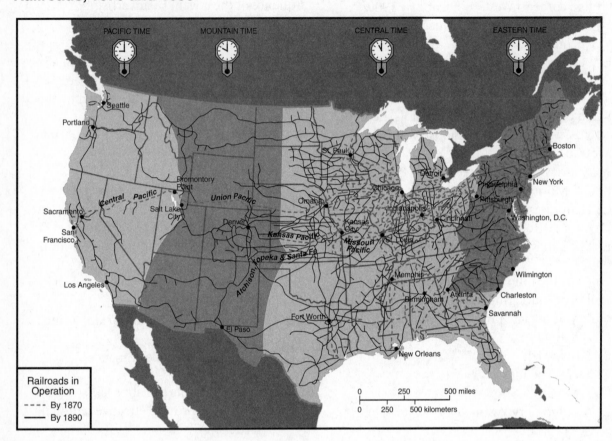

Free-Response Question

> How did the railroad industry pioneer the economic developments of the late nineteenth century?

ANSWERS AND EXPLANATIONS

Multiple-Choice Questions

▌ **1. (A) is correct.** During the last third of the nineteenth century America's transportation system developed tremendously with the construction of tens of thousands of miles of railway, along with a large influx of immigrants (potential consumers) and the growth of family business empires (e.g., Carnegies, Morgans and Rockefellers).

2. (C) is correct. Henry Bessemer developed a process in the late 1850s in England that resulted in a more durable and uniform quality steel.

3. (D) is correct. The first Wal-Mart was not opened until 1962 in Rogers, Arkansas.

4. (A) is correct. The second half of the 1800s saw a dramatic increase in industrialization worldwide and a decrease in the importance of agriculture. Steel became the critical component to the economy of the late 1800s because steel was a stronger and more durable metal compared to iron, and it was also necessary for the production of reliable railroads.

5. (C) is correct. A dramatic increase of patents means that there was a dramatic increase in the number of new things that we invented during the late nineteenth century. These new inventions, such as the typewriter, telephone and electric lighting, tended to be significant in nature. However, even if they weren't significant in nature, with well over a half million new patents from 1850 to 1899 there were bound to be dramatic changes with that many new inventions.

6. (D) is correct. Advertising provided companies with a means to inform the public. The public were informed about products that they had not considered using or needing, but once informed of the product it became a necessary item. The advent of advertising also allowed producers to reach new customers that had been isolated by geography or lack of population base. This new interest and access made Americans into consumers of these newly available products and this increased the demand for these goods.

7. (B) is correct. During the nineteenth century women's place was seen as in the home, "queen of a little house—no matter how humble—where there are children rolling on the floor." When women did find employment outside of the home, they were traditionally hired into positions that were comparable to the types of duties that they would be responsible for in the household (e.g., textiles, cooking and cleaning).

8. (A) is correct. The Knights of Labor was far more successful in terms of membership than its leadership could have ever imagined or managed. In the 1880s its membership was more than 700,000 people spread out all across the country. Actions that were against its national policy, such as strikes in St. Louis and Kansas City, illustrated this inability of the national leadership to control its large membership. In 1886, Jay Gould's Texas and Pacific Railway crushed a Knights of Labor strike that not only showed the ineffectiveness of the national leadership, but also caused the membership and the public to begin to grow disillusioned with the Knights of Labor and unions in general. By 1890, the Knights of Labor had decreased to about 100,000 members.

9. (C) is correct. The Haymarket Square riot was a confrontation between police and strikers in Chicago. During the protests a number of policemen and civilians were injured and killed, which caused public sympathy to swing to the employers and against unions in general.

10. (C) is correct. In the early 1880s, Congress decided to build the first transcontinental railway. The Union Pacific Railroad Company was contracted to start in Nebraska and build westward, while the Central Pacific Railroad

Company would start at the Pacific Coast and build eastward. On May 10, 1869 the two lines met at Promontory, Utah, where a golden spike was hammered in by the presidents of both companies.

Free-Response Essay Sample Response

How did the railroad industry pioneer the economic developments of the late nineteenth century?

The railroad was a critical component of the American economy during the late nineteenth century. There were two main reasons why the railroad industry was responsible for many of the economic developments during this time period. The first reason was quite simple, with the construction of almost 200,000 miles of new railroads during the second half of the nineteenth century, the steel and iron industries prospered as the main components required for building railways. The significant increase in the need for steel and iron caused dramatic surges in the size of these industries.

The second reason was the fact that an increase in the amount of railroads allowed producers of just about every product a dramatically improved transportation system. The transcontinental railroad allowed goods to be moved from coast to coast, over terrain that had been difficult to navigate by other methods. It increased the speed of moving goods by almost seven times. The increase in the speed of moving goods allowed new goods to be moved about, such as cattle from Texas and fruit from Florida, which had never been transported about the country before. This meant that the railroad opened up new markets and created an increase in the number of consumers available to all industries.

In addition to these two main reasons, there were other factors that contributed to the importance of the railroad industry to the American economy, such as the end of the self-sufficient community and the direct access to both producers and markets. However, the requirements of the railroad and the improved access to markets for producers made the railroad industry critical to the American economy during the late nineteenth century.

CHAPTER 19

Toward an Urban Society, 1877–1900

The development of **American cities** radically altered the nation's social environment and problems.

The Lure of the City

In the late nineteenth century, people flocked to the city, drawn by the hope of economic opportunity and the promise of a more exciting life.

- Between 1870 and 1900, cities grew on the base of a new technology of metal-frame skyscrapers, electric **elevators**, **streetcar systems**, and green **suburbs**, producing an increasingly stratified and fragmented society.
- Cities were no longer **"walking cities"** and as the middle class moved out, immigrants and working class poured in.
- **Immigrants from abroad** joined rural Americans in search of jobs in the nation's cities. These newcomers to the city were often forced to live **in tenement houses** with primitive, if any, sanitation facilities.
- The **"new" immigrants** turned to their families, churches, schools, and ethnic organizations to endure the economic and social stresses of industrial capitalism.
- **Between 1877 and 1890**, 6.3 million people immigrated to the United States, most from **southern and eastern Europe**.
- **Immigrant families** were mostly close-knit **nuclear families**. They depended on **immigrant associations** for their social safety net, and communities were built around institutions like churches and schools.
- **Political "machines"** provided some needed services for these immigrants while enriching themselves through exploiting the gullibility of the cities' newest residents, exemplified by William M. Tweed, "Boss Tweed," of New York.

Social and Cultural Change, 1877–1900

The rapid development of an urban society transformed America. How people lived, what and how they ate, and how they took care of their health all changed.

- **Victorian morality, manners, and mores**—usually describing strict standards of dress, manners, and sexual behavior—declined in the face of rapid changes.
- **Manners and mores** were different for the middle- and upper-classes than they were for the lower socio-economic classes.
- **This period saw the rise of organized spectator sports**, which supplemented traditional leisure activities such as concerts, fairs, the circus, and even croquet.

- **Technology** brought a variety of new forms of leisure and entertainment.
- **Economic changes** also produced **new roles for women and the family**.
- **Working-class families** no longer toiled together but did maintain the strong ties needed to survive the urban industrial existence.
- **Middle-class families** became more isolated; homemakers attempted to construct **a sphere of domesticity** as a haven from rampaging materialism of the outside world.
- **Families** became smaller as the birthrate fell dramatically.
- **Americans also began to change their views about women**, demonstrating a limited but growing acceptance of **working women, divorce, sexuality, and women's rights** and related causes.
- **With the development of childhood as a distinct time of life**, Americans placed greater emphasis on **education** with a **structured curriculum** and a **longer school day**.
- **The South** lagged behind in most educational changes.
- **Colleges** grew in number and expanded in size, broadened their curriculum, developed the **first American graduate schools**, and provided more educational **opportunities for women**, but still provided little opportunity for **African Americans** and other minorities.

The Stirrings of Reform

In spite of the period's **"Social Darwinism,"** increasing numbers of Americans proposed the need for reforms.

- **Henry George** launched critical studies of the new urban America with his book *Progress and Poverty*. While his reforms were not adopted, many began to ask the same questions, recognizing as George did the need for reform.
- **Social thinkers** challenged the tenets of Social Darwinism with a new emphasis on the influence of **environmental deprivation** on poverty.
- **Churches** established missions in the inner cities and began to preach the **"Social Gospel"** to encourage those with means to help those in need.
- **New professional social workers**, many of them women, established **settlement houses** to improve slum conditions by providing education, training and other social services, and by working to abolish child labor. Best known is **Jane Addams and the Hull House in Chicago**.

Multiple-Choice Questions

1. The journalist who exposed *How the Other Half Lives* in urban tenements was
   - (A) John Root.
   - (B) James Whitcomb Riley.
   - (C) Samuel Lane Loomis.
   - (D) James E. Ware.
   - (E) Jacob Riis.

2. If an American became ill in the 1870s,
   - (A) hospital insurance would cover the cost of the illness.

   - (B) home care would be the accepted form of treatment.
   - (C) there was little help from the medical profession.
   - (D) recent medical discoveries would guarantee recovery.
   - (E) they would probably die.

3. Most Americans in the 1880s
   - (A) no longer held religious beliefs.
   - (B) believed the school was the center of life.

(C) were church-attending Protestants.

(D) had few moral standards.

(E) were Catholic.

4. The Comstock Law

(A) prohibited the sale of liquor.

(B) ended corruption in politics.

(C) ended segregation in the South.

(D) legislated public morality.

(E) never made it through Congress.

5. The most famous of the urban political bosses in the late nineteenth century was

(A) William Tweed.

(B) Henry George.

(C) Jane Addams.

(D) Dwight L. Moody.

(E) James McManes.

6. The common-law doctrine of *femme couverte*

(A) was revised to adapt to the changes of the period.

(B) provided women with freedom in their marriages.

(C) brought women new political rights.

(D) was strongly supported by women.

(E) was central to the idea of the "New Woman."

7. As a result of the *Plessy v. Ferguson* decision,

(A) African American education was to be separate but equal to white education.

(B) integration of schools was to occur with deliberate speed.

(C) illiteracy among school age children would be eradicated.

(D) *de facto* segregation could no longer occur.

(E) teachers at black schools were paid the same as their counterparts at white schools.

8. Booker T. Washington

(A) believed African Americans should fight for equal rights.

(B) had little hope for the future of African Americans in American society.

(C) believed that self-help was the best plan for African Americans.

(D) emphasized the importance of higher education for African Americans.

(E) founded the National Association for the Advancement of Colored People.

9. The Social Darwinists

(A) believed the laws of nature applied to society.

(B) were active reformers in the late nineteenth century.

(C) had enormous influence on American society.

(D) raised important questions about the conditions of society.

(E) stressed society's responsibility to aid the poor.

10. According to Henry George,

(A) modern society was perfect.

(B) there was a wide gulf between rich and poor.

(C) little could be done to alleviate the problems of the poor.

(D) a graduated income tax would solve the nation's problems.

(E) the poor in America were making real progress.

Free-Response Question

What was the purpose of the Settlement House movement? Evaluate its objectives and methods.

ANSWERS AND EXPLANATIONS

Multiple-Choice Questions

▌ **1. (E) is correct.** In 1890, Jacob Riis wrote "Be a little careful, please! The hall is dark and you might stumble.…Here where the hall turns and dives into utter darkness is…a flight of stairs. You can feel your way, if you cannot see it. Close? Yes! What would you have? All the fresh air that enters these stairs comes from the hall-door that is forever slamming.…Here is a door. Listen! That short, hacking cough, that tiny helpless wail—what do they mean?…The child is dying of measles. With half a chance it might have lived; but it had none. That dark bedroom killed it."

▌ **2. (B) is correct.** There were few hospitals and no health insurance during the 1870s. Advances in medicine, particularly in the areas of surgical procedures made home care not only a more acceptable form of treatment, but also a more effective form of treatment.

▌ **3. (C) is correct.** In the late 1870s approximately nine-tenths of the population of the United States was white, primarily from the Anglo-Saxon countries of northern Europe. During the Reformation of the 1500s and 1600s, these were the same countries that began to break away from the Catholic Church and form Protestant denominations. These were the people who made up a majority of Americans in the 1880s. In fact, approximately eight out of every ten Americans who went to church were Protestants.

▌ **4. (D) is correct.** The Comstock Law of 1873 was passed by Congress at the urging of Anthony Comstock and his Society for the Suppression of Vice. The purposes of these laws were to prohibit the printing or distribution of obscene material, in effect legislating what was and was not moral in the eyes of society.

▌ **5. (A) is correct.** William Tweed became the political boss of Tammany Hall in New York in the late nineteenth century. In this position, he was ultimately responsible for the building of the New York City Courthouse, the creation of Central Park, and the initial backing for the Brooklyn Bridge.

▌ **6. (A) is correct.** *Femme couverte* meant that wives were in essence property of their husbands. They had no legal standing when it came to earning money, owning property or raising children. During the 1890s, many states began to revise the doctrine to allow women to control their own earnings and inherit property. During this time period divorce laws were also modernized to allow for the woman to have sole or joint custody of children upon divorce.

▌ **7. (A) is correct.** The United States Supreme Court decision in the case of *Plessy v. Ferguson* in 1896 allowed the southern states to maintain a school system that was segregated based upon race. The decision specifically stated, however, that these separate systems had to be equal in quality.

▌ **8. (C) is correct.** Washington believed "that the agitation of questions of social equality [was] the extremist folly" and that African Americans should focus on economic gains by going to school, learning skills and working their way up the ladder.

■ **9. (A) is correct.** The concept of Social Darwinism is the application of Charles Darwin's theory of evolution and principle of national selection to society. Darwin believed that animals would evolve or adapt to their environment or would fail to exist in that environment. Social Darwinism is basically the idea that humans, like animals, were subjected to the concept of "survival of the fittest."

■ **10. (B) is correct.** In Henry George's *Progress and Poverty* of 1879, George argued that there was a great divide between the wealthy and the poor and that this divide was based largely upon the fact that the wealthy owned land. He argued that land was the basis of wealth and because it increased in value without any effort, that land should be taxed to provide revenues to aid the poor.

Free-Response Essay Sample Response

What was the purpose of the Settlement House movement? Evaluate its objectives and methods.

The Settlement House movement was undertaken by the youthful, idealist, and mostly middle class. Its purpose was to form settlements in the slums and experience the problems that these individuals hoped to address. As Lillian Wald stated in *The House on Henry Street* (1915), "We were to live in a neighborhood…identify ourselves with it socially, and, in brief, contribute to our citizenship."

The objectives of the movement, while quite ideal, were rather noble for the class of people who undertook them. Composed of largely middle- or upper-class young adults, the movement sought to study, educate, provide health care, and generally raise the level of living conditions for the largely immigrant population that lived in these slums.

Largely unsuccessful in making a meaningful difference in the lives of the majority of the poor it looked to assist, the small number of these Settlement Houses that did provide basic citizenship education, a clean bathtub, or a local reading, only catered to a fraction of the people who lived in the neighborhood. Few of the Settlement Houses offered programs for blacks, which along with immigrants new to the United States, made up the majority of the population of these inner cities.

Seen as outsiders by many of the impoverished, those involved with the Settlement House movement were met with mistrust and even disdain. This statement summarizes the overall effectiveness of the movement.

CHAPTER 20

Political Realignments in the 1890s

Economic depression dominated the 1890s and reshaped political alignments and attitudes.

Politics of Stalemate

America's white male voters of the 1870s and 1880s (the bulk of the electorate) displayed keen interest in partisan politics. Southern states increasingly disfranchised black men.

- **Democrats** emphasized **decentralized** power.
- **Republicans** emphasized a **more active national government**, but the closeness of electoral politics and disillusionment with Civil War centralization stalemated national government. Elections depended on a few key "swing" states.
- **It is noteworthy** that 140 years later, the platforms of the two political parties have virtually changed hands.
- **Most governmental action and reform**, and especially with the new regulatory commissions and bureaus, occurred at the **state and local level**.
- **Between 1880 and 1900**, American presidents succeeded in reasserting the authority of their office.
- **The presidency had been weakened** considerably by the **Johnson impeachment, the Grant scandals, and the electoral controversy of 1876**. By the late 1890s, they had laid the basis for the powerful **modern presidency**.

Republicans in Power: The Billion-Dollar Congress

In **1888**, the Republicans broke the **electoral stalemate** by winning control of the presidency and both houses of Congress.

- **Holding the controlling majority** of government, the Republicans enacted significant legislative programs, **the McKinley Tariff, the Sherman Antitrust Act and the Sherman Silver Purchase Acts.**
- **Americans rejected that activism** by crushing the Republicans in the elections of **1890** and, especially in the Midwest, Democrats gained new power.

The Rise of the Populist Movement

By the summer of 1890, **Farmers' Alliance** organizers were recruiting huge numbers of unhappy farmers, sometimes at the rate of 1,000 a week.

- **Populism** surged as a response to an agrarian sense of social and economic loss that was not altogether realistic.

- **Farmers organized the Grange and the Farmers' Alliance** in pursuit of the reforms of the **Ocala Demands**. Later, the Populist party adopted much of the same platform as the Ocala Demands.
- **In the South**, the Alliance enjoyed considerable success within the Democratic party; in the North and West, it successfully ran many of its own candidates.
- **In 1892**, the Alliance led in the formation of the **Populist party**, which collected over one million votes for its 1892 presidential candidate, but the party then began to lose strength.
- **Major planks of the Populists' presidential platform** were later incorporated into law.

The Crisis of the Depression

Grover Cleveland and the Democratic party swept the election of **1892** but then faced a severe depression following the Panic of 1893.

- **The economy slumped into a crisis** as banks failed at record rates, factories and mines shut down, and millions were out of work. The next year worsened, and the economic crisis became more than a temporary hitch.
- **The depression** led to protests demanding relief for workers and farmers, including a march on Washington by **Coxey's Army** and the **Pullman Strike**, which shut down the railroads of the West and produced the **Socialist leader Eugene Debs**.
- **President Cleveland** defeated the strike with a violent confrontation between federal troops and a mob of people unconnected with the strike.
- **The depression also led** to a strike of **bituminous coal mines** by the new **United Mine Workers**. The violence which followed pitted workers against capital but also divided the "old" mostly English and Irish miners and the "new" miners from Southern and Eastern Europe.
- **President Cleveland** blamed the depression on the **Sherman Silver Purchase Act** and led its repeal in 1893, which split and (in combination with the depression) wrecked the Democratic party.
- **Thus, the depression** led to a **new Republican supremacy**, and made the Democratic party little more than a southern, sectional party.

Changing Attitudes

The depression also changed the country's traditional social views. Many Americans now saw **poverty as a failure of the economy** rather than the individual, so they demanded **reforms** to help the poor and unemployed, an important step toward national authority and activism.

- **"Everybody Works but Father"** More women and children worked at jobs made available to them because they were paid less than men.
- **Realistic and naturalistic writers** portrayed everyday life in a new, sometimes deterministic manner, including, for example, **Mark Twain, William Dean Howells, Stephen Crane, Frank Norris, and Theodore Dreiser**.

The Presidential Election of 1896

The Republican dominance initiated in 1894 continued with the victory of the **Republican William McKinley over the Democrat William Jennings Bryan**.

- **Silver** became a central, symbolic issue.
- **Many believed silver's free coinage** could end the depression; it also came to represent the interests of the common people, especially farmers in the West.
- **McKinley and the Republicans** promised a return to the **gold standard**, which they claimed would end the depression.
- **Although split over silver**, the **Democrats endorsed free silver** and nominated William Jennings Bryan after he captured the convention with the oratory of his **"Cross of Gold"** speech.
- **McKinley won the election handily**, as both the Democrats and the People's party nominated Bryant, but each chose a different vice-president, effectively dividing the vote.
- **The People's party vanished after 1896.**

The McKinley Administration

The new government enjoyed prosperity, raised the tariff, demonetized silver, and prodded its party to shift from promoting to regulating industrialism. By the time of **McKinley's assassination and Theodore Roosevelt's ascent to the presidency**, the Republican party had clearly emerged as the dominant party, as Americans rallied to reform the system that had produced the depression of the 1890s.

Multiple-Choice Questions

1. Why were Americans fascinated by politics during the Gilded Age?
   - (A) Women and men were voting for the first time.
   - (B) African Americans were able to use their newly won suffrage.
   - (C) The quality of political candidates was excellent.
   - (D) Most Americans saw it as a form of entertainment.
   - (E) Cash incentives made people eager to vote.

2. Which of the following did NOT determine party loyalty in the late nineteenth century?
   - (A) ethnic background
   - (B) political ideology
   - (C) religious beliefs
   - (D) Civil War loyalties
   - (E) class

3. Which of the following was NOT part of the Republican Party's platform in the post-Civil War period?
   - (A) high protective tariffs
   - (B) civil rights legislation
   - (C) subsidies to railroads
   - (D) decentralized government power
   - (E) promotion of moral progress

4. The *Wabash* decision stated that
   - (A) states could regulate only intrastate commerce.
   - (B) states could jointly regulate interstate commerce.
   - (C) only the federal government could regulate intrastate trade.
   - (D) private property was the sanctity of the individual.
   - (E) states could regulate both intrastate and interstate commerce.

5. The Sherman Antitrust Act
   - (A) was vague and at the mercy of the Courts.
   - (B) had little effect on antitrust policy.
   - (C) was only concerned with regulating railroads.
   - (D) did not have criminal penalties for violators.
   - (E) was used aggressively by the Justice Department.

6. The case *United States v. E. C. Knight*
   (A) strengthened the regulatory powers of the federal government.
   (B) provided stronger regulation over manufacturing.
   (C) had little effect on national policy.
   (D) gave the Supreme Court an opportunity to uphold and strengthen the Sherman Antitrust Act.
   (E) narrowed the definition of trusts and monopolies.

7. The major objective of the Alliance Movement was
   (A) to form a social organization for farmers.
   (B) to organize and politicize the American farmer.
   (C) to ensure equal distribution of wealth.
   (D) to elect Democrats and Republicans who represented the farmers.
   (E) to protect farmers against greedy cattle ranchers.

8. Which of the following was NOT a consequence of the Pullman strike?
   (A) The Supreme Court provided an anti-labor weapon.
   (B) Grover Cleveland won public support for his actions.
   (C) The Supreme Court endorsed the use of injunctions in labor disputes.
   (D) Eugene V. Debs rose to national prominence.
   (E) The workers had their demands met.

9. William McKinley was elected president in
   (A) 1884.
   (B) 1888.
   (C) 1892.
   (D) 1896.
   (E) 1900.

10. The major issue of the election of 1896 was
    (A) currency.
    (B) tariffs.
    (C) patronage.
    (D) regulation of the railroads.
    (E) race relations.

Free-Response Question

Is it correct to assume the election of 1896 was a turning point in American political history? Explain.

ANSWERS AND EXPLANATIONS

Multiple-Choice Questions

▌ **1. (D) is correct.** The political campaigns of the Gilded Age included numerous social events, such as rallies, parades, picnics, and torchlight processions—events in which the whole community could become involved. For this reason, the majority of Americans saw politics as a form of mass entertainment, almost sport-like.

▌ **2. (B) is correct.** The politics of the late nineteenth century was still dominated by the Civil War generation. The differences in Civil War loyalties, ethnic background, religious beliefs and even class were not only important in determining party loyalty, but were also still very strong and seldom changed. Political ideology, however, was no longer an important factor in party loyalties and this trend would continue until later in the twentieth century.

▌ **3. (D) is correct.** It was the Democratic Party of the late nineteenth century that believed that government should be kept local and small. The Republican Party believed in protective tariffs and subsidies to railroads as a means of economic growth. They were responsible for legislative and constitutional protections for civil rights and saw the role of government to promote moral progress and material wealth for Americans.

▌ **4. (C) is correct.** In 1886, the United States Supreme Court in *Wabush, St. Louis, & Pacific Railway Co. v. Illinois* decided that states could not regulate commerce outside of the borders of their own state. This meant that only the federal government could regulate trade between states.

▌ **5. (A) is correct.** One of the more important pieces of legislation during the 1890s, the Sherman Antitrust Act was rarely used by the Justice Department to regulate business combinations. As an example of the vagueness of the legislation, in its first use in the *United States v. E.C. Knight*, the court's interpretation of the legislation rendered it almost completely ineffective.

▌ **6. (E) is correct.** In the case of *United States v. E.C. Knight*, the courts made the distinction between commerce and manufacturing as it pertained to the E.C. Knight Co. It determined that E.C. Knight Co., which controlled 98% of all sugar refining in the United States, was a manufacturer and not subject to the Sherman Antitrust Act. This distinction, that a manufacturer does not constitute commerce, narrowed the federal government's definition of trusts and monopolies under the Sherman Antitrust Act.

▌ **7. (B) is correct.** Originally a social organization, the Alliance Movement became a force in American politics. Rejecting the traditional Republican and Democratic parties, the Alliance Movement began to back those who wanted to take control of the two existing parties and, in some cases, even formed their own political parties.

▌ **8. (E) is correct.** The Pullman strike was put down by the army after President Grover Cleveland obtained a court injunction from the Supreme Court due to the disruption to the mail system. While the public supported Cleveland's action, the reality was that the court injunction would be a powerful antilabor weapon for business to use. Jailed for his actions during the Pullman strike, Eugene V. Debs gained national recognition and upon his release from jail worked to build the Socialist Party of America.

▌ **9. (D) is correct.** Grover Cleveland won the elections of 1884 and 1892, while Benjamin Harrison was elected to office in 1888. William McKinley was elected President in 1896. He was re-elected to the same post in 1900.

▌ **10. (A) is correct.** Known as the "Battle of the Standards," the major issue of the election of 1896 was which precious metal should be used to back American currency as its standard. McKinley and the Republicans supported maintaining the use of the gold standard, while Bryan and the Democrats supported the free coinage of silver.

Free-Response Essay Sample Response

Is it correct to assume the election of 1896 was a turning point in American political history? Explain.

Prior to the election of 1896 party loyalties, which had been rooted in Civil War traditions, were based upon ethnic and religious differences, along with class distinctions. These loyalties were also remarkably strong. However, the election of 1896 saw the emergence of new voting patterns for the first time in American political history.

The main issue of the election of 1896 was the free coinage of silver. After suffering through the depression since 1893, a large segment of the American population wanted U.S. Mints to coin all silver offered to it. The people of the South and the West, even the farming regions of New York and New England, believed that the more silver that was coined would translate into more money that would be in circulation. Additional money in circulation would mean more business for everyone: farm prices would rise, laborers would go back to work, closed factories would open, and the United States would even assert its independence by bucking the worldwide trend of using only the gold standard.

However, the people of the Northeast, the Midwest and four border states sided with gold and the Republican candidate, William McKinley. In addition to the silver-gold standard debate, the Democratic candidate William Jennings Bryan summoned voters to a traditional America. With the election of 1896 marking a turning point in traditional voter intentions, this appeal failed to resonate with the voters.

CHAPTER 21

Toward Empire

As the **American frontier** "closed," many in America pushed for new frontiers of an empire for exploration, settlement, and new markets.

America Looks Outward

In contrast to prior expansion into contiguous territories intended for settlement and annexation, the United States in the 1890s acquired island colonies intended as **naval bases** and **commercial outposts** for the expansion and protection of American markets.

- **Stimulated by a closing frontier and an expanding economy** at home, the United States became increasingly interested in the **worldwide scramble for colonies** in the latter nineteenth century.
- **Advocates of Anglo-Saxon racial superiority** exhorted expansion of U.S. trade and dominion as both an American duty and destiny in "civilizing" the less advanced regions of the world.
- **American policy-makers** sought to avoid entanglements in Europe during this era while expanding American trade (and perhaps territory) in Latin American and Asia.
- **The United States** reasserted the **Monroe Doctrine** and promoted **Pan-American** interests.
- **The Hawaiian and Samoan Islands** attracted Americans primarily as stepping stones to the valuable trade of the Far East.
- **American residents in Hawaii** instigated a revolution and the creation of a republican government in **1893**, but the United States resisted annexation of the islands until 1898.
- **Acquiring a naval station in Samoa in 1878**, the United States divided the island chain with Germany in 1899.
- **Captain Alfred Thayer Mahan**, naval strategist and historian, convinced many Americans of the need for an **expanded navy** to guarantee the nation's wealth and power.
- **Benjamin F. Tracy, secretary of the navy** under President Benjamin Harrison, pushed Congress to begin a build-up program that would move the United States **from twelfth** among world navies in 1889 **to third** in 1900.

War with Spain

The brief war with Spain increased American confidence as well as dramatically enlarged the United States' empire. The United States would become the dominant force in the twentieth century.

- **In 1895**, economic depression and discontent with Spanish rule led **to revolution in Cuba**.
- **Spain responded** with a policy of brutal repression. Exaggerated accounts of Spanish atrocities by **America's "yellow press"**; the publication of a letter insulting President McKinley from the Spanish ambassador in Washington; and **the sinking of the American battleship *Maine*** in Havana harbor all contributed to a growing clamor for United States intervention in the war on behalf of Cuban independence.
- **Dissatisfied with Spain's response** to Cuban and American demands, **President McKinley called for war in April 1898**.
- **Congress and the American public** responded enthusiastically to war. More soldiers volunteered to fight than could be trained, fed, or equipped.
- **The war lasted only ten weeks** and resulted in relatively few American deaths (more to tropical diseases than battle), prompting the soon-to-be secretary of state **John Hay's famous observation of the conflict as "a splendid little war."**
- **Many of the units that fought** in the war were **National Guard** units, and they mirrored many of the changes in American society.
- **Certain that African American men** could resist tropical diseases, United States military officials recruited them as soldiers. Although subjected to segregation and discrimination, these **"smoked Yankees"** (as the Spanish troops referred to them) responded bravely and played a crucial role in the American invasion and takeover of Cuba.
- **American military operations** began with a stunning naval victory directed by Commodore George Dewey over the Spanish fleet in **Manila Bay**, resulting in the **U. S. occupation of the Philippine Islands**.
- **In the Caribbean**, the United States invaded Cuba, **captured Santiago**, occupied **Puerto Rico**, and destroyed Spain's only remaining battle fleet, forcing **Spain's surrender in August 1898**. Only 379 Americans died in battle, but more than 5,200 died of disease or accidents.

Acquisition of Empire

The treaty ending the **Spanish-American War** called for Spanish recognition of **Cuban independence**; Spanish cession of **Puerto Rico, Guam, and the Philippine Islands to the United States**; and U.S. payment of **$20 million to Spain**. Promptly submitted to the Senate for ratification, the treaty set off a storm of debate throughout the country.

- **Members of an Anti-Imperialistic League** argued that American acquisition of colonies would prove to be undemocratic, costly, and potentially harmful to the interests of labor and racial harmony.
- **Proponents of imperialism** repeated the economic, strategic, and intellectual arguments justifying American expansionism. The Senate ratified the treaty in February 1899, with only two votes to spare.
- **Demanding independence**, Filipino insurgents led by **Emilio Aguinaldo** fought a guerrilla war against American takeover of the islands. Proving much more difficult and costly than the war against Spain, the **Philippine-American War**

(1899–1902) convinced American leaders of the need to prepare the island archipelago for eventual self-government.

▌ **From 1901 to 1904**, the Supreme Court ruled that the Constitution does not "follow the flag" and that Congress could extend American constitutional provisions to territories as it saw fit.

▌ **Cuba was granted "independence,"** but forced to include the **Platt Amendment** in her constitution, allowing for **special United States privileges**, including the right of intervention.

▌ **By the end of the nineteenth century**, outside powers had carved **China** into spheres of influence, threatening to reduce or even eliminate American economic interests there. During the **Boxer Rebellion**, through a series of diplomatic notes in 1899–1900 urging an **"Open Door"** in China, **Secretary of State John Hay** boldly proclaimed a policy that preserved for China some semblance of national authority over its territory and trade, and thus commercial opportunities equal to other foreign powers for the United States. From 1867 to 1900, the United States had transformed itself from a relatively isolationist nation to one of world power.

Multiple-Choice Questions

1. Theodore Roosevelt resigned from his position as _____ to organize the Rough Riders.
   (A) vice president
   (B) secretary of defense
   (C) assistant secretary of defense
   (D) secretary of the navy
   (E) assistant secretary of the navy

2. Josiah Strong
   (A) fostered the concept of the righteousness of American expansion.
   (B) believed that only missionary work should be done overseas.
   (C) had little regard for the theories of Charles Darwin.
   (D) hindered American expansion through his religious teachings.
   (E) thought foreign trade was unimportant.

3. The Treaty of Washington in 1871
   (A) created a breach in Anglo-American relations.
   (B) showed the diplomatic skills of Hamilton Fish.
   (C) allowed Grant to extend American influence in Asia.
   (D) provided for the negotiation of American Civil War claims against Great Britain.
   (E) both B and D

4. During the Cleveland administration, which nation did the United States replace as the major power in Latin America?
   (A) Germany
   (B) Great Britain
   (C) Venezuela
   (D) Mexico
   (E) Spain

5. Why did the United States increase its interest in Hawaii after the Civil War?
   (A) There was intense pressure by American missionaries.
   (B) There was a fear of German influence in the region.
   (C) The economic and military value of the islands increased.
   (D) American political leaders believed the islands could be a model for expansionism.
   (E) Native Hawaiians appealed to the United States for help.

6. In their approaches to the Cuban rebellion against Spain,
   (A) President Cleveland was generally neutral while President McKinley favored the insurgents.
   (B) President Cleveland wanted to intervene on behalf of the insurgents but McKinley wanted neutrality.
   (C) both Presidents Cleveland and McKinley wanted war with Spain.
   (D) both Presidents Cleveland and McKinley were totally neutral.
   (E) both Presidents Cleveland and McKinley opposed any involvement with Spain or Cuba.

7. By 1897, Spain
   (A) was unwilling to meet any American demands.
   (B) tried to avoid a confrontation with the United States.
   (C) supported the polices of General Weyler.
   (D) seemed determined to maintain control at all costs.
   (E) agreed to give up Cuba rather than go to war.

8. The Philippine-American War was
   (A) a minor event for Americans.
   (B) more costly than the Spanish-American War.
   (C) fought in a traditional manner.
   (D) never completely resolved.
   (E) over before the Spanish-American War.

9. According to the Supreme Court,
   (A) U.S. possessions should be given formal privileges.
   (B) U.S. possessions should be given fundamental rights.
   (C) no rights should be given to U.S. possessions.
   (D) Congress should determine the rights of U.S. possessions.
   (E) "the Constitution followed the flag."

10. In which of the following territories did the native inhabitants receive United States citizenship in 1900?
    (A) Guam
    (B) Hawaii
    (C) Puerto Rico
    (D) the Philippines
    (E) Alaska

Free-Response Question

Why was the Spanish-American War "a splendid little war" for the United States? What effect did it have on American society?

ANSWERS AND EXPLANATIONS

Multiple-Choice Questions

▊ **1. (E) is correct.** When war broke out between the United States and Spain in 1898, against the advice of colleagues, Roosevelt resigned as Assistant Secretary of the Navy to enlist and with a friend formed the First United States Volunteer Cavalry, also known as the Rough Riders.

▊ **2. (A) is correct.** Strong believed that the Anglo-Saxon people were God's chosen race and that it was their duty to expand in order to export both their trade and their religion to other inferior peoples.

▊ **3. (E) is correct.** The Treaty of Washington was one of the first peaceful settlements of an international dispute that had been settled by the United States. Through the patient and skillful negotiations of Secretary of State Fish, the United States was able to repair the relationship with Britain that had been strained during the Civil War.

■ **4. (B) is correct.** During the Cleveland administration, Great Britain became involved in disputes in both Venezuela and British Guiana. The United States took the side of both Latin American countries and in the end, the British backed down and the United States was left as the dominant power in the Western Hemisphere.

■ **5. (C) is correct.** The Hawaiian islands were a natural "Crossroads of the Pacific" for American goods that were destined for Asian markets and Asia goods that were imported into the United States. In addition to its economic importance, the islands of Hawaii were of great military value, being centrally located between the United States and the Asian military power of Japan. Being closer to the United States than to Japan, it was feared that the islands could play a stronger military role for the Japanese against the United States in future aggressions.

■ **6. (A) is correct.** Cleveland was against the annexation of Cuba and therefore feared that the island nation may become unstable without an imperial overlord. For these reasons, he tried to remain neutral during the dispute, even offering to mediate a peaceful settlement between the insurgents and Spain. McKinley, on the other hand, favored the cause of the insurgents and took steps to ensure that there was a peaceful resolution to the conflict or that there would be American assistance for the insurgents.

■ **7. (B) is correct.** A change of government in Spain in 1897 led the Spanish to begin negotiations with the United States in order to find a peaceful solution to their problem with Cuba.

■ **8. (B) is correct.** Four times as many American soldiers fought in the Philippine-American Wars than did in the Spanish American War. The same comparison saw more than 12 times the number of soldiers killed during the Philippine-American Wars than were killed during the Spanish American War.

■ **9. (D) is correct.** In the cases *De Lima* v. *Bidwell*, *Dooley* v. *United States*, and *Downes v. Bidwell*, the Supreme Court asserted that Congress had the ability to extend whatever constitutional provisions that it saw fit to annexed territory.

■ **10. (B) is correct.** In 1900, the United States granted American citizenship, along with an elective legislature and an appointed governor from Washington to Hawaii.

Free-Response Essay Sample Response

Why was the Spanish-American War "a splendid little war" for the United States? What effect did it have on American society?

As far as wars go, the Spanish American War was a relatively happy occasion. With few casualties and numerous victories during the ten-week period of the war, the newspapers in the United States were able to write a "good news" story almost every day. The war itself allowed the United States to show the gains that it had made in its navy, which was fast becoming one of the strongest in the world. It also allowed the army to begin the process of modernizing itself after thirty years of neglect following the Civil War.

On the home front, towns all across America took ownership of the units of volunteers that had come from their hometowns. These "hometown" units were simply an extension of the community, largely due to the high number of volunteers that answered McKinley's call in 1898. Communities sent food, clothing and even local doctors to these hometown units.

At the end of the war, the United States saw itself in possession of an island empire that stretched throughout the Caribbean and across the Pacific. At home, the discrimination against African Americans, especially the black units that were stationed at southern posts, continued in the southern states as it had during the war. However, American society was upbeat as the United States had proved itself among the military leaders in the world, complete with its modern navy and overseas empire.

CHAPTER 22

The Progressive Era

In late 1902, writers for *McClure's Magazine* introduced a new type of journalism, investigating and exposing the problems caused by rapid industrialization and urbanization. These journalists, dubbed **"muckrakers"** by Theodore Roosevelt, contributed to a broad reform movement called **"progressivism."**

▌ **From the mid-1890s through World War I**, progressives challenged the status quo and sought changes in the nation's society, politics, economy, culture, and environment.

The Changing Face of Industrialism

In spite of persistent problems of poverty, disease, and racism, a new century and generally improved economic conditions brought a sense of optimism to Americans.

▌ **The emergence of mammoth business** enterprises from 1895 to 1915 led to inevitable changes in managerial attitudes, business organization, and worker roles.

▌ **In 1913, Henry Ford established a moving assembly line** to mass produce his standard automobile, **the Model T.** By dramatically reducing the time and costs of production, Ford managed to **lower prices** and expand sales and profits.

▌ **Standard Oil** began a national trend among American big businesses toward **oligopoly** (rule of the few) by swallowing up smaller competitors.

▌ **By 1909**, nearly one-third of the nation's manufactured goods were produced by only one percent of the industrial companies.

▌ **Massive business mergers and reorganizations** touched off a national debate over what the national government could and/or should do about the trusts. Many progressives as well as business leaders generally favored **moderate reforms** that would promote economic progress while protecting private property.

▌ **Assembly line production** caused management to focus on speed and product rather than on the worker.

▌ **Frederick Winslow Taylor** introduced principles of **"scientific management"** to extract maximum efficiency.

▌ **The industrial system** promoted worker productivity, but jobs became increasingly monotonous and dangerous. A **1911 fire at the Triangle Shirtwaist Company** in New York City killed 146 people and focused national attention on unsafe working conditions.

Society's Masses

The mass production of goods in America allowed greater consumption and required a larger work force. Women, African Americans, Mexican Americans, and immigrants played significant roles in the nation's economic expansion and sought to improve their individual as well as group conditions.

▍ **Farmers benefited from greater production** and expanding urban markets.

▍ **Improved roads and mail services** diminished rural isolation and brought farmers into the larger society.

▍ **In 1900, one-fifth of all adult women worked**, but most earned only meager wages.

▍ **Women of color** had even fewer job opportunities or protections.

▍ **Continuing use of child labor** provoked public indignation and led women reformers to lobby for federal protection of maternal and infant health.

▍ **Progressive reforms** seemed barely to touch the lives of **African Americans.** Few belonged to unions, obtained adequate education, or earned pay equal to that of white workers in the same jobs.

▍ **African-American leader W. E. B. DuBois** rejected the gradualist approach urged by **Booker T. Washington** and began the **Niagara Movement** for racial justice and equality, resulting in the creation of the **National Association for the Advancement of Colored People (NAACP) in 1910.**

▍ **The "new" immigration of southern and eastern Europeans** continued in the early twentieth century. Employers used **"Americanization"** programs in attempts to fashion dutiful habits among foreign workers.

▍ **After 1910**, large numbers of Mexicans fled to the United States.

Conflict in the Workplace

Long hours, low pay, and the impersonal and unsafe conditions of factory jobs led to an increase of worker strikes, absenteeism, and union membership. Mindful of workers' problems and fearful of potential violence, progressives urged labor reforms.

▍ **The most successful union**, the **American Federation of Labor (AFL)**, restricted membership to skilled male workers and limited its agenda to issues of wages and working conditions. **The Women's Trade Union League (WTUL)** led the effort to organize women workers and promote their interests. The militant **International Workers of the World (IWW)** urged labor solidarity and called for social revolution.

▍ **Some business leaders used violence and police action** to keep workers in line. Others learned to consider workers' job satisfaction and safety as well as pay as means to promote productivity and improve public relations.

A New Urban Culture

The first two decades of the twentieth century saw a general improvement in the quality of life for many Americans.

▍ **Average life expectancies for Americans** increased dramatically. By 1920, fewer than one-half of all Americans lived in rural areas.

▍ **Rising urban affluence** led to outlying suburbs, and major cities used zoning as a technique to shape growth and, often, extend racial and ethnic segregation.

▍ **Changing work rules and increasing mechanization** from 1890 to 1920 gradually allowed American workers **greater leisure time** for play and enjoyment of the arts.

- **Mass entertainment** consisted of sports events, vaudeville, and later, movies as well as phonograph records of the new types of music: ragtime, blues, and jazz.
- **In the fine arts,** Americans sought new forms and styles of expression, reflecting the period's pervading call for change and progress. The nation's urban centers, especially New York City and Chicago, attracted painters, writers, poets, dancers, and musicians interested in artistic experimentation. These artists joined with a generation of people in the fields of politics, journalism, science, education, and a host of others in hopes of progressive change.

Multiple-Choice Questions

1. Henry Ford showed that enormous revenues could come from
   (A) cheap, low-quality goods.
   (B) an emphasis on craft methods of production.
   (C) low-volume, high-quality production.
   (D) small unit profit on a large volume of sales.
   (E) high-priced luxury goods.

2. Frederick W. Taylor's management methods emphasized
   (A) keeping the employee happy.
   (B) creating a comfortable working environment.
   (C) trusting the employee's willingness to work.
   (D) the enforcement of work standards and cooperation.
   (E) allowing the worker to develop the best solutions to problems.

3. Which one of the following is an incorrect match?
   (A) Henry Ford: mass production
   (B) Ida Tarbell: muckraker
   (C) Booker T. Washington: Niagara Movement
   (D) J. P. Morgan: finance
   (E) George W. Bellows: realist painting

4. This organization led the fight for equal rights and education.
   (A) WCTCU
   (B) NAACP
   (C) Wobblies
   (D) ACTUC
   (E) SNCC

5. Between 1900 and 1920, women
   (A) increasingly found medical careers open to them.
   (B) increasingly found professional careers closed to them.
   (C) received considerable support in their quest for careers.
   (D) found opportunities for careers equal to those of men.
   (E) taught in colleges and universities in increasing numbers.

6. In the first decade of the twentieth century, the American Federation of Labor
   (A) became increasingly radical.
   (B) remained devoted to the interests of skilled craftsmen.
   (C) included more and more unskilled workers.
   (D) lost its place as the largest American union.
   (E) aligned itself with management of America's largest corporations.

7. In terms of worker relations, Henry Ford
   (A) was generally behind the times.
   (B) showed little concern for his workers.
   (C) used trickery and brute force to achieve his aims.
   (D) developed a poor image that limited his choice of workers.
   (E) tried many innovations.

8. The greater leisure time available to workers resulted from
   (A) the advent of flexible work schedules.
   (B) a decrease in the length of the work week.
   (C) a rise in unemployment.
   (D) longer work breaks.
   (E) increased use of machines and automation.

9. A popular form of entertainment that drew from the immigrant experience was
   (A) the band concert.
   (B) ragtime.
   (C) vaudeville.
   (D) jazz.
   (E) the minstrel show.

10. Using your own knowledge and the following graph, between 1898 and 1903, the American economy saw

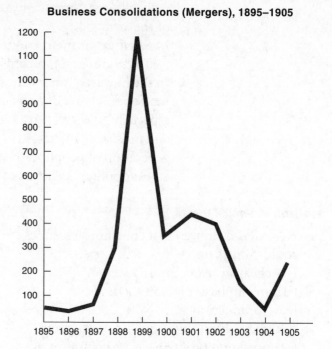

Business Consolidations (Mergers), 1895–1905

   (A) an increase in the number of smaller businesses.
   (B) greater competition among all businesses.
   (C) a wave of mergers and consolidations.
   (D) the outlawing of trusts.
   (E) meager overall business growth.

Free-Response Question

Describe Henry Ford's theory of production, profit, and labor relations.

ANSWERS AND EXPLANATIONS

Multiple-Choice Questions

▌ **1. (D) is correct.** After failing to make much profit with high priced automobiles, in 1907 Ford lowered the prices of his cars and sales soared. This lesson of the modern economy, that smaller unit profits on large numbers of sales means enormous revenues, was one that would sustain Henry Ford for the remainder of his career.

▌ **2. (D) is correct.** In his book *The Principles of Scientific Management*, Taylor argued that through the enforcement of standards, best practices, and co-operation management would be able to control the workplace.

▌ **3. (C) is correct.** The Niagara Movement rejected Booker T. Washington's approach that self-help was the best plan for African Americans. Instead, the Niagara Movement supported militant action to achieve equal rights and education for African American youth.

▌ **4. (B) is correct.** This organization, which was created by W.E.B. Du Bois in 1910, fought for equal rights by pressuring employers and labor unions and governments on behalf of African Americans. It also fought for political rights, such as voting, for African Americans and against segregation.

▌ **5. (B) is correct.** The number of women in colleges and universities declined during this period and many women found that professions like medicine and science were closed to them. However, with more women than men graduating from high school, many women found careers in clerical work after they completed studies from new business schools that were opening.

▌ **6. (B) is correct.** While the American Federation of Labor increased dramatically at the turn of the twentieth century, it remained devoted to the interests of skilled craftsmen by seeking to limit entry into the crafts and protect worker prerogatives.

▌ **7. (E) is correct.** Ford was known for his innovations in worker relations. Concepts such as doubling the wage rate for common labor, the eight hour work day and a personnel department allowed Ford to have his pick of the labor force.

▌ **8. (B) is correct.** The average workweek for manufacturing laborers in 1920 was 51 hours. This had decreased by nine hours over the previous thirty years.

▌ **9. (C) is correct.** Vaudeville expressed variety of city life by using skits, songs, comics, acrobats and magicians to show an earthiness that was new to mass audiences.

▌ **10. (C) is correct.** The graph above indicates the tremendous increase in the number of mergers and consolidations during the period 1898 to 1900 and relatively high numbers from 1900 to 1903.

Free-Response Essay Sample Response

Describe Henry Ford's theory of production, profit, and labor relations.

In American industrial society, Henry Ford was a leader in his field. His industrial practices revolutionized the way that business was conducted in the United States during the early 1900s.

In terms of production, Henry Ford took the concept of mass production (that had been originally conceived of by Ransom E. Olds) and copied techniques that he had witnessed in meat packing facilities, where the product moves along an assembly line and at each stop experts perform the necessary functions for the item to move to the next stage. In 1913, Ford set up a moving assembly line in his Michigan plant and significantly reduced the time it took to manufacture an automobile.

In his early years, Henry Ford priced his automobiles like many others, continually raising the prices as much as the market would allow. However, after a particularly poor year Ford lowered the price dramatically in 1907 and sales of his automobiles skyrocketed. He learned very quickly that he was able to make a greater profit by selling a high number of automobiles at a low margin, compared to a smaller number of automobiles at a high margin. Based on these lessons, he stated "I am going to democratize the automobile. When I'm through everyone will be able to afford one, and about everyone will have one."

On the labor relations front, on January 5, 1914, Henry Ford announced the five-dollar day. This was double the wage rate for common labor that had been traditionally paid. He also decreased the length of the work day from nine hour to eight hours and established a personnel department, which was designed to place workers in jobs that were appropriate to their individual skill sets. These gains gave Ford his pick of the industrial workforce as people flocked to apply for positions in his plants.

It was in these three areas; production, profit, and labor relations where Henry Ford modernized the field of industry and allowed his company to become a leader in American business. The effects of Henry Ford's influences continue to the present day.

CHAPTER 23

From Roosevelt to Wilson in the Age of Progressivism

Despite trying to continue with Roosevelt's basic policies and directions, Taft's presidency was far from smooth, and a bitter rift developed between the two men and within their party.

The Spirit of Progressivism

Despite philosophical differences, **progressives** held to several basic tenets. Being optimistic about human nature, they sought to **humanize and regulate big business.** Progressives believed in the necessity of **educated intervention** in people's lives and an **active role by all levels of government** to manifest reform. They believed in **reforming the environment** though scientific and moral approaches.

- **Between 1890 and 1920**, a large number of **national professional societies** of accountants, architects, doctors, lawyers, etc. were formed.
- **Groups of concerned professionals put pressure** on city governments and businesses to dramatically improve conditions. These **social workers** collected data on urban conditions, wrote books and pamphlets, and **sought recognition as a distinct field** within the social sciences.
- **Many reform-conscious women** dedicated themselves to the **crusade to abolish alcohol and** its evils from American life. Promoted by superb organizational efforts under the **Women's Christian Temperance Union** and the **Anti-Saloon League**, these reformers succeeded in winning passage of the **Prohibition Amendment to the U.S. Constitution**.
- **With more college-educated women**, numerous organizations were started to promote the rights and welfare of American women. After long delays, the **suffragists** succeeded in gaining passage of the **Nineteenth Amendment**.
- **Women progressives** also worked to **regulate child and female labor**.
- **The Socialist party** made some progress, doubling in membership between 1904 and 1908, and elected many local officials.

Reform in the Cities and States

Due to various factors, **voter turnout dropped sharply** in the quarter century after 1900. Many people turned to interest groups and professional and trade associations to promote their respective concerns.

- **Stressing efficiency and results**, substantial reform movements within city governments spread across the nation. Using new corps of experts, city officials constructed **model governments** that pushed through scientifically based policies.

Galveston, Texas, and Cleveland, Ohio, were among the cities implementing new policies and regulation of corrupt practices.

▊ **States across the nation formed regulatory commissions**, especially for utilities, transportation, and business. The most famous reform governor of the Progressive Era was **Robert LaFollette** of Wisconsin.

▊ In 1912, Congress added the **Seventeenth Amendment** to the Constitution to provide for the **direct elections** of U.S. Senators.

▊ **Under the "Wisconsin Idea,"** LaFollette improved education and workers' compensation, lowered railroad rates, and brought forth the **first state income tax.**

The Republican Roosevelt

As McKinley's successor, **Roosevelt** brought a new spirit of enthusiasm and aggressiveness to the presidency. Early in his administration, Roosevelt appeared to support racial progress, but later retreated in the face of growing criticism.

▊ **Distinguishing between "good" and "bad" trusts**, Roosevelt sought to protect the former and regulate the latter.

▊ **To regulate corporations**, Congress created the **Department of Commerce and Labor with a Bureau of Corporations**. The president also pursued regulation through antitrust suits, most notably against **J. P. Morgan's Northern Securities Company** and the **American Tobacco Company.**

▊ **Viewing the federal government as an impartial "broker"** between labor and management, Roosevelt pressured the coal companies to settle their differences with the **United Mine Workers** or face executive intervention.

Roosevelt Progressivism at Its Height

Easily winning in his bid for reelection with 57 percent of the vote, Roosevelt readied himself for more reform.

▊ **Roosevelt moved into other areas of reform** in his second term. The powers of the **Interstate Commerce Commission** were strengthened by passage of the **Hepburn Act**.

▊ After the publication of Upton Sinclair's *The Jungle*, **the Meat Inspection Act and the Pure Food and Drug Act** answered the public demand for regulation of the food and drug industry. These laws significantly increased the safety of the nation's food and drug supply.

▊ **The president** significantly broadened the concept and **policy of conservation of natural resources.** He increased the **amount of land in preserves** from 45 million acres to almost 195 million acres, and pushed for **national parks and forests.**

The Ordeal of William Howard Taft

▊ **Failing to heal the Republican Party rift over the tariff**, Taft accepted the compromise bill, **the Payne-Aldrich Act**, which angered progressives.

▊ **Taft supported the attempt** by Secretary of Interior **Ballinger to sell a million acres of public land** to a syndicate headed by **J. P. Morgan.**

▊ **The Mann-Elkins Act**, which further strengthened the Interstate Commerce Commission, and the **Sixteenth Amendment, authorizing income taxes**, were positive accomplishments of an otherwise decisive administration. Supporting competition within the business world and using the "rule of reason" against unfair trade practices by corporations, Taft further alienated himself from his former mentor Roosevelt.

▌ **Taft** controlled the party machinery and captured the Republican nomination in the election of 1912.

▌ **Roosevelt**, in another bid for the White House, organized the progressive Republicans under his Bull-Moose banner. But the Democrats, in nominating the scholarly **Governor Woodrow Wilson** and in taking advantage of the split Republican Party, captured the presidency.

Woodrow Wilson's New Freedom

Despite his lack of political experience, Wilson seized the progressive initiative and pushed landmark legislative successes through Congress. The **Underwood Tariff** substantially reduced rates and levied a modest income tax. **The Federal Reserve Act** centralized banking and created the **Federal Reserve Board** to regulate interest rates and the money supply. The **Clayton Antitrust Act** brought about much needed improvements in regulating trusts, outlawed interlocking directorates, and created the **Federal Trade Commission**.

Multiple-Choice Questions

1. Which of the following was NOT characteristic of progressivism?
   (A) It sought radical changes in American life.
   (B) It meant to humanize and regulate big business.
   (C) Its members were fundamentally optimistic about human nature.
   (D) Its members were willing to intervene in other people's lives.
   (E) It emphasized the role of the environment in human development.

2. Women gained the right to vote through the
   (A) Eighteenth Amendment.
   (B) Nineteenth Amendment.
   (C) Twenty-First Amendment.
   (D) Twelfth Amendment.
   (E) Twentieth Amendment.

3. The Mann-Elkins Act of 1910
   (A) displeased Theodore Roosevelt.
   (B) balanced progressive and conservative demands.
   (C) angered conservatives.
   (D) pleased no one.
   (E) angered the public.

4. The 1910 election was significant because
   (A) the Republicans suffered tremendous losses in Congress.
   (B) the Democratic Party maintained its control of Congress.
   (C) Taft gained additional power as president.
   (D) a third party appeared.
   (E) it was a major victory for the Republicans.

5. The Sixteenth Amendment
   (A) established civil rights guidelines.
   (B) authorized the direct election of senators.
   (C) gave women the vote.
   (D) authorized an income tax.
   (E) extended the franchise to eighteen-year-olds.

6. In 1912, Roosevelt's New Nationalism
   (A) demanded a stronger role for the president and government.
   (B) called for tighter immigration laws.
   (C) represented a repudiation of progressivism.
   (D) was readily accepted by all Progressives.
   (E) was resolutely anti-trust.

7. Woodrow Wilson won the election of 1912 because
   - (A) he was more popular than Roosevelt.
   - (B) of the split in the Republican Party.
   - (C) of the support of Taft.
   - (D) he won the support of the Socialists.
   - (E) he won the support of Progressives.

8. The Clayton Antitrust Act of 1914
   - (A) outlawed trusts.
   - (B) prohibited interlocking directorates and unfair trade practices.
   - (C) was opposed by the labor movement.
   - (D) was supported by big business.
   - (E) died in committee.

9. The Adamson Act of 1916
   - (A) dealt with the problem of race relations.
   - (B) was designed to help the farmer.
   - (C) was an antilabor measure.
   - (D) imposed the eight-hour day on railroads.
   - (E) finally ended child labor in the United States.

10. The president who invited Booker T. Washington to the White House was
   - (A) Theodore Roosevelt.
   - (B) William McKinley.
   - (C) William Howard Taft.
   - (D) Woodrow Wilson.
   - (E) Franklin D. Roosevelt.

Document-Based Question

What were the main issues, ideas, and events of the Progressive Era during the period 1900–1915? In your answer, draw on your knowledge of the time period as well as the information contained in the documents.

DOCUMENT 1 Source: Mother Jones, *The March of the Mill Children*, 1903

In the spring of 1903 I went to Kensington, Pennsylvania, where seventy-five thousand textile workers were on strike. Of this number at least ten thousand were little children. The workers were striking for more pay and shorter hours. Every day little children came into Union Headquarters, some with their hands off, some with the thumb missing, some with their fingers off at the knuckle. They were stooped little things, round-shouldered and skinny. Many of them were not over ten years of age, although the state law prohibited their working before they were twelve years of age.

The law was poorly enforced and the mothers of these children often swore falsely as to their children's age. In a single block in Kensington, fourteen women, mothers of twenty-two children all under twelve, explained it was a question of starvation or perjury. That the fathers had been killed or maimed at the mines.

DOCUMENT 2 Source: Lincoln Steffens, *The Shame of the Cities*, 1904

The Philadelphia machine isn't the best. It isn't sound, and I doubt if it would stand in New York or Chicago. The enduring strength of the typical American political machine is that it is a natural growth—a sucker, but deep-rooted in the people. The New Yorkers vote for Tammany Hall. The Philadelphians do not vote; they are disfranchised, and their disfranchisement is one anchor of the foundation of the Philadelphia organization.

The machine controls the whole process of voting, and practices fraud at every stage. The assessor's list is the voting list, and the assessor is the machine's man.…The assessor pads the list with the names of dead dogs, children, and non-existent persons.

The repeating is done boldly, for the machine controls the election officers, often choosing them from among the fraudulent names; and when no one appears to serve, assigning the heeler ready for the expected vacancy. The police are forbidden by law to stand within thirty feet of the polls, but they are at the box and they are there to see that the machine's orders are obeyed and that repeaters whom they help to furnish are permitted to vote without "intimidation" on the names they, the police, have supplied.…

DOCUMENT 3   Source: Upton Sinclair, *The Jungle*, 1905

The fertilizer works of Durham's lay away from the rest of the plant. Few visitors ever saw them, and the few who did would come out looking like Dante, of whom the peasants declared that he had been into hell. To this part of the yards came all the "tankage" and the waste products of all sorts; here they dried out the bones,—and in suffocating cellars where the daylight never came you might see men and women and children bending over whirling machines and sawing bits of bone into all sorts of shapes, breathing their lungs full of the fine dust, and doomed to die, every one of them, within a certain definite time. Here they made the blood into albumen, and made other foul-smelling things into things still more foul-smelling. In the corridors and caverns where it was done you might lose yourself as in the great caves of Kentucky. In the dust and the steam the electric lights would shine like far-off twinkling stars— red and blue-green and purple stars, according to the color of the mist and the brew from which it came. For the odors in these ghastly charnel houses there may be words in Lithuanian, but there are none in English. The person entering would have to summon his courage as for a cold-water plunge. He would go on like a man swimming under water; he would put his handkerchief over his face, and begin to cough and choke; and then, if he were still obstinate, he would find his head beginning to ring, and the veins in his forehead to throb, until finally he would be assailed by an overpowering blast of ammonia fumes, and would turn and run for his life, and come out half-dazed.

DOCUMENT 4   Source: Jane Addams, *Ballots Necessary for Women*, 1906

Unsanitary housing, poisonous sewage, contaminated water, infant mortality, the spread of contagion, adulterated food, impure milk, smoke-laden air, ill-ventilated factories, dangerous occupations, juvenile crime, unwholesome crowding, prostitution and drunkenness are the enemies which the modern cities must face and overcome would they survive. Logically, its electorate should be made up of those who can bear a valiant part in this arduous contest, those who in the past have at least attempted to care for children, to clean houses, to prepare foods, to isolate the family from oral dangers, those who have traditionally taken care of that side of life which inevitably becomes the subject of municipal consideration and control as soon as the population is congested. To test the elector's fitness to deal with this situation by his ability to bear arms is absurd. These problems must be solved, if they are solved at all, not from the military point of view, not even from the industrial point of view, but from a third which is rapidly developing in all the great cities of the world—the human welfare point of view.

DOCUMENT 5   Source: Theodore Roosevelt, The New Nationalism, 1910

Practical equality of opportunity for all citizens, when we achieve it, will have two great results. First, every man will have a fair chance to make himself all that in him lies; to reach the highest point to which his capacities, unassisted by special privilege of his own and unhampered by the special privilege of others, can carry him, and to get for himself and his family substantially what he has earned. Second, equality of opportunity means that the commonwealth will get from every citizen the highest service of which he is capable. No man who carries the burden of special privileges of another can give to the commonwealth that service to which it is fairly entitled.…

It has become entirely clear that we must have government supervision of the capitalization, not only of the public service corporations, including, particularly, railways, but of all corporations doing an interstate business. I do not wish to see the nation forced into the ownership of the railways if it can be possibly avoided, and the only alternative is thoroughgoing and effective regulation, which shall be based on a full knowledge of all the facts, including a physical valuation of property.…

Combinations in industry are the result of an imperative economic law which cannot be repealed by political legislation. The effort at prohibiting all combination has substantially failed. The way out lies, not in attempting to prevent such combinations, but in completely controlling them in the interest of the public welfare.

DOCUMENT 6   Source: Woodrow Wilson, The New Freedom, 1913

Mr. Roosevelt attached to his platform some very splendid suggestions as to noble enterprises which we ought to undertake for the uplift of the human race;…If you have read the trust plank in that platform as often as I have read it, you have found it very long, but very tolerant. It did not anywhere condemn monopoly, except in words; its essential meaning was that the trusts have been bad and must be made to be good. You know that Mr. Roosevelt long ago classified trusts for us as good and bad, and he said that he was afraid only of the bad ones. Now he does not desire that there should be any more of the bad ones, but proposes that they should all be made good by discipline, directly applied by a commission of executive appointment. All he explicitly complains of is lack of publicity and lack of fairness; not the exercise of power, for throughout that plank the power of the great corporations is accepted as the inevitable consequence of the modern organization of industry. All that it is proposed to do is to take them under control and deregulation.

Shall we try to get the grip of monopoly away from our lives, or shall we not? Shall we withhold our hand and say monopoly is inevitable, that all we can do is to regulate it? Shall we say that all we can do is to put government in competition with monopoly and try its strength against it? Shall we admit that the creature of our own hands is stronger that we are? We have been dreading all along the time when the combined power of high finance would be greater that the power of government.

DOCUMENT 7   Source: Herbert Croly, from *Progressive Democracy*, 1914

Proposals for the regulation of public utility companies, which would then have been condemned as examples of administrative autocracy, are now accepted without serious public controversy. Plans of social legislation, which formerly would have been considered culpably "paternal," and, if passed at the solicitation of the labor unions, would have been declared unconstitutional by the courts, are now considered to be a normal and necessary exercise of the police power. Proposed alterations in our political mechanism, which would then have been appraised as utterly extravagant and extremely dangerous, are now being placed on the headlines of political programs and are being incorporated in state constitutions.

DOCUMENT 8   Source: Picture of jumpers from the burning Triangle Shirtwaist Company building, 1911

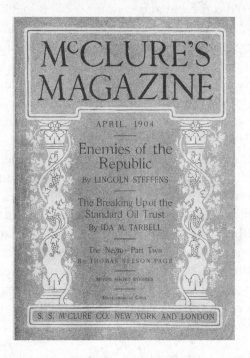

Free-Response Question

> *Examine Theodore Roosevelt's actions as president, discussing his reputation as a "trustbuster." Was that reputation deserved or undeserved?*

ANSWERS AND EXPLANATIONS

Multiple-Choice Questions

▌ **1. (A) is correct.** The changes that the Progressives sought in American society were not seen as radical changes, only updates to keep the United States abreast of the changes in society. Some of these changes included the regulation of big business, intervention into the lives of American citizens, and the ability to change the person by changing the environment. These changes reflected the Progressives' optimism in the people of the United States.

▌ **2. (B) is correct.** The Nineteenth Amendment, passed in 1920, gave women the right to vote in elections in the United States.

▌ **3. (B) is correct.** The progressives were pleased with the regulatory requirements of the law, while the conservatives saw the creation of a Commerce Court as beneficial to their own interests.

▌ **4. (A) is correct.** For the first time since 1894, the Republicans had lost control of both the House of Representatives and the Senate. In total, the Republicans had lost fifty-eight seats in the House and ten seats in the Senate.

▌ **5. (D) is correct.** Initiated by the Congress, the Sixteenth Amendment of 1913 authorized the collection of income tax for the first time in American history.

■ **6. (A) is correct.** Roosevelt's New Nationalism called for national solutions to national problems, and the only institutions that were in a position to achieve this were the office of the presidency and the federal government. In order to accomplish this, both institutions had to play a stronger role.

■ **7. (B) is correct.** By splitting the votes in most states, Roosevelt and Taft allowed Democratic candidate Wilson to win a substantial number of electoral votes without actually winning a majority of the popular vote.

■ **8. (B) is correct.** The Clayton Act of 1914 was passed in response to the Pujo Committee which had discovered that, through interlocking directorates, the Morgan-Rockefeller corporate empire controlled one tenth of the nation's wealth. The Act was designed to prohibit such interlocking directorates and other unfair trade practices.

■ **9. (D) is correct.** Threatened by a railroad strike in 1916, Wilson passed the Adamson Act which imposed an eight hour day on interstate railroads and established a federal commission to study the railroad problem.

■ **10. (A) is correct.** In 1901, Theodore Roosevelt invited Booker T. Washington to dinner at the White House. This act was protested by many southerners, including one newspaper that stated the invitation was "a crime equal to treason."

Document-Based Question Sample Response

What were the main issues, ideas, and events of the Progressive Era during the period 1900–1915? In your answer, draw on your knowledge of the time period as well as the information contained in the documents.

The Progressive Era from 1900–1915 was one of the most intensive periods of social reform in American history. Issues which came to the fore during that time period included child labor, improving conditions for workers, and controlling the big business monopolies of the day.

Working conditions during this time period were not good for many workers. Child labor was common, and working conditions for children were often unhealthy. **(DOCUMENT 1)** Children often had to work because the family needed the money, so many children were not in school. Working conditions for adults were often not any better. The Chicago meat packing houses were infamous for their dangerous and unsanitary conditions. **(DOCUMENT 3)**

Political corruption was also rampant during this period. Governments in many cases at this time simply did not or could not deal with issues such as immigration or industrialization. This was particularly true of government at the city and state level. Much of this void was filled by corrupt political machines. The people who controlled these machines used the political process to enrich themselves and enhance their own power. Some of the "muckraking" writers of the time used their writing as a way of exposing these abuses. **(DOCUMENTS 2 AND 9)** Women still did not have the vote on a national level at this time. Many, such as Jane Addams, felt that women should be given the vote and that this would help uplift the political process and help to solve some of the pressing issues of the day. **(DOCUMENT 4)** On a national level, the Progressive Era often wrestled with the issue of the large trusts of the day. Theodore Roosevelt felt that the trusts should be regulated, whereas Woodrow Wilson leaned more towards breaking them up and restoring small business competition. **(DOCUMENTS 5 AND 6)** Herbert Croly refers to the changed political landscape because of the Progressive Movement—essentially a precursor to the modern idea of "big government" liberalism. **(DOCUMENT 7)** One of the most important events of the day was the 1911 Triangle Shirtwaist Company fire which, in addition to killing over 140 people, provided the impetus for modernizing building codes, and the legislation that came out of it was an early precursor of the New Deal of the 1930s. **(DOCUMENT 8)**

Free-Response Essay Sample Response

Examine Theodore Roosevelt's actions as president, discussing his reputation as a "trustbuster." Was that reputation deserved or undeserved?

During his seven years in office, Theodore Roosevelt initiated twenty-five antitrust indictments. Compared to his successor, William Taft, who initiated almost twice as many in four years, this was not a significant amount. However, in addition to the strict numbers that history has recorded, the actions of Roosevelt while he was President also sent a clear message that his reputation as a trustbuster was undeserved.

During his early years as President, Roosevelt saw the large corporations as a necessary component of the industrial growth of the nation. While he was mistrustful of the effects that these giant corporations could have on the local community, he was not against trusts, only those who needed to be controlled due to predatory practices. In fact, he believed that government action was not required because the press and public opinion would uncover such practices and pressure corporations to abandon them.

The turning point appears to have been the creation of the Bureau of Corporations and the antitrust suit brought against the Northern Securities Company under the Sherman Antitrust Act. In this case, the Supreme Court upheld the suit and dissolved the company. Roosevelt then brought suits against other trusts, such as the beef trust, the American Tobacco Company, the Du Pont Corporation, the New Haven Railroad, and Standard Oil. However, even during these suits Roosevelt was still quite friendly to many of these giant corporations: allowing them additional access to the President and allowing them to clearly violate the antitrust measures when he felt that it was for the good of the national economy.

In the end, Roosevelt largely maintained his beliefs from the early years of his presidency that trusts didn't necessarily need to be dissolved, only regulated to ensure that they were kept inside the bounds of fair business practices.

CHAPTER 24

The Nation at War

In 1915, the British steamship *Lusitania* was sunk by a German submarine off the coast of Ireland, with 1200 fatalities. The tragedy embroiled the United States more deeply in the European crisis, and despite Wilson's commitment to peace and neutrality, **America went to war in 1917**.

A New World Power

▌ **The strong desire for an isthmian canal to connect the two oceans** led to a major departure in U.S.-Latin American relations.

▌ **President Roosevelt**, convinced that America should achieve a more active international status, intervened in affairs in **Colombia-Panama** to secure the **canal zone**, and in 1914, the canal was completed. **The Hay-Bunau-Varilla Treaty** gave the United States control of the canal zone and guaranteed the independence of Panama.

▌ **With American interests entrenched in the Caribbean**, the president issued the **Roosevelt Corollary to the Monroe Doctrine** to allow for American intervention in Latin America when necessary.

▌ **In the Far East**, Roosevelt sought to normalize relations with **Japan** after that rising power's military **victory over Russia**. In 1908, Roosevelt sent the enlarged naval fleet around the world, with a stop in Tokyo, as a show of strength.

▌ **Under President Taft**, American business and financial interests were extended abroad through **"dollar diplomacy."**

Foreign Policy Under Wilson

Confident of his own abilities and extremely idealistic, **President Wilson** foresaw a world free from the threats of militarism, colonialism, and war.

▌ **President Wilson and Secretary of State William Jennings Bryan** sought to apply a policy of human rights and national integrity to Latin America, but practical considerations softened Wilson's idealism.

▌ **Revolution and lingering political instability** caused Wilson to become embroiled in Mexican political turbulence. Incapable of bringing progressive reform or political stability and uncertain as to whom to support, Wilson used military intervention to track down the revolutionary **Pancho Villa**.

Toward War

The assassination of **Austro-Hungarian Archduke Franz Ferdinand** set into motion a chain of events that by August 1914 had brought the major European nations to war.

- **At the outset of war**, Wilson envisioned the nation's role as that of a peacemaker and pillar of democracy.
- **Americans were sharply divided in sentiment**, but they accepted **neutrality** as the desirable course. A majority of Americans sympathized with the British and French and considered **German aggression** largely responsible for the war.
- **Despite occasional British blockades and German U-boat warfare**, American goods flooded European ports especially in Britain and France, resulting in great profits at home and increasing commercial ties with the Allies.
- **Germany's use of the dreaded submarines** posed a direct threat to American shipping. The sinking of the *Lusitania* outraged Americans and forced President Wilson to pressure the German government.
- **After the French steamer *Sussex* was sunk**, German **Kaiser Wilhelm** issued a pledge promising that German submarines would only target enemy naval vessels.
- **The "preparedness" advocates** led by Theodore Roosevelt called for readiness in case of war and spoke out **against pacifist sentiment** in the country.
- **Wilson ran successfully for reelection in 1916** against the Republican candidate **Charles Evans Hughes**. Winning by a very narrow margin, Wilson continued to pledge his commitment to peace.
- **In January 1917**, Wilson called upon the European nations to submit to a **"peace without victory"** and a peace between equals, but renewed German submarine attacks severely threatened relations with the United States.
- **Public indignation against Germany** soared after the exposure of the **Zimmermann telegram**, which encouraged a Mexican war against the United States, and a Mexican-German alliance in such a case. Prompted by continued sinking of American ships, **Wilson at last demanded military intervention**.

Over There

- **Wilson selected "Black Jack" Pershing** to lead the **American Expeditionary Force (AEF)**, and in **May 1917**, Congress passed the **Selective Service Act** which eventually drafted some two million men into the army.
- **A massive German offensive** was launched in **March 1918** against Western Europe, but the American-supported Allied lines held, and in autumn, German forces were in headlong retreat. **In November, Germany agreed to armistice terms**. Within the month, Austria-Hungary, Turkey, and Bulgaria also were finished.

Over Here

All resources of the economy and society were needed to fight the war, and the whole country mobilized for war.

- **At home, the Committee on Public Information** launched a **propaganda** campaign to evoke hatred for Germany. Wilson encouraged repression against anti-war sympathizers and enforced the **Sedition Act** against those who opposed the war effort. A postwar **"Red Scare"** of fear, hatred, and persecution of suspected communists began at home.
- **The War Industries Board** was established to oversee all aspects of industrial production. **Herbert Hoover** headed the **Food Administration**, and the **Fuel**

Administration rationed coal and oil and imposed **daylight savings time**. Government involvement in American life had never been greater.

▌ **Liberty bonds** were sold, and taxes on individuals and corporations were boosted.

▌ **The war fastened the partnership between labor and government**, and union membership swelled to more than four million by 1919. **The War Labor Board** standardized wages and hours and protected the rights of workers to organize and collectively bargain.

▌ **Women and African Americans** found economic opportunities that had never before existed.

▌ **Growing competition for jobs** led to an increase in racial tensions.

The Treaty of Versailles

England and France reluctantly submitted to much of Wilson's idealistic plans for world peace.

▌ **Wilson's lofty goals for a lasting peace** included national self-determination in Europe and a **League of Nations**. Some of Wilson's important principles were sacrificed, however, as **enormous reparations** were heaped upon Germany, and the doctrine of self-determination was not always manifested in the legitimization of new nations.

Multiple-Choice Questions

1. The Hay-Bunau-Varilla Treaty
   (A) gave Colombia's permission for the building of the Panama Canal.
   (B) gave the United States control of the Panama Canal Zone.
   (C) transferred rights to the Panama Canal from France to the United States.
   (D) ended hostilities with Mexico in 1914.
   (E) gave the United States control of the Philippines.

2. Taft's policy of "dollar diplomacy"
   (A) promoted American financial and business interests abroad.
   (B) was aimed, primarily, at helping underdeveloped countries.
   (C) resulted in less American influence in Latin America.
   (D) had little influence on American national security interests.
   (E) helped establish American prestige in Asia.

3. In his approach to foreign affairs, Wilson could be described as
   (A) a militarist.
   (B) a moralist.
   (C) being primarily concerned with economic matters.
   (D) a global strategist.
   (E) a pacifist.

4. At the beginning of World War I, Americans
   (A) showed little interest in the conflict.
   (B) sided strongly with the British.
   (C) were eager to enter the conflict.
   (D) sided strongly with the Germans.
   (E) generally accepted neutrality.

5. At the beginning of World War I, Great Britain
   (A) respected American neutrality.
   (B) made few attempts to influence American policy.
   (C) sought the military aid of the United States.

(D) sought to restrict American trade with Germany.

(E) briefly considered surrender.

6. The 1915 German sinking of the _____ cost 128 American lives and enraged the American public.

(A) *Sussex*

(B) *Arabic*

(C) *Reuben James*

(D) *Lusitania*

(E) *Queen Mary*

7. The Zimmermann Telegram

(A) announced Germany's European war aims.

(B) pledged Germany's intention to end the war peacefully.

(C) proposed an alliance between Germany and Mexico.

(D) had little effect on America's move toward war.

(E) hinted at an alliance between Germany and Canada.

8. In forming his delegation for the Paris Peace Conference, Wilson

(A) wanted a group he could control.

(B) readily sought advice from his Republican opponents.

(C) tried to create a bipartisan group.

(D) included only his personal friends.

(E) was turned down by several prominent Republicans.

9. One of Wilson's major goals at Paris was

(A) to punish Germany for starting the war.

(B) to recompense the British and French for their great losses.

(C) to found a League of Nations to enforce peace.

(D) to bring the Russians to the peace table.

(E) to see the Eiffel Tower.

10. The _____ were fourteen Republican senators who steadfastly opposed every aspect of the League of Nations.

(A) mild reservationists

(B) strong reservationists

(C) irreconcilables

(D) irreparables

(E) curmudgeons

Free-Response Question

Although the United States officially adopted a policy of neutrality at the beginning of World War I, there was considerable pressure on the government to alter that stance. What were the key sources of that pressure?

ANSWERS AND EXPLANATIONS

Multiple-Choice Questions

▊ 1. **(B) is correct.** The Hay-Bunau-Varilla Treaty, which was negotiated in 1903 by U.S. Secretary of State John Hay, allowed the United States to control the Panama Canal Zone and in return the United States supported Panamanian independence and provided annual fees to Panama for control of the canal.

▊ 2. **(A) is correct.** "Dollar diplomacy" was designed to create economic ties in Latin American countries where military ones had previously existed. The Monroe Doctrine and the Roosevelt Corollary required military intervention in order to work. However, "dollar diplomacy" promoted American financial and business interests in Latin America. The end result was the same: American influence in Latin America. The only difference was the method used to achieve that influence.

3. (B) is correct. President Wilson had little experience in or knowledge of foreign affairs upon assuming the office. His approach to matters of foreign policy exhibited this, for example, his statement "The force of America is the force of moral principle." This moral diplomacy led Wilson on an idealistic and unsuccessful presidency with regards to foreign policy.

4. (E) is correct. With the exception of its foreign policy in Latin America, the United States did not typically become involved in the problems of other countries. Many Americans felt that since the initial German advance had been stopped by the British and the French, there was little need for the United States to become involved in a war half way around the world.

5. (D) is correct. At the start of the war, Britain sought to limit all supplies from reaching Germany through the use of naval blockades. This meant that American ships destined for Germany were routinely stopped and in many instances their cargo was confiscated. While the United States protested such moves, the British rarely responded.

6. (D) is correct. On May 7, 1915 a German U-boat sunk the British steamship the Lusitania off the coast of Ireland.

7. (C) is correct. On February 25, 1917, the British government privately gave President Wilson a telegram intercepted from Arthur Zimmermann, the German foreign minister, to the German ambassador in Mexico. The telegram had proposed an alliance between Germany and Mexico in the event that the United States entered the war. The Germans offered the government of Mexico financial support and recovery of territory that it had lost to the United States.

8. (A) is correct. In selecting the delegation that would accompany him to the Paris Peace Conference, President Wilson overlooked prominent Republicans and others who opposed his Fourteen Points for Peace. Instead, he selected individuals that he would be able to exert influence over while sitting at the peace table.

9. (C) is correct. During the Paris Peace talks, Wilson would eventually trade most of the fourteen points in his peace plan. The only point that he was unwilling to move from was the creation of a League of Nations, a multi-national body whose purpose was to arbitrate disputes that threatened peace.

10. (C) is correct. These individuals, who were led by Senator William E. Borah of Idaho, were against the League of Nations on any grounds. Unlike other Senators who would have ratified the Treaty of Versailles with certain reservations attached, these fourteen Senators were steadfast in their opposition to the Treaty on the basis of the League of Nations.

Free-Response Essay Sample Response

Although the United States officially adopted a policy of neutrality at the beginning of World War I, there was considerable pressure on the government to alter that stance. What were the key sources of that pressure?

There were a number of sources of pressure for the United States to abandon its policy of neutrality and enter the War on the side of the Allies. While many of these sources were in direct relation to actions taken by those already involved in the war, others were historic in nature.

At the outset of the war, the new weapon of the U-boat or submarine proved to be a main source of pressure upon America to join the war. While the Germans made a commitment not to sink American ships as a part of their submarine campaign, the sinking of the *Falaba*, the *Lusitania*, the *Arabic*, and the *Sussex* gave the pro-war forces in the United States much ammunition to pressure President Wilson towards war. Many groups within the United States saw these actions as leading us down an eventual path to war and that the United States should begin preparedness for that eventuality. Others, however, argued that any attempt at military readiness would just bring us closer to war and should not even be contemplated.

While these events were convincing, there was also a general sentiment among Americans that sympathized with the Allies and blamed the war on the Germans. Sharing a common language and institutions with the British, along with admiring English literature, customs and laws, the Americans also remembered when the French had come to their aid during the Revolutionary War. On the other hand, the Germans appeared to be arrogant and militaristic and this further cemented American feelings towards both sides. These feelings were challenged by groups from both sides who utilized propaganda in the United States to win the hearts and minds of Americans to their own side.

The diplomatic pressure from the British to assist in their war effort, along with negotiations with the German government to keep the United States out of the war, were additional factors that weighed upon Wilson's decision on whether or not to take the United States to war. In the end, it was a British intercept of a German telegram to the Mexicans asking them to join the war and attack the United States that eventually lead the Americans to drop their position of neutrality in 1917. However, the pressure had been building from many domestic sources for three years to make that very decision.

CHAPTER 25

Transition to Modern America

The 1920s were marked by rapid economic and urban growth as well as rapid social change, inspiring tensions as rural America resisted the ensuing changes.

The Second Industrial Revolution

Based on mass production, the moving assembly line, and the marketing of consumer goods, the economy of the 1920s experienced phenomenal growth.

▎ **The automobile industry**, one of the most important inceptions of the 1920s, significantly changed American culture.

▎ **Henry Ford's** revolutionary application of the **assembly line** in his manufacturing process allowed prices to fall, guaranteeing an affordable car for virtually every American family.

▎ **The corporation** (run by a professionally trained manager) dominated the businesses of the 1920s, and brought conformity to a wide variety of industrial and commercial pursuits.

▎ **The entertainment industry** boomed in the 1920s via radio and cinema.

▎ **A consumer-oriented economy** emerged that was driven by the new ideas of **marketing** and advertising.

▎ **Despite the progress**, some elements of the economy fared poorly, notably **farmers, union members, and minorities**.

City Life in the Jazz Age

Still another important feature of the 1920s was the rapid rise of the city and the consequent changes in society.

▎ **Women** continued to work outside of the home in increasing numbers.

▎ **Families** changed as a result of **falling birthrates**, **rising divorce rates**, and the flowering **feminist movement**.

▎ **The cultural revolution known as the "Roaring Twenties"** also prompted the rise of organized crime, spectator sports, and a **sexual revolution**.

▎ **Frustrated with the materialism of mass culture**, many literary figures wrote scathing criticisms of this new era. Others lived in self-exile in Europe. **African American authors** in America, however, found energy and inspiration in the **Harlem Renaissance**.

▎ **Insecurity** in the face of all this social upheaval caused rural and small-town America to react and rally against the dominance of the city.

▎ **Tradition-minded Americans** feared the specter of **bolshevism or anarchism** and tried to eliminate **radicalism** from American life, abusing civil liberties in the process.

- **Many associated alcohol with alien cultures** and the new urban ways, and, therefore, tried to implement **prohibition** of the manufacture, sale, or transportation of alcoholic beverages.
- **Prohibition enforcement was lax**, and there was wide-spread non-compliance with the new laws.
- **Some even joined such groups as the ominously reinvigorated Ku Klux Klan** in order to preserve what they thought was sacred and pure and to limit the rights of blacks, aliens, non-protestants, and anyone who refused to conform to their standards.
- **Nativists** successfully restricted **foreign immigration** and Congress passed a series of laws aimed at limiting immigration, especially from southern and eastern Europe and Asia.
- **Some Americans found solace** and security in supporting **fundamentalist Christianity** or in opposing **theories of evolution** being taught in the public schools. In 1925, John Scopes was convicted of teaching the theory of evolution in violation of Tennessee law (known as the **Scopes Monkey Trial**).

Politics of the 1920s

Rural-urban tensions dominated the politics of the 1920s.

- **During this period**, the Republicans dominated the White House with three popular presidents: **Harding, Coolidge, and Hoover.**
- **In this era**, the Republican Party passed a program of higher tariffs, lower taxes, and spending cuts.
- **The Democrats were divided on rural-urban issues**, but were gaining strength among the new immigrant voters of the big cities.
- **The election of 1928** symbolized the decade, pitting **Democrat Al Smith**, a Catholic, urban, "wet" son of immigrants, against **Republican Herbert Hoover**, an old-stock, "dry" Protestant from Iowa.
- **Hoover won easily** and then presided over the worst **depression** in American history.
- **During the 1920s**, America struggled to enter the modern era.
- **The economics of mass production** and the politics of urbanization drove the country forward, but the persistent appeal of individualism and rural-based values held it back.
- **Americans achieved greater prosperity** than ever before, but the prosperity was unevenly distributed. Further, as the outbursts of nativism, ethnic and racial bigotry, and intolerance revealed, prosperity hardly guaranteed generosity or unity.

Multiple-Choice Questions

1. Crucial to the growth of the automobile industry in the 1920s was
   - (A) new buyer financing techniques.
   - (B) marketing.
   - (C) the long life of the new automobile.
   - (D) the new method of financing the industry.
   - (E) greater disposable income.

2. The revolution in consumer goods
   - (A) disguised the decline of many traditional industries.
   - (B) epitomized the growth of all areas of the economy.
   - (C) was a short-term factor in the American economy.

(D) aided all other kinds of industry.

(E) helped fuel growth in the railroad industry.

3. Labor unions in the 1920s were NOT weakened by
   (A) their conservative leadership.
   (B) management's attempt to portray them as radical.
   (C) intensive government intervention in labor affairs.
   (D) injunctions.
   (E) "yellow-dog" contracts.

4. The most visible symbol of the new cities of the 1920s was
   (A) the new literature of the period.
   (B) the skyscraper.
   (C) the home appliance.
   (D) mass transit.
   (E) the department store.

5. The impact of the Nineteenth Amendment on women was
   (A) to thrust women into the political arena.
   (B) to dramatically increase the number of women in government.
   (C) to take women out of the home.
   (D) less than women had hoped.
   (E) to unite women politically.

6. The Red Scare of 1919
   (A) was a relatively harmless event.
   (B) was an outgrowth of the intense nationalism of World War I.
   (C) resulted from the very real threat of Russian Bolshevism.
   (D) demonstrated the tolerance of the American people.

(E) began as a movement in France that quickly found its way to America.

7. Prohibition
   (A) bred a profound disrespect for the law.
   (B) did little to decrease drinking.
   (C) was most effective among the upper classes.
   (D) made it almost impossible to obtain alcohol in the United States.
   (E) began at the national level.

8. The immigration legislation of the 1920s
   (A) had no lasting effect.
   (B) was opposed by the large corporations.
   (C) encouraged immigration from underdeveloped countries.
   (D) was the most enduring achievement of the rural counterattack.
   (E) was quickly repealed in the 1930s.

9. The famous evolution trial of 1925 involved biology teacher
   (A) John Scopes.
   (B) Clarence Darrow.
   (C) H. L. Mencken.
   (D) William Jennings Bryan.
   (E) Jerome Lawrence.

10. The chief figure in the Teapot Dome scandal was
    (A) Albert Fall.
    (B) Harry Daugherty.
    (C) J. Frank Norris.
    (D) Calvin Coolidge.
    (E) Gifford Pinchot.

Free-Response Question

Discuss the tension between new and changing attitudes with traditional attitudes.

ANSWERS AND EXPLANATIONS

Multiple-Choice Questions

1. (B) is correct. As the number of car owners increased due to the increase in the amount of disposable income that individuals possessed, marketing became crucial to the growth of the automobile industry. Automobile makers began to heavily rely upon advertising and annual model changes, hoping to increase interest in their products.

2. (A) is correct. While consumer goods, such as automobiles and other widgets boomed, traditional industries declined. The railroad was poorly managed and facing competition from the newly formed trucking industry. The coal industry was being replaced by petroleum products and cotton was facing competition from synthetic fibers.

3. (C) is correct. During the 1920s, there was very little government intervention in the economy. Unlike previous generations, which had sought to regulate both the practices of labor and big business, the governments of the 1920s allowed businesses to prosper.

4. (B) is correct. With dramatic increases in their population and smaller increases in their geography, American cities were forced to build up (as opposed to out). While urban sprawl still occurred, high land prices made skyscrapers attractive to developers during the 1920s.

5. (D) is correct. With no single issue to galvanize the women's movement around, the Nineteenth Amendment effectively hindered the movement from making other significant gains that many women had hoped would follow the extension of the franchise.

6. (B) is correct. The Bolshevik movement and its communist principles rubbed against the grain of an America that was experiencing post-war prosperity. This, along with the intense sense of nationalism throughout the United States, was successful in achieving a unity of American sentiment in the form of fear of the unknown.

7. (A) is correct. Unpopular in urban areas and with the working class, prohibition was effective in rural areas and with those unable to afford the high prices of bootlegged alcohol. However, it was seen by most as a way for the wealthy to exclude others from their alcoholic social events and would only serve to breed disrespect for the law, and government in general.

8. (D) is correct. In the eyes of many in the United States, the 1920s was a time when the moral fiber of the United States was being torn away. There were many initiatives that were pushed by rural America, such as prohibition. However, the immigration legislation of the 1920s was one of the few lasting achievements of these rural reformers.

9. (A) is correct. Chicago defense attorney Clarence Darrow was responsible for defending John Scopes, a high school biology teacher who was being charged with violating Tennessee's law that forbade the teaching of Darwin's theory of evolution. William Jennings Bryan was the chief witness against Scopes, while H.L. Mencken was a reporter who covered the trial.

■ **10. (A) is correct.** Albert Fall was the Secretary of the Interior under President Warren Harding and one of two individuals that was largely responsible for the downfall of his administration. Two oil promoters gave Fall $400,000 in loans and bribes to help them secure leases on naval oil reserves in California and Wyoming.

Free-Response Essay Sample Response

Discuss the tension between new and changing attitudes with traditional attitudes.

In many ways the period known as the "Jazz Age" was a time of conflict. Many different forces were at work in American society.

Politically, the Republican Party was in control. Presidents Warren Harding, Calvin Coolidge, and Herbert Hoover took a "hands-off" approach to government and business. Calvin Coolidge was particularly known for his quiet and laid back approach to governing.

On the surface, the economy was booming. Industrial production grew, wages rose, as did the stock market. However, there were economic problems under the surface. Both the farm and industrial economies were producing more than could be consumed, setting the stage for the collapse that would occur later. Stock prices were not based on actual corporate values. Consumers had done much buying and investing on credit and were eventually unable to sustain the amount of debt they had accumulated.

This was also the time of Prohibition. While Prohibition did initially reduce the amount of alcohol consumed, the main effect over time was a rise in crime and gangsters. Prohibition was eventually repealed in 1933 during the Great Depression.

The Scopes trial was a famous event of the 1920s. John Scopes, a high school biology teacher was arrested in Tennessee for teaching about evolution. This was against Tennessee law at the time. Although he was convicted, the trial pitted science against religion, North against South, cities against rural areas, and the forces of modernism against older cultural values.

Other tensions were at work as well. A resuscitated Ku Klux Klan was at the peak of its power. However, the African American community in Harlem was experiencing what is known as the Harlem Renaissance. This was particularly so in the areas of art, literature, and music, and was exemplified by the works of poets like Langston Hughes and Countee Cullen.

There was a women's movement and a youth culture during the 1920s. Many women took jobs during World War I and did not leave them after the war. New hair and clothing styles for women were considered rebellious for the time. Many young people experienced previously unheard of freedom due to the growth of the automobile. Many danced new dances like the Charleston to jazz music and spoke using new words for the time, such as "copacetic" and "hot diggety dog!" Much of the music and terminology came from the African American community. Youth and female behavior of the time often caused much consternation among the older generation and more conservative elements of society.

CHAPTER 26

Franklin D. Roosevelt and the New Deal

After a great rise in the stock market, the 1929 crash brought about an economic depression, which had to be addressed by Hoover, and then, more successfully, by Franklin Delano Roosevelt.

The Great Depression

The economy of the United States collapsed after 1929, creating the single worst fiscal panic and era of unemployment in the nation's history.

- **From 1927 to 1929**, the stock market experienced a sharp increase known as the **great bull market**, caused by easy credit, inflated currency, and **margin loans**.
- **This bubble burst** in the fall of 1929 in the **stock market crash**.
- **This was the start of a decade of terrible economic conditions**, and few escaped its impact.
- **Eventually**, the **Great Depression** became the worst downturn in the nation's history.

Fighting the Depression

Ending the depression became the most important political issue of the 1930s, as first a Republican president and then a Democrat tried to achieve economic recovery.

- **President Hoover emphasized voluntary solutions** to the economic ills of the nation, using federal resources only minimally though he was inadvertently involving the government more and more.
- **His efforts** failed to stop the deteriorating health of business.
- **In 1932 the voters overwhelmingly elected Franklin D. Roosevelt**, former governor of New York, to the presidency in a landslide.
- **With a clear understanding of the responsibilities of political leadership**, Roosevelt asserted his authority with the **banking crisis**. After this success, he proceeded to pass several significant reforms in **the first three months of his initial term**.
- **Roosevelt** pushed several acts through Congress that attempted to provide immediate help to the hungry and homeless, as well as provide aid to the farmers.
- **Roosevelt** implemented many new **work relief programs** to not only spur the economy but also to keep people from starving and restore their self-respect.
- **Work relief projects** also generated needed jobs for new schools, parks, and other public projects.

Roosevelt and Reform

After pressure developed for more fundamental reform, Roosevelt responded by suggesting permanent changes in the economic arrangements and institutions of the United States.

- **Several critics** complained about the **New Deal** and the still-ailing economy, suggesting more radical reforms were in order.
- **In response to criticism**, Roosevelt secured passage of the **Social Security Act**, which provided only modest pensions and unemployment insurance.
- **The president also supported legislation (the Wagner Act)** that guaranteed the rights of **workers to organize and bargain collectively**, then endorsed a law that provided for **maximum hours and a minimum wage**.

Impact of the New Deal

Roosevelt's program, **known as the New Deal**, succeeded in improving some, if not all, elements of American society.

- **The New Deal resulted in a dramatic increase in union membership**, especially among the unskilled who worked in the nation's steel and automobile industries, the mines and other factories.
- **With only a few exceptions**, the New Deal did not address the problems of the **nation's minorities**.
- **Some New Deal Programs actively discriminated** against blacks and Hispanics. **Native Americans** fared somewhat better.
- **For most women** the Depression caused a **worsening of their position** in the economy.
- **Women's wages** were lower if they did work and more than 20 percent were unemployed throughout the decade.

End of the New Deal

After five years of significant success, Roosevelt could no longer secure passage of new reforms and his New Deal came to an end.

- **Roosevelt and his party won a landslide victory** in the elections of **1936** against forces from the right and the left, but several factors combined to close the New Deal.
- **Roosevelt's effort to reorganize the Supreme Court** so that it would act more favorably on his programs failed in Congress; a significant coalition that opposed the president resulted.
- **Huey Long**, a senator from Louisiana, founded the "Share the Wealth" movement in 1934. To make "every man a king," Long advocated a drastic redistribution of wealth.
- **The recession of 1937** and the unsuccessful **"Purge of '38"** revived the Republican party and strengthened opposition to Roosevelt's programs in Congress.
- **The New Deal did not cure the problems of the Depression**, nor did it radicalize the nation's economy. But it did have a **positive psychological impact** on the public, made **some permanent reforms**, and left the **Democratic Party** as the majority party for decades.

Multiple-Choice Questions

1. The most striking characteristic of the stock market in 1929 was
   (A) investors' obsession with speculation.
   (B) the downward trend of its major stocks early in the year.
   (C) the government's desire to carefully regulate it.
   (D) the fact that the great majority of wage-earning Americans were so heavily involved in it.
   (E) its steady advancement through the decade, culminating in record levels in 1929.

2. Hoover believed that unemployment relief would
   (A) be in accord with previous government policies during economic crises.
   (B) bring about inflation.
   (C) promote domestic unrest.
   (D) be the most beneficent if it came from private charities.
   (E) be a sign of weakness.

3. The Reconstruction Finance Corporation was designed to
   (A) loan money to financial institutions to prevent bankruptcies.
   (B) stimulate the growth of new business.
   (C) give direct "doles" to the unemployed.
   (D) provide direct loans to homeowners.
   (E) fund the construction of cheap housing for the growing number of homeless Americans.

4. Franklin D. Roosevelt and his advisers believed that to restore purchasing power to farmers, production should be
   (A) cut.
   (B) increased.
   (C) redistributed.
   (D) expropriated.
   (E) monitored.

5. Roosevelt's Hundred Days banking legislation was designed to
   (A) support strong banks and eliminate the weaker ones.
   (B) decrease government regulation of U.S. banks.
   (C) allow the government to take over the banking system.
   (D) give bankers a place in his government.
   (E) merge smaller banks with larger ones.

6. Franklin D. Roosevelt's initial New Deal legislation was surprisingly
   (A) radical.
   (B) liberal.
   (C) inflationary.
   (D) conservative.
   (E) unsuccessful.

7. The Hundred Days refers to
   (A) the period between Roosevelt's election and his inauguration.
   (B) the period immediately after Roosevelt's first inauguration.
   (C) the last three months of the 1932 campaign.
   (D) the final days of the Hoover administration.
   (E) the worst period of the Great Depression.

8. The Tennessee Valley Authority (TVA) was designed to
   (A) bring modernization and jobs to desolate areas of the upper rural South.
   (B) help support the continued control of electrical power by private companies.
   (C) alienate conservationists.
   (D) test the authority of the Supreme Court.
   (E) win votes in a largely Republican area.

9. Huey Long advocated
   (A) higher taxes for every income level.
   (B) "sharing the wealth."

(C) more conservative measures to control the economy.

(D) cutting the taxes of the wealthy.

(E) nationalization of the banking system.

10. The Social Security Act of 1935
    (A) was a fundamentally conservative measure.
    (B) provided immediate stimulus to the economy.
    (C) provided a guaranteed income for all Americans over the age of 65.
    (D) was financed by a special tax on corporations.
    (E) was strictly a federal program.

Document-Based Question

Discuss the Great Depression and its impact on the United States. In your answer, draw on your knowledge of the time period as well as the information in the documents below.

DOCUMENT 1 Source: Francis Perkins and the Social Security Act, 1935

The process of recovery is not a simple one. We cannot be satisfied merely with makeshift arrangements which will tide us over the present emergencies. We must devise plans that will not merely alleviate the ills of today, but will prevent, as far as it is humanly possible to do so, their recurrence in the future. The task of recovery is inseparable from the fundamental task of social reconstruction.

Among the objectives of that reconstruction, President Roosevelt in his message of June 8, 1934, to the Congress placed "the security of the men, women and children of the Nation first." He went on to suggest the social insurances with which European countries have had a long and favorable experience as one means of providing safeguards against "misfortunes which cannot be wholly eliminated in this man-made world of ours."

It has taken the rapid industrialization of the last few decades, with its mass-production methods, to teach us that a man might become a victim of circumstances far beyond his control, and finally it "took a depression to dramatize for us the appalling insecurity of the great mass of the population, and to stimulate interest in social insurance in the United States." We have come to learn that the large majority of our citizens must have protection against the loss of income due to unemployment, old age, death of the breadwinners and disabling accident and illness, not only on humanitarian grounds, but in the interest of our National welfare. If we are to maintain a healthy economy and thriving production, we need to maintain the standard of living of the lower income groups in our population who constitute 90 per cent of our purchasing power.

DOCUMENT 2   Source: Franklin Roosevelt, First Inaugural Address, 1933

Our greatest primary task is to put people to work. This is no unsolvable problem if we face it wisely and courageously. It can be accomplished in part by direct recruiting by the Government itself, treating the task as we would treat the emergency of a war, but at the same time, through this employment, accomplishing greatly needed projects to stimulate and reorganize the use of our natural resources.

Finally, in our progress toward a resumption of work we require two safeguards against a return of the evils of the old order: there must be a strict supervision of all banking in credits and investments, so that there will be an end to speculation with other people's money; and there must be provision for an adequate but sound currency.

DOCUMENT 3   Source: Mrs. Henry Weddington, letter to President Roosevelt, 1938

I really don't know exactly how to begin this letter to you. Perhaps I should first tell you who I am. I am a young married woman. I am a Negro....I believe that you are familiar with the labor situation among the Negroes, but I want you to know how I and many of us feel about it and what we expect of you. My husband is working for the W.P.A. doing skilled labor. Before he started on this we were on relief for three months. We were three months trying to get relief. While trying to obtain relief I lost my unborn child. I believe if I had sufficient food this would not have happened. My husband was perfectly willing to work but could not find it. Now I am pregnant again. He is working at Tilden Tech. School where there are more white than colored. Every month more than one hundred persons are given private employment and not one of them are colored. It isn't that the colored men are not as skilled as the white, it is the fact that they are black and therefore must not get ahead.

We are citizens just as much or more than the majority of this country....We are just as intelligent as they. This is supposed to be a free country regardless of color, creed or race but still we are slaves....Won't you help us? I'm sure you can. I admire you and have very much confidence in you. I believe you are a real Christian and non-prejudiced. I have never doubted that you would be elected again. I believe you can and must do something about the labor conditions of the Negro.

DOCUMENT 4   Source: Map of the Great Depression

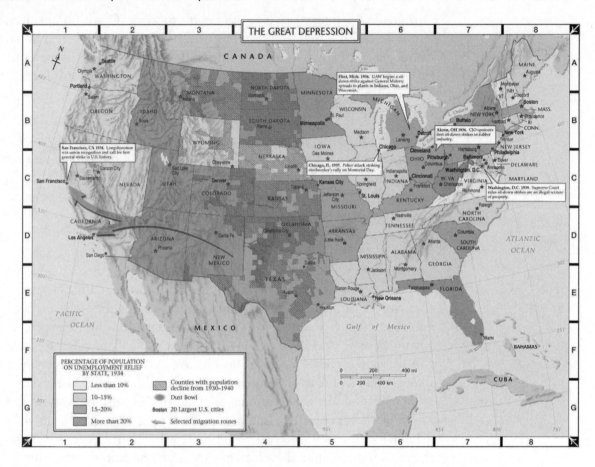

DOCUMENT 5   Source: Great Depression unemployment chart

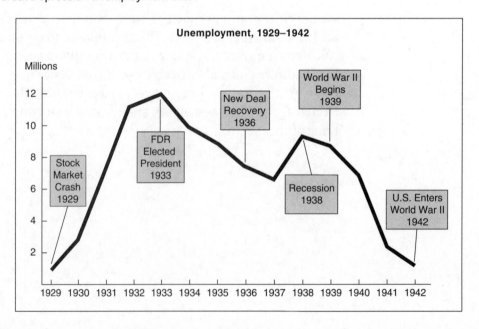

DOCUMENT 6   Source: Breadline during the Great Depression

DOCUMENT 7   Source: Chart of bank failures during the Great Depression

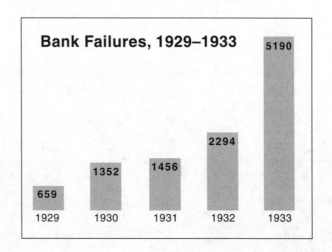

DOCUMENT 8   Source: NRA Poster

DOCUMENT 9   Source: Dust storm, May 1934

DOCUMENT 10   Source: CCC workers

DOCUMENT 11   Source: PWA map

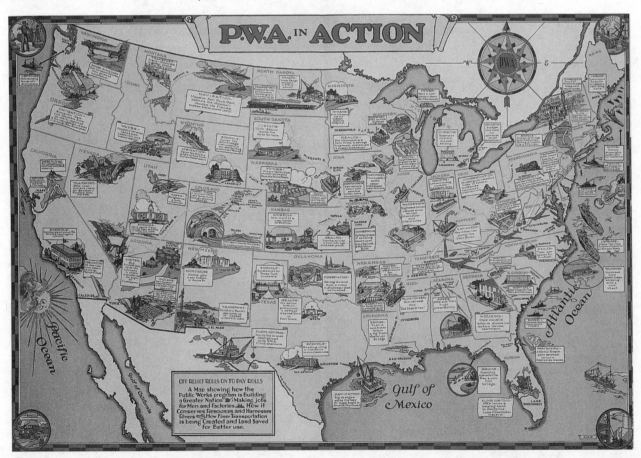

DOCUMENT 12 Source: Court-packing scheme cartoon

Free-Response Question

> Using the following image and your own knowledge, analyze the economic impact of the Great Depression on the daily lives of citizens.

ANSWERS AND EXPLANATIONS

Multiple-Choice Questions

1. (A) is correct. Investors of the 1920s speculated about the "next big thing" to the point that it drove increased investment during the mild recession of 1927 and covered the true sense of where the market was and where it should be.

2. (D) is correct. Hoover did not believe in unemployment relief from the federal government. Instead he felt that relief should come from private charities and local government. He felt that the federal government had an obligation to maintain the proud character of its citizens and that direct relief would undermine this.

3. (A) is correct. In 1932, Hoover established the Reconstruction Finance Corporation which was designed to loan money to financial institutions to prevent bankruptcies. Critics pointed out that while Hoover was against direct relief for Americans, he was not above providing hand-outs to big business.

4. (A) is correct. By creating fewer products, the demand for that product would increase. As the demand for the product increased, the price would begin to increase and farmers would begin to see some additional purchasing power. This was the strategy that was included in Roosevelt's New Deal to try and assist the agricultural industry.

5. (A) is correct. Within his first eight days in office, Roosevelt had passed the first step in his New Deal. This measure was designed to protect the banking industry by supporting those banks that could maintain a profitable business, while removing from the industry those that could not. With the support of both houses of Congress, he was able to restore some measure of confidence in the banking industry.

6. (D) is correct. The banking measures of the New Deal, which could have gone as far as nationalizing the entire industry, were quite conservative. The banks were able to maintain their private ownership, with government support as opposed to being owned directly by the government, which would have been a much more radical change.

7. (B) is correct. These first "Hundred Days" of the Roosevelt presidency saw the passage of fifteen separate pieces of legislation that would form the basis of the New Deal and begin to pull the United States out of the depths of the Great Depression.

8. (A) is correct. The Tennessee Valley Authority was designed to create a series of dams in seven states along the Tennessee River to control floods, ease navigation and produce electricity. The production of electricity created a supply of cheap power that resulted in industrial growth in the poverty-stricken upper South.

9. (B) is correct. Long was a modern Robin Hood who advocated extremely high taxes on the wealthy in order to create programs that would support the poor.

10. (A) is correct. Compared to the $200 per month that many of the supporters of the left in the Democratic party had pushed for, the $10–$85 per month was quite conservative given the majority that the Democratic Party held in Congress.

Document-Based Question Sample Response

Discuss the Great Depression and its impact on the United States. In your answer, draw on your knowledge of the time period as well as the information in the documents.

The Great Depression of the 1930s was one of the largest economic collapses in world history. Its impact on the United States was enormous.

Much of the impact was in the area of government. By the 1930s the economy had changed from what it had been in the 19th century. The old economic philosophy of laissez-faire did not fit the new economic reality. The Social Security Act of 1935 was the first time the Federal government acknowledged direct responsibility for the welfare of its citizens. It provided for old age payments and unemployment insurance which would help to ameliorate the impact of future economic slowdowns. **(DOCUMENT 1)** Franklin Roosevelt recognized this new reality, and in his first inaugural address made clear that the old American notion of a limited role for government in the economy was no longer valid in this new situation. **(DOCUMENT 2)**

The Depression affected the American people directly, and it affected everyone. However, minority groups, particularly African-Americans, were hit harder than most. **(DOCUMENT 3)** The Depression hit the entire country, although its impact varied from area to area. It sparked one of the biggest migrations in American history as people, especially from the Midwest, moved in search of jobs. **(DOCUMENT 4)** The Midwest was particularly hard hit because the farming techniques of the day created the dust bowl, which drove many farmers out. **(DOCUMENT 9)** The impact of the Great Depression can be measured in the bank failures and the enormous breadlines of the day. **(DOCUMENTS 6 AND 7)**

Government responded in many ways. These included work programs such as the CCC and PWA which directly put people on the government payroll doing public works projects. **(DOCUMENTS 10 AND 11)** The NRA tried to reduce business competition so businesses could keep prices up, and gave working people the right to unionize so wages could be kept up. **(DOCUMENT 8)** Not everyone favored the New Deal programs. Many were declared unconstitutional by the Supreme Court. This caused FDR to try and expand the number of Justices on the Court. Many people did not support this, and his plan failed. **(DOCUMENT 12)** The national unemployment rate was about 25% during the worst of the Depression. As the chart shows, the problem of unemployment was not fully solved until World War II in the 1940s. **(DOCUMENT 5)**

Using the following image and your own knowledge, analyze the economic impact of the Great Depression on the daily lives of citizens.

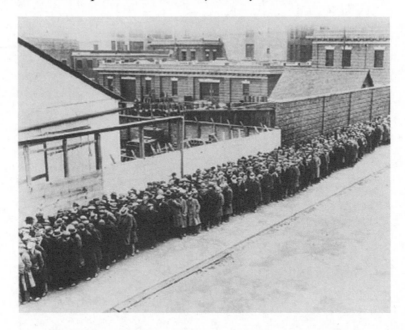

The Great Depression was a time when helplessness was as virulent as a cold. Economically the Great Depression meant that overproduction led to a cut back in jobs which led to less consumer spending which led to a further cutback until the whirling chasm of economic turmoil encompassed the lives of citizens. There were long lines for government subsidized food stations as seen in the above image. These stations served as a refueling station for hope yet also symbolized the fall from grace as former millionaire investors waited for their free coffee.

The daily lives of citizens were held up looking for jobs, trying to afford food for their families as the price plummeted for labor related activities. It was only after the public service projects completed under Roosevelt did change start to occur. Because unemployment was rampant and prices were rock bottom the citizens had to etch out a life for themselves by any means necessary. This later orchestrated the rise of organized crime bosses such as Al Capone who offered more money than many would see in weeks for a simple run for whiskey at Windsor, Ontario.

In conclusion, the economic impact of the Great Depression on the daily lives of citizens was vast. Rampant unemployment led to loss of self-respect. Many attempted to make a basic living either through looking for work or turning to a life of crime.

CHAPTER 27

America and the World, 1921–1945

After remaining primarily **isolationist** through the 1920s, in the 1930s, the United States became increasingly involved in world affairs and took a leading role in maintaining world order.

Retreat, Reversal, and Rivalry

In the 1920s, the United States followed a foreign policy that was narrow, cautious, and self-centered.

- **Regarding Europe**, American policy makers insisted on **payment of war debts** without allowing access to American markets and, thus, the dollars necessary to pay those debts.
- **In Latin America**, the United States continued to **seek economic advantages**, but did so with more friendly tactics than had previous administrations.
- **Dollar diplomacy** slowly replaced **gunboat diplomacy** in the Latin American region.
- **In Asia**, the United States continued on a confrontational course with **Japan**.
- **Japan expanded in China** and soon into other areas of Asia.

Isolationism

Because of the **Great Depression** and the fear of another European war, the United States followed an **isolationist policy** in the 1930s.

- **Looking back at World War I as a meaningless effort**, many Americans sought security in **pacifism and legal neutrality**. They wanted a way to ensure that the United States would not be drawn into a European conflict. Young people especially wanted to avoid war.
- **A series of neutrality laws** tried to limit the ways that Americans could be drawn into a conflict.
- **Events in Europe** made this isolationist posture increasingly unrealistic and difficult to maintain, and the neutrality acts became harder to support.

The Road to War

From 1939 to 1941, the United States moved ever closer to war as the nation's sympathy and support went to England and France.

- **As the war worsened in Europe**, President Roosevelt pushed the country closer to participation.

- **Roosevelt** clearly favored the Allied cause and convinced Congress to relax the strict neutrality acts in order to aid the British. Roosevelt asked for a peace time draft, and began the Lend-Lease program to get war supplies to the British.
- **Japan continued to expand in Asia**, especially into British and French colonies.
- **A surprise attack by the Japanese on Pearl Harbor** plunged the nation into war.

Turning the Tide Against the Axis

In both Europe and Asia the early days of the war were discouraging for Americans, although several factors developed that allowed the Allies to halt the advance of the **Axis** powers.

- **The alliance of the United States and Britain** was a genuine coalition with unified command and strategy, while the Soviet Union took the worst fury of the **German** *blitzkrieg*.
- **The United States and Britain** first invaded **North Africa** and then **Italy**, while the **Soviet Union** stopped the Germans at **Stalingrad**.
- **In Asia**, the United States Navy gained control of the central Pacific by July of 1942.

The Home Front

The war wrought vast changes in American society and ended the decade of depression. The need for **war materials** was met by American industries working at full capacity. A **War Production Board** was formed to answer the complex logistical concerns. Incomes rose for workers and farmers.

- **The war motivated millions to migrate**, creating problems in housing and family life, but offering opportunities to African Americans, Hispanic Americans, and women.
- **Another important problem** was the **relocation of Japanese Americans** into concentration camps.
- **Roosevelt and the Democrats** maintained power and won wartime elections.

Victory

After the offensives of the Axis powers had been stopped, the war ended quickly.

- **The Germans** were thoroughly defeated and forced to surrender unconditionally.
- **The alliance** between the **United States** and the **Soviet Union** ended. The two countries had far different goals concerning the rebuilding of **postwar Europe**.
- **Though the war in Europe was over**, the war in the Pacific continued until President Harry S. Truman ordered the **dropping of two atomic bombs on Japan**.

Multiple-Choice Questions

1. The supporters of the Kellogg-Briand Pact hoped to
   - (A) achieve immediate international disarmament.
   - (B) establish a Franco-American mutual defense pact.
   - (C) initiate the process toward the outlawing of war.
   - (D) establish a formal alliance between the United States and France.
   - (E) achieve a quick military build-up.

2. The Clark Memorandum of 1930
   - (A) ordered U.S. marines into Nicaragua.
   - (B) repudiated the Roosevelt Corollary to the Monroe Doctrine.
   - (C) ordered the blockade of Venezuela.
   - (D) closed the Panama Canal.
   - (E) established large plantations under U.S. control in northern Panama.

3. The signatories of the Five Power Treaty at the Washington Conference in 1921 agreed to limit the size of their
   - (A) armies.
   - (B) navies.
   - (C) air force.
   - (D) munitions factories.
   - (E) occupational ground forces.

4. The Good Neighbor Policy promised Latin American countries
   - (A) more U.S. military involvement in their affairs.
   - (B) less U.S. interest in Latin America.
   - (C) easy U.S. loans with low rates of interest.
   - (D) closer ties with each other.
   - (E) a cooperative, rather than paternalistic, relationship with the United States.

5. In 1931, the illusion of peace was shattered by the Japanese invasion of
   - (A) Korea.
   - (B) Malaysia.
   - (C) the Philippines.
   - (D) Manchuria.
   - (E) Siberia.

6. The dictator of Fascist Italy was
   - (A) Francisco Franco.
   - (B) Antonio Gramsci.
   - (C) Adolfo Colavita.
   - (D) Fiorello LaGuardia.
   - (E) Benito Mussolini.

7. Britain and France responded to initial German aggression by
   - (A) attempting to appease Hitler.
   - (B) immediately threatening war.
   - (C) establishing a military alliance with the Soviet Union.
   - (D) seizing German territory.
   - (E) blockading German ports.

8. With the outbreak of war in Europe in 1939, Franklin D. Roosevelt
   - (A) immediately declared war on Germany.
   - (B) declared American neutrality.
   - (C) loaned massive quantities of war supplies to France and England.
   - (D) warned Germany that if France were attacked, the United States would declare war.
   - (E) made a secret pact with the French.

9. The Lend-Lease Act of 1941
   - (A) ensured the British easier access to American war supplies.
   - (B) placed restrictions on which materials the United States could ship to Great Britain.
   - (C) encountered almost no opposition from American congressmen.
   - (D) was proposed by American isolationists.
   - (E) was approved but never implemented.

10. The American fleet at Pearl Harbor was caught by surprise when Japan attacked because
   - (A) American intelligence had not been able

to break the Japanese code.

(B) of faulty radar equipment.

(C) of human miscalculations and mistakes.

(D) Roosevelt conspired to get the United

States into the war by provoking a Japanese attack.

(E) American intelligence had incorrectly decoded an intercepted message.

Free-Response Question

Assess the various responses of the United States to the military aggression of Japan, Germany, and Italy in the 1930s.

ANSWERS AND EXPLANATIONS

Multiple-Choice Questions

1. (C) is correct. The supporters of the Kellogg-Briand Pact, especially those in the United States, had hoped that this would be the first step in getting all nations to agree not to use war as an instrument of national policy. In reality, the Pact was a toothless document that had no provisions for enforcement.

2. (B) is correct. The Clark Memorandum stated that the United States had no right to intervene in neighboring states unless it was to protect American lives or property under international law. This was opposite of the Roosevelt Corollary, which allowed the United States to intervene if a country was having internal economic problems.

3. (B) is correct. Isolated from countries like France, Japan, Britain and Italy with oceans on either side of it, the United States sought to limit the size of national navies for its own protection in the Five Power Treaty.

4. (E) is correct. Roosevelt's beliefs on foreign policy in Central and South America was not one of economic and political dominance, but one of co-operation and friendship. He felt that these measures would be more effective than threats and armed interventions.

5. (D) is correct. The spirit of the Nine Power Treaty and the Kellogg-Briand Pact was violated in September, 1931 when Japan invaded Manchuria.

6. (E) is correct. In 1922, Benito Mussolini came to power in Italy, imposing a fascist regime and aggressive foreign policy upon the peninsula nation.

7. (A) is correct. During the 1930s, the governments of Britain and France followed a policy of appeasement towards Hitler and Germany. The basic concept was that if the French and British made concession that they would be able to appease Hitler and avoid another war.

8. (B) is correct. While the United States would eventually declare war on Germany and supply the French and British with war supplies, when Germany invaded Poland on September 1, 1939, Roosevelt proclaimed America's neutrality.

9. (A) is correct. The Lend-Lease Act of 1941 allowed the United States to provide war supplies to any nation that was deemed "vital to the defense of the United States." In asking Congress for approval, Roosevelt stated that America should become the "greatest arsenal of democracy."

10. (C) is correct. The Japanese attack on Pearl Harbor caught the United States by surprise largely because American officials believed that the Japanese were receptive to a negotiated settlement. The United States had the ability to decode Japanese messages faster than the Japanese were able to decode the messages themselves, yet officials in the government were unable to decipher the manipulation that the Japanese were undertaking.

Free-Response Essay Sample Response

Assess the various responses of the United States to the military aggression of Japan, Germany, and Italy in the 1930s.

During the 1930s, the United States responded to military aggression by isolating itself in matters of foreign affairs. After having taken steps throughout the early 1920s to ensure world security, the United States backed away from the notion of collective security and allowed aggressive nations, such as Japan, Germany and Italy, to reign unchecked.

One of the first instances of this sense of isolationism came in 1931, when Japan, in violation of the Nine Power Treaty and the Kellogg-Briand Pact, invaded Manchuria. Aside from issuing a statement that the United States would not recognize Manchuria as part of the Japanese empire, the American government did not take any additional action.

Later in that same decade, as Hitler seized Austria and made demands upon the Sudetenland, U.S. President Roosevelt backed the meeting of the leaders of France, Britain and Germany in Munich. The American President even expressed support for the British policy of appeasement. Six months later, when Hitler seized the remainder of Czechoslovakia, the isolationists blocked moves by Roosevelt for neutrality revisions.

Even at the outbreak of war in Europe in 1939, the United States was only able to provide cash and carry amendments to their arms embargo for England and France to take advantage of. Throughout the 1930s, the United States retreated from the responsibility of collective security in Europe and Asia and isolated itself from world affairs up until it began to threaten its own democracy and security.

CHAPTER 28

The Onset of the Cold War

Postwar antagonism gradually led the **United States** and the **Soviet Union** into the **Cold War**. The contrasts between the countries were dramatically represented in their leaders: **Truman**, who believed in the innate goodness of America, and **Stalin**, the hard-headed realist who was determined to protect Russia's wartime conquests.

The Cold War Begins

At the Potsdam Conference in Yalta, Russia and the United States split over three issues: control of Europe, postwar economic aid, and the control of atomic weapons.

▌ **The Allies** first took sides over the division of Europe, with each side intent on imposing its values in the areas liberated by its military.

▌ **The division of Germany** between the **West** (where the U.S., Britain, and France exercised authority) and the **East** (under the Soviets) was most crucial.

▌ **The U.S. decision to end lend-lease aid** and to ignore a Soviet request for a loan convinced Stalin of **Western hostility**.

▌ **The United States** proposed only a **gradual abolition of nuclear arms**, thus preserving America's atomic monopoly, while the Soviets proposed immediate nuclear disarmament.

▌ **Attempts to agree** on mutual reduction of atomic weapons failed.

Containment

U.S. foreign policy leaders initiated a **major departure** in American foreign affairs from the traditional policy of **isolationism** to one of **containment**, arguing that only strong and sustained resistance could halt **Soviet expansionism**. The **Truman Doctrine** marked an informal declaration of cold war against the Soviet Union.

▌ **In 1947, President Truman asked Congress for money** for aid to **Greece** and **Turkey**, thereby assuming what had been Great Britain's role as leading power in the eastern Mediterranean.

▌ **The American government also decided to contain Soviet influence** by **financing postwar European recovery** as a check on communist power. The plan paid rich dividends by helping the **industrial revival** in Western Europe and ending the threat that all Europe might drift into the communist orbit. The Cold War had cut Europe in half—the **Iron Curtain** separated the two sides.

▌ **In 1949, the United States entered into the North Atlantic Treaty Organization (NATO)** with ten European nations and Canada, a pact for collective self-defense.

▌ **When the Russians blockaded the western access to Berlin**, the Truman government responded with an airlift, which maintained the American position in that German city.

The Cold War Expands

In the late 1940s and the early 1950s, the Cold War expanded. Both sides built up their military might, and diplomatic competition spread from Europe to Asia.

▊ **Committed to winning the growing conflict with Russia**, the American government unified its armed services and initiated a massive military buildup, especially in its **air force**.

▊ **The National Security Act** created the **Department of Defense**, the **CIA**, and the **National Security Council**.

▊ **In Asia**, the United States consolidated its Pacific sphere, but failed to avert the Chinese civil war in which **Mao Tse-tung** and the communists drove **Chiang Kai-shek and the Nationalists** from the mainland to **Formosa** (renamed **Taiwan**).

▊ **The showdown for the Cold War in Asia** came in June 1950, when communist **North Korea** invaded **South Korea**, perhaps without Soviet approval, leading to war. The U.S. secured UN support for a **police action** to defend South Korea.

▊ **An attempt to drive the communists out of North Korea failed** and the war settled into a stalemate near the **38th parallel**.

The Cold War at Home

President Truman tried unsuccessfully to revive the New Deal reform tradition after World War II.

▊ **Truman's apparent lack of political vision** and his fondness for **appointing cronies** to high office were major weaknesses. Truman found himself caught between **union demands for higher wages** and the **public demand that consumer prices be kept down**.

▊ **The president benefited from Thomas Dewey's passive campaign** and the indecisiveness of the Republican Congress and won the **1948 presidential election**.

▊ Fear of communists led to a **government loyalty program** and unrelenting investigations by the **House Un-American Activities Committee**. Former State Department official **Alger Hiss** was convicted of perjury after allegations of espionage. Thousands of government workers were dismissed by the **Loyalty Review Board** for dubious memberships. Following Soviet detonation of an atomic bomb, **Julius and Ethel Rosenberg** were executed for conspiring with the Soviets.

▊ **Senator Joseph McCarthy** engaged in tireless pursuits of communist conspirators. McCarthy directed his accusations everywhere, from the State Department to the U.S. Army. Fearful of arousing suspicion, would-be opponents remained quiet.

▊ **Promising to clean up corruption** and to bring the Korean War to an honorable end, **Dwight Eisenhower** won election as president in **1952**. Eisenhower succeeded in reaching agreement with the North Koreans for **an armistice in 1953**. McCarthy's unfounded accusations led to public humiliation and censure following Senate hearings in 1954.

Eisenhower Wages the Cold War

Together with Secretary of State **John Foster Dulles**, President Eisenhower tried to bring the Cold War under control.

- **Eisenhower refused pleas for American assistance** from the French in their attempts to reestablish colonial control in **Indochina**. Following an international conference dividing Vietnam in 1954, the U.S. later offered support to the anti-communist government of **Ngo Dinh Diem in Saigon**.
- **When Egypt's Nasser seized control of the Suez Canal in 1956**, England and France retaliated with an **invasion** of Egypt. Both the U.S. and the Soviet Union supported a UN resolution calling for their withdrawal.
- **In 1958**, the U.S. intervened temporarily in **Lebanon** to secure establishment of a stable government.
- **During the 1950s**, the U.S. worked behind the scenes through the **CIA** on many fronts: to place the **Shah of Iran** in control of that country, to overthrow a leftist regime in **Guatemala**, and to oppose the **Castro regime in Cuba**.
- **Eisenhower's efforts** to end the nuclear arms race failed.
- **Soviet launching of** *Sputnik* intensified U.S. fears.
- **Stalin's successor**, **Nikita Khrushchev**, first agreed and later refused to meet with Eisenhower after an American spy plane was shot down by the Soviets.

Multiple-Choice Questions

1. The fundamental disagreement at the beginning of the Cold War involved the question of
   (A) who would control postwar Europe.
   (B) sharing the secrets of atomic weapons.
   (C) free elections in Western Europe.
   (D) whether Truman or Stalin would lead postwar alliances.
   (E) who would control post-war Japan.

2. The Soviet Union first learned of the American atomic bomb
   (A) from Franklin D. Roosevelt.
   (B) through conversations between Truman and Stalin.
   (C) from the British and French.
   (D) through the use of espionage.
   (E) when the first one was dropped on Japan.

3. George Kennan's "containment" policy proposed
   (A) long-term neutrality for the United States with respect to European affairs.
   (B) a series of aggressive maneuvers toward the Soviet Union.
   (C) American vigilance regarding Soviet expansionist tendencies.
   (D) restrictions on American expansionist plans.

   (E) keeping nuclear weapons information a closely guarded secret.

4. The Truman Doctrine was developed as a response to problems in
   (A) Greece.
   (B) Italy.
   (C) North Africa.
   (D) southeast Asia.
   (E) Turkey.

5. The Truman Doctrine
   (A) marked an informal declaration of war against the U.S.S.R.
   (B) promised warmer U.S.-Soviet relations.
   (C) emphasized the idea of economic aid to western Europe.
   (D) was proposed as an alternative to containment policy.
   (E) was an extension of the Monroe Doctrine.

6. The Marshall Plan proposed
   (A) the infusion of massive amounts of American capital in Western Europe.
   (B) the rearming of Germany.
   (C) a massive military buildup in Europe.
   (D) a series of Western military alliances.
   (E) the division of Germany.

7. Overall, the Marshall Plan
   - (A) did little to halt Soviet encroachment in Western Europe.
   - (B) failed as an economic measure.
   - (C) received wholehearted support from the Soviets.
   - (D) generated a broad industrial recovery in Western Europe.
   - (E) had no effect on the U.S. economy.

8. The North Atlantic Treaty Organization
   - (A) received little support from European nations.
   - (B) represented a departure from traditional American isolationism.
   - (C) was perceived as nonthreatening by the Soviets.
   - (D) continued the old American tradition of involvement in European alliances.
   - (E) was opposed by the United Nations secretary-general.

9. NATO
   - (A) had the effect of easing U.S.-Soviet tensions.
   - (B) intensified Soviet fears of the West.
   - (C) involved only the United States and major Western European powers.
   - (D) failed to radically affect European military strategy.
   - (E) relied exclusively on European forces.

10. Truman's handling of the Berlin Blockade
    - (A) was an important factor in his victory in the election of 1948.
    - (B) showed his indecisiveness in confronting the Soviet threat.
    - (C) caused many to question his leadership abilities.
    - (D) led the Soviets to view him as a weak president.
    - (E) angered American citizens.

Document-Based Question

What were the major issues and events of the Cold War during the period 1945–1960? In your answer, draw on your knowledge of the time period involved as well as the information contained in the documents below.

DOCUMENT 1   Source: Division of Europe after World War II

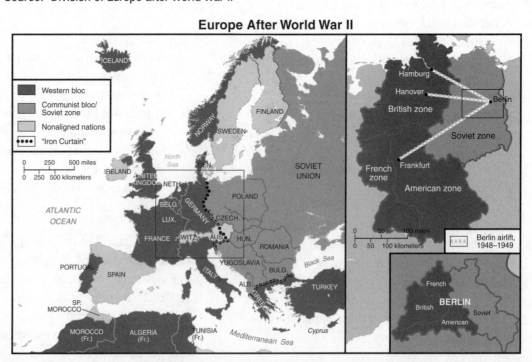

Europe After World War II

DOCUMENT 2 Source: George F. Kennan, The Long Telegram, 1946

We have here a political force committed fanatically to the belief that with the US there can be no permanent *modus vivendi*, that it is desirable and necessary that the internal harmony of our society be disrupted, our traditional way of life be destroyed, the international authority of our state be broken, if Soviet power is to be secure.

DOCUMENT 3 Source: Berlin Airlift, 1948–1949

DOCUMENT 4 Source: Harry Truman, The Truman Doctrine, 1947

At the present moment in world history nearly every nation must choose between alternative ways of life. The choice is too often not a free one.

One way of life is based upon the will of the majority, and is distinguished by free institutions, representative government, free elections, guaranties of individual liberty, freedom of speech and religion, and freedom from political oppression.

The second way of life is based upon the will of a minority forcibly imposed upon the majority. It relies upon terror and oppression, a controlled press and radio, fixed elections, and the suppression of personal freedoms.

I believe that it must be the policy of the United States to support free peoples who are resisting attempted subjugation by armed minorities or by outside pressures.

I believe that we must assist free peoples to work out their own destinies in their own way.

DOCUMENT 5 Source: George Marshall, The Marshall Plan, 1947

The truth of the matter is that Europe's requirements for the next three or four years of foreign food and other essential products—principally from America—are so much greater than her present ability to pay that she must have substantial additional help or face economic, social, and political deterioration of a very grave character....

Aside from the demoralizing effect on the world at large and the possibilities of disturbances arising as a result of the desperation of the people concerned, the consequences of the economy of the United States should be apparent to all. It is logical that the United States should do whatever it is able to do to assist in the return of normal economic health in the world, without which there can be no political stability and no assured peace. Our policy is directed not against any country or doctrine but against hunger, poverty, desperation, and chaos. Its purpose should be the revival of a working economy in the world so as to permit the emergence of political and social conditions in which free institutions can exist.

DOCUMENT 6 Source: Ronald Reagan, Testimony Before the House Un-American Activities Committee, 1947

The Committee met at 10:30 A.M. [October 23, 1947], the Honorable J. Parnell Thomas (Chairman) presiding.

THE CHAIRMAN: The record will show that Mr. McDowell, Mr. Vail, Mr. Nixon, and Mr. Thomas are present. A Subcommittee is sitting.

Staff members present: Mr. Robert E. Stripling, Chief Investigator; Messrs. Louis J. Russell, H. A. Smith, and Robert B. Gatson, Investigators; and Mr. Benjamin Mandel, Director of Research.

MR. STRIPLING: As a member of the board of directors, as president of the Screen Actors Guild, and as an active member, have you at any time observed or noted within the organization a clique of either Communists or Fascists who were attempting to exert influence or pressure on the guild?

MR. REAGAN: Well, sir, my testimony must be very similar to that of Mr. [George] Murphy and Mr. [Robert] Montgomery. There has been a small group within the Screen Actors Guild which has consistently opposed the policy of the guild board and officers of the guild, as evidenced by the vote on various issues. That small clique referred to has been suspected of more or less following the tactics that we associated with the Communist Party.

MR. STRIPLING: Would you refer to them as a disruptive influence within the guild?

MR. REAGAN: I would say that at times they have attempted to be a disruptive influence.

MR. STRIPLING: You have no knowledge yourself as to whether or not any of them are members of the Communist Party?

MR. REAGAN: No, sir, I have no investigative force, or anything, and I do not know.

MR. STRIPLING: Has it ever been reported to you that certain members of the guild were Communists?

MR. REAGAN: Yes, sir, I have heard different discussions and some of them tagged as Communists.

MR. STRIPLING: Would you say that this clique has attempted to dominate the guild?

MR. REAGAN: Well, sir, by attempting to put over their own particular views on various issues...

DOCUMENT 7   Source: Telegram from Joe McCarthy to President Truman, 1950

In a Lincoln Day speech at Wheeling Thursday night I stated that the State Department harbors a nest of communists and communist sympathizers who are helping to shape our foreign policy. I further stated that I have in my possession the names of 57 communists who are in the State Department at present.

DOCUMENT 8   Source: National Security Council Memorandum Number 68, 1950

Two complex sets of factors have now basically altered this historical distribution of power. First, the defeat of Germany and Japan and the decline of the British and French Empires have interacted with the development of the United States and the Soviet Union in such a way that power has increasingly gravitated to these two centers. Second, the Soviet Union, unlike previous aspirants to hegemony, is animated by a new fanatic faith, antithetical to our own, and seeks to impose its absolute authority over the rest of the world. Conflict has, therefore, become endemic and is waged, on the part of the Soviet Union, by violent or non-violent methods in accordance with the dictates of expediency. With the development of increasingly terrifying weapons of mass destruction, every individual faces the ever-present possibility of annihilation should the conflict enter the phase of total war.

On the one hand, the people of the world yearn for relief from the anxiety arising from the risk of atomic war. On the other hand, any substantial further extension of the area under the domination of the Kremlin would raise the possibility that no coalition adequate to confront the Kremlin with greater strength could be assembled. It is in this context that this Republic and its citizens in the ascendancy of their strength stand in their deepest peril....

DOCUMENT 9   Source: Protest against the execution of Julius and Ethel Rosenberg

DOCUMENT 10   Source: Korean War map, 1950–1953

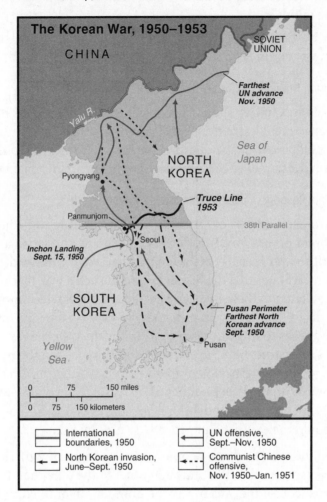

The Korean War, 1950–1953

CHINA

SOVIET UNION

Farthest UN advance Nov. 1950

Yalu R.

Sea of Japan

NORTH KOREA

Pyongyang

Truce Line 1953

Panmunjom

38th Parallel

Inchon Landing Sept. 15, 1950

Seoul

SOUTH KOREA

Pusan Perimeter Farthest North Korean advance Sept. 1950

Yellow Sea

Pusan

0   75   150 miles

0   75   150 kilometers

International boundaries, 1950

UN offensive, Sept.–Nov. 1950

North Korean invasion, June–Sept. 1950

Communist Chinese offensive, Nov. 1950–Jan. 1951

DOCUMENT 11   Source: Hydrogen bomb test, 1952

DOCUMENT 12   Source: 1950s family bomb shelter

DOCUMENT 13   Source: Defense spending, 1945–1960

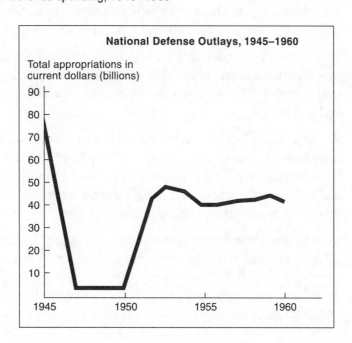

National Defense Outlays, 1945–1960

Total appropriations in
current dollars (billions)

But threats, new in kind or degree, constantly arise.

Of these, I mention two only.

A vital element in keeping the peace is our military establishment. Our arms must be mighty, ready for instant action, so that no potential aggressor may be tempted to risk his own destruction.

Our military organization today bears little relation to that known by any of my predecessors in peacetime, or indeed by the fighting men of World War II or Korea.

Until the latest of our world conflicts, the United States had no armaments industry. American makers of plowshares could, with time and as required, make swords as well. But now we can no longer risk emergency improvisation of national defense; we have been compelled to create a permanent armaments industry of vast proportions. Added to this, three and a half million men and women are directly engaged in the defense establishment. We annually spend on military security more than the net income of all United States corporations. This conjunction of an immense military establishment and a large arms industry is new in the American experience. The total influence—economic, political, even spiritual—is felt in every city, every Statehouse, every office of the Federal government. We recognize the imperative need for this development. Yet we must not fail to comprehend its grave implications. Our toil, resources and livelihood are all involved; so is the very structure of our society.

In the councils of government, we must guard against the acquisition of unwarranted influence, whether sought or unsought, by the military-industrial complex. The potential for the disastrous rise of misplaced power exists and will persist.

We must never let the weight of this combination endanger our liberties or democratic processes. We should take nothing for granted. Only an alert and knowledgeable citizenry can compel the proper meshing of the huge industrial and military machinery of defense with our peaceful methods and goals, so that security and liberty may prosper together.

Akin to, and largely responsible for the sweeping changes in our industrial-military posture, has been the technological revolution during recent decades.

Free-Response Question

Describe the Korean problem (1950–1953) and the UN response to it.

ANSWERS AND EXPLANATIONS

Multiple-Choice Questions

▌ **1. (A) is correct.** The Soviets were mindful of past invasions from the west through Poland and were intent on ensuring a friendly government in that country. The Americans, however, believed in the principle of self-determination for all peoples, including the people of Poland. Poland is the most commonly used example of the disagreements over who would control a postwar Europe.

▌ **2. (D) is correct.** While the first official notice that the United States gave to the Soviet Union regarding their creation of an atomic bomb was at the Potsdam Conference when Truman told Stalin, the Soviets had an extensive network of spies in the United States and had known about the project and had begun one of their own as early as 1943.

▌ **3. (C) is correct.** The containment policy was designed to stop the expansion of the Soviet Union and its influence through strong and sustained resistance.

▌ **4. (A) is correct.** There was a civil war going on in Greece between the British-supported government and communist guerrillas. In 1947, the British government informed the Americans that they were no longer able to support the democratically elected government in Greece. Fearing Soviet involvement in the civil war, the United States acted.

▌ **5. (A) is correct.** The Truman Doctrine stated that the United States was committed to opposing any internal subversion or external aggression by the Soviet Union in an attempt to contain the Soviets and communism in general. This meant that the United States would be in conflict with the Soviet Union.

▌ **6. (A) is correct.** The basis of the Marshall Plan was that if a country could achieve economic well being, that there was little chance that communist ideology would be a threat in that country. By channeling large amounts of money into the countries of Western Europe, the United States effectively stopped any interest that may have been brewing in communist ideologies.

▌ **7. (D) is correct.** By the 1950s, most of Western Europe had become self-sustaining in an economic sense. This was less than a decade after the end of the war. Compared to the success (or lack thereof) of Germany to achieve this type of economic upswing after World War I, it can easily be seen that the Marshall Plan was successful in these countries.

▌ **8. (B) is correct.** Leading up to and at the beginning of both World Wars, the United States was reluctant to become involved in wars that involved only European countries and their colonies. However, with the creation of NATO and the American commitment to militarily assist any NATO member, the United States took a drastic change of direction in their traditional foreign policy stance.

▌ **9. (B) is correct.** The creation of the twelve-member military alliance of NATO made the Soviet Union nervous about the organization being offensive in nature. This was especially true after West Germany became a member of NATO in the 1950s.

▌ **10. (A) is correct.** As the nation rallied around its President during a time of crisis, Truman's handling of the Berlin Blockade showed his leadership ability and the electorate gave that ability a vote of confidence.

Document-Based Question Sample Response

What were the major issues and events of the Cold War during the period 1945–1960? In your answer, draw on your knowledge of the time period involved as well as the information contained in the documents below.

The Cold War was a dangerous and uncertain time in American history. It began right at the close of World War II. Many events, both domestic and foreign, shaped American history during this period.

As World War II drew to a close, many decisions had to be made. One decision that the Allies made was to allow the Soviets to be the first into Berlin. Because the Soviets had taken many casualties in the war, the Americans and British felt it important to let them get into Berlin first. However, this action resulted in the de facto division of Europe after the war into a communist east and non-communist west. Although Berlin was in the communist zone, it was also divided into communist and non-communist areas. **(DOCUMENT 1)**

Many Americans were concerned about the growth of Soviet power and the spread of Communism, and were convinced that the Soviets were out to destroy America and the west. **(DOCUMENT 2)** The Soviets did make an unsuccessful attempt to get the western powers out of Berlin by blockading it. This effort was defeated by the Berlin Airlift of 1948–1949. **(DOCUMENT 3)** President Truman felt that containing the spread of communism should be the focus of American foreign policy and instituted the Truman Doctrine as the means for implanting that concept. **(DOCUMENT 4)** There was also a great deal of concern about the condition of Europe after the war; many felt that unless we helped much of Europe could go communist. The Marshall Plan was implemented in order to help prevent that from coming about. **(DOCUMENT 5)**

The threat of communism in this time period had other impacts as well. Because of the nuclear arms race at the time, the hydrogen bomb was developed. **(DOCUMENT 11)** Many were nervous about the growth of Soviet power and felt that it may lead to unending conflict between two opposing systems forever. **(DOCUMENT 8)** The United States fought a three-year-long war in Korea in order to prevent South Korea from going communist. **(DOCUMENT 10)** The Cold War in this time period had a great impact at home as well. Many were fearful and nervous about communists in our government. Senator Joe McCarthy stirred up a lot of fear in this regard, as did the House Un-American Activities Committee. **(DOCUMENTS 6 AND 7)** Many Americans also built bomb shelters in their own homes to try and protect themselves against the possibility of a Soviet nuclear attack. **(DOCUMENT 12)** One of the most significant episodes of the time was the execution of the Rosenbergs, who were convicted of spying for the Soviet Union. There was much controversy over their execution. **(DOCUMENT 9)** Defense spending increased greatly for much of this period as a result of the military pressure that the United States felt itself to be under. **(DOCUMENT 13)** Finally, the fear that the Cold War had stirred up, as well as the growing power of industry and the military, concerned many in the country, including President Eisenhower, who issued a warning about this during his last days in office. **(DOCUMENT 14)**

Free-Response Essay Sample Response

Describe the Korean problem (1950–1953) and the UN response to it.

Korea had been divided into two sections "temporarily," but an agreement on unification was unable to be reached. Both the north and the south wanted to be in control. This created a great deal of political tension in the region as the communist-supported north and the American-supported south intensified their feud.

This atmosphere of tension heightened to its climax when the North Korean army launched a military strike against South Korea, pushing the southern forces all the way back to a small area of Korea near Pusan. This was a flagrant violation of United Nations policy and their response to it was to send in United Nations soldiers, with the U.S. forces.

The United Nations response, organized by General Douglas MacArthur, came in the form of a daring attack at Inchon, near Seoul. This surprised the communist forces and they were quickly pushed out of South Korea. At this point, the UN mandate had been fulfilled but the South Korean leader (as with some of the other forces, such as the United States) still continued to push. They forced the North Koreans back to the Yalu River. While this did leave South Korea in control, it also upset China. The Chinese stated that any further military action near their border would lead to a Chinese response. Several days later, the Chinese forces pushed America, UN and South Korean troops back to the 38th parallel.

At this point, the UN's involvement yet again increased. However, this involvement was diplomatic as opposed to military. The UN truce was negotiated to end the Korean conflict where it had begun, at the 38th parallel. Although nothing was truly resolved with this issue, as Korea continues to be divided to the present day, it did indicate the ability of the UN, when backed by major powers, to enforce its policy.

CHAPTER 29

Affluence and Anxiety

In postwar America, new affluence replaced the poverty and hunger of the Great Depression, and people flocked to the suburbs to escape the city and to raise their growing families.

The Postwar Boom

An intensified **demand for consumer goods** and **heavy government spending** stimulated economic growth from the late 1940s through the 1950s. Although the rate of economic growth slowed in the second half of the 1950s, most Americans had far **more real income during this era than ever before**.

▮ **By 1950**, production caught up with demand and the gross national product reached a point 50 percent higher than in 1940.

▮ **The Baby Boom** and expanding **suburbia** stimulated consumerism as fear of another depression dissipated. Slowdowns in economic growth occurred in the second half of the decade, but **higher pay and shorter hours** remained as permanent standards in the American workplace.

▮ **The newly affluent postwar generation** shed their identities to live in **look-alike homes** and embrace the new **culture of the suburbs**. Life in these communities depended on the **automobile**.

▮ **Homemaking and child rearing** became primary vocations of suburban women.

The Good Life?

Despite an abundance of material goods, many Americans questioned the quality of their lives.

▮ **Among the institutions that flourished in the postwar years** was organized religion.

▮ **A tremendous increase** in the number of **school-aged children** created an enormous **strain** on local school districts.

▮ **The number of young adults attending college** increased precipitously.

▮ **At home, television** became the most popular entertainment medium—a safe conveyor of the consumer culture.

▮ **Critics like David Riesman, C. Wright Mills, and Jack Kerouac** found fault with the blandness, conformity, corporate dehumanization, and loss of individuality of the 1950s.

▮ **The Soviet launching of an orbiting satellite (Sputnik)** caused panic among Americans in 1957 and heightened concern and self-assessment that the nation had lost its unquestioned supremacy in the world. Congress responded with the National Defense Education Act—with an emphasis on science and math in the schools.

Farewell to Reform

Growing affluence removed the urgency for social and economic change.

▌ **In the wake of his 1948 electoral victory**, **President Truman** tried to push for too many reforms too soon.

▌ **Although he failed to get congressional and public support** for the **"Fair Deal,"** Truman's spirited efforts did prevent Republicans from repealing New Deal social legislation.

▌ **When Dwight Eisenhower was elected in 1952**, moderation based upon **fiscal conservatism**, encouragement of **private initiative**, and **reduction of federal programs** became the theme. His administration's legislative record (which consisted of **extending Social Security benefits** and creating the **Department of Health, Education, and Welfare**) was relatively modest.

▌ **One significant accomplishment, the Highway Act of 1956**, created the modern **interstate** system.

The Struggle over Civil Rights

The Cold War helped to arouse national conscience in favor of civil rights for African Americans.

▌ **Although benefiting economically** from World War II, blacks continued to live in blighted neighborhoods and to be actively segregated from white society.

▌ **Although President Truman had failed to push his civil rights package** through Congress over **southern opposition**, he did succeed in adding civil rights to the liberal agenda, and most importantly, in **desegregating the armed forces**.

▌ **The Supreme Court** took the lead in reversing the late nineteenth century's **"separate but equal"** decisions.

▌ In *Brown* v. *Board of Education of Topeka,* the Court ordered the nation's public schools to **admit African American students for the first time**.

▌ **President Eisenhower sent troops into Little Rock, Arkansas**, to enforce the ruling but lack of overall presidential support weakened the desegregation process.

▌ **A permanent Civil Rights Commission** was established to protect voting rights.

▌ **In Montgomery, Alabama, Rosa Parks and Dr. Martin Luther King Jr.** led successful boycotts against the city's segregated bus system.

▌ **Drawing from sources such as Gandhi**, King refined the concept of **passive resistance**.

▌ **In 1960, "sit-ins" and other demonstrations** succeeded in desegregating many public facilities.

Multiple-Choice Questions

1. The individual who invented the concept of mass construction of suburban homes was
   (A) William Levitt.
   (B) C. Wright Mills.
   (C) William Douglas.
   (D) William Whyte.
   (E) Charles Newcastle.

2. The great economic growth of the late 1940s and early 1950s resulted from
   (A) radically new industrial production methods.
   (B) government decisions to remove federal regulations on business.

(C) great consumer demand and heavy defense spending.

(D) government success in balancing the budget.

(E) across-the-board wage increases.

3. The new American suburbs of the 1950s
   (A) showed a surprising occupational diversity among inhabitants.
   (B) were inhabited primarily by the middle class.
   (C) allowed only upper-class inhabitants.
   (D) were mainly inhabited by lower-class families.
   (E) were open to all races and religions.

4. According to the social critic C. Wright Mills, the real villain in American society in the 1950s was
   (A) the Soviet Union.
   (B) the corporation.
   (C) the labor union.
   (D) the university.
   (E) the government.

5. The launching of the Soviet *Sputnik* in 1957
   (A) led to a massive reformation in American education.
   (B) was widely praised by American citizens.
   (C) proved Soviet technological superiority.
   (D) was a hoax.
   (E) was a disaster.

6. President Harry Truman's domestic program was known as the
   (A) New Deal.
   (B) New Frontier.
   (C) Square Deal.
   (D) Great Society.
   (E) Fair Deal.

7. Eisenhower's legislative record could be characterized as
   (A) impressive, particularly in terms of social programs.
   (B) oriented toward much heavier government spending.
   (C) very modest.
   (D) in the tradition of Roosevelt and Truman.
   (E) radical.

8. In Congress, which one of the following Democrats did President Eisenhower have to work most closely with during the 1950s?
   (A) John Dulles
   (B) Robert Taft
   (C) Sam Rayburn
   (D) Dean Acheson
   (E) John Carmichael

9. The one significant legislative achievement of the Eisenhower years was the
   (A) Social Security Act.
   (B) Highway Act of 1956.
   (C) Taft-Hartley Act.
   (D) Fair Employment Act.
   (E) Truth in Advertising Act.

10. In its decision in *Brown v. Board of Education of Topeka*, the Supreme Court
    (A) refused to rule on the question of segregation.
    (B) declared separate educational facilities to be inherently unequal.
    (C) continued to support the doctrine of separate but equal.
    (D) ruled that the NAACP's case had no merit.
    (E) ordered federal funding of new schools and universities to meet growing needs.

Free-Response Question

Discuss the impact of Sputnik *on the United States.*

Multiple-Choice Questions

▌ **1. (A) is correct.** In 1947, William Levitt announced that he was going to build two thousand rental houses in a former potato field on Long Island, just outside of Manhattan. Using mass production techniques, Levitt built these houses, and thousands more, to allow people to move out of crowded city apartments into larger homes that were still fairly close to the city center.

▌ **2. (C) is correct.** Throughout the late 1940s and early 1950s Americans were busy spending money. Not having enough money to buy things during the Great Depression and then not having enough things to spend money on during World War II, beginning in 1945 Americans were able to become the great consumers that they had been during the 1920s. Along with a government that was spending $40 billion a year on defense during the Cold War and Korean War, these factors led to great economic growth in the United States.

▌ **3. (A) is correct.** The additional purchasing power of a new middle class in the United States allowed housing developments in the suburbs to be composed of almost every walk of life. It was entirely possible for a doctor or lawyer to be living next door to a salesclerk or plumber. There was little regard for the traditional distinctions of ancestry, education or religion.

▌ **4. (B) is correct.** In his books, *White Collar* in 1951 and *Power Elite* in 1956, Mills stated that the corporation was the villain by depriving office workers of their own identities and imposing an impersonal discipline through manipulation and propaganda.

▌ **5. (A) is correct.** After the launching of the Soviet satellite *Sputnik* in 1957, the American Congress passed the National Defense Education Act, which authorized federal financing in scientific and foreign language programs in the nation's schools and colleges.

▌ **6. (E) is correct.** Following in the footsteps of Roosevelt's New Deal, President Truman wanted to continue with the social reform that had begun during the Great Depression. Proposing programs such as an increase to the minimum wage, a broadening of Social Security, a new program of national medical insurance, and federal aid to education, all began part of Truman's Fair Deal.

▌ **7. (C) is correct.** Passive when it came to domestic issues, Eisenhower preferred to delegate authority to advisors when dealing with Congress. A strong believer in the separation of powers, Eisenhower rarely lobbied Congress for action on legislative items that he favored. Finally, the Democratic control of both houses of Congress from 1954 onwards made it difficult for Eisenhower to find allies in the Congress to push his own agenda through the legislative process.

▌ **8. (C) is correct.** Sam Rayburn was the Democratic Speaker of the House of Representatives. President Eisenhower had to rely upon Rayburn, and Senate Majority Leader Lyndon B. Johnson, for legislative action after 1954.

▌ **9. (B) is correct.** The Highway Act allowed for the creation of a 41,000 mile interstate highway program that would cost the federal government an estimated $25 billion. This interstate highway would revolutionize the way that goods were transported to markets, along with how Americans traveled for leisure.

10. **(B) is correct.** In 1954, Chief Justice Earl Warren accepted the arguments of NAACP lawyer Thurgood Marshall that separate schools did profound psychological damage to African American children when he declared that "separate educational facilities are inherently unequal."

Free-Response Essay Sample Response

Discuss the impact of Sputnik *on the United States.*

During the 1950s, there existed a fear in American society that has been dubbed the "Red Scare." This fear of communism and the Soviet Union led to witch hunts at home and dictated almost every foreign policy action taken by the United States in the post-World War II period. The launching of the Soviet satellite *Sputnik* added to the sense of paranoia that existed throughout the United States.

The race for space was seen simply as an extension of the arms race. After the successful explosion of an atomic bomb by the Soviet Union in 1949, the United States became obsessed with maintaining a military and strategic advantage over their Cold War enemy. At the time that *Sputnik* appeared in the sky, the United States had been involved in a satellite program of its own and the Soviet *Sputnik* was seen as the Soviet Union beating the United States. This sense of defeat deepened when the Americans' first attempt at launching a satellite into outer space blew up on the launch pad.

Within the year the United States had launched a much smaller, but scientifically superior satellite of its own, *Explorer*, into orbit. However, the national embarrassment and sense of fear that existed within American society prompted President Eisenhower to embark upon a national space program and the creation of NASA. Changes were also made to the education system in an attempt to make up the lost ground that Americans perceived existed. Finally, a national commission was appointed to look at national objectives for the next decade to bring the United States back to its position of unquestioned primacy in the eyes of the world.

Whether real or imagined, the fear of the day and the sense of paranoia that most Americans felt towards the Soviet Union meant that the impact of the Soviet satellite *Sputnik* on the United States was dramatic. The next five years saw the people and government of the United States embark upon a soul searching journey to find its way back into the top position in the eyes of their fellow nations.

CHAPTER 30

The Turbulent Sixties

Under Presidents **Kennedy and Johnson**, the continued American involvement in **Vietnam** led to escalation and, eventually, stalemate.

Kennedy Intensifies the Cold War

In foreign affairs, **John F. Kennedy** surrounded himself with the "best and brightest," young, aggressive advisors determined to invoke a hard-line approach to the Soviet Union.

- **Kennedy also launched two new strategies:** to give America the flexible response needed to meet any challenge, and to create a successful first-strike capability.
- A **"superpower" stalemate** that developed in **Berlin** left Germany divided between the East and the West.
- **Kennedy reacted to Soviet statements** with a combination of **financial aid**, **technical assistance**, and **counterinsurgency** in order to build strong, stable, Western democracies in the less-developed areas of Asia.
- **Kennedy gave his approval to a CIA** plan to topple **Castro** by using Cuban exiles as invasion troops.
- **The Bay of Pigs landing** proved to be an utter disaster, and Kennedy took responsibility for the failure.
- **In 1962**, the United States faced a much more serious issue regarding the **installation of nuclear missiles in Cuba**. Kennedy refused to bargain on the missiles and boldly ordered a **quarantine of Cuba** as the world braced for a possible nuclear showdown.
- **Premier Khrushchev backed down**, but the Russians went on a crash nuclear buildup to achieve parity with the United States. Some positive results followed: a **limited test ban treaty** signed in 1963, a **hot line** to speed communication between the nuclear antagonists, and a **policy of conciliation** replaced that of confrontation.

The New Frontier at Home

John F. Kennedy took advantage of **television debates** and a national sense of dissatisfaction to narrowly defeat the Republican candidate **Richard Nixon** for the presidency in **1960**.

- **Because the conservative coalition** stood firmly against education and health care proposals, much of the **New Frontier** languished in Congress.
- **The greatest stimulus to economic growth** came from increased appropriations for defense and space. Kennedy's chief economic advisor, **Walter Heller**, called for major tax cuts to stimulate consumer spending

- **The president's solution to the problem of civil rights** was to exert leadership rather than depend on congressional action.
- **Responding to Dr. King's continued campaign for racial justice** in Birmingham and his eloquent speech from the Lincoln Memorial in 1963, Kennedy decided to take the offensive and **push for civil rights legislation**.
- **The Warren-led Supreme Court** made far-reaching decisions that improved the rights of accused criminals, and brought about more equitable reapportionment in legislative redistricting.

"Let Us Continue"

Vice President Lyndon Johnson moved quickly to fill the void left by Kennedy's assassination.

- **Although lacking Kennedy's charm and charisma**, Johnson possessed far greater ability than his predecessor in dealing with Congress.
- **Johnson succeeded** in achieving passage of Kennedy's **civil rights measures**.
- **The Civil Rights Act of 1964** was a landmark in the advance of African American freedom and equality.
- **Convinced of the detrimental societal effects of poverty**, Johnson declared an unconditional **"war on poverty"** and set up the new **Office of Economic Opportunity**. In **1964**, Johnson soundly defeated the hawkish Republican **Barry Goldwater** and was elected to his own term in office.
- **Announcing his "Great Society,"** the president pushed for **Medicare** and **Medicaid** assistance and for federal aid to public education. The **Voting Rights Act** encouraged great increases in African American voter registration.

Johnson Escalates the Vietnam War

Lyndon Johnson shared Kennedy's Cold War view and inherited his military and diplomatic problems.

- **In Vietnam the United States had supported the South** Vietnamese regime of **Ngo Dinh Diem** against communist insurgents.
- **Kennedy had sent military advisors** and substantial military and economic aid.
- **Full-scale American involvement began under Johnson in 1965**, after the **Gulf of Tonkin resolution** by Congress gave the president the power to take the offensive.
- **Refusing to call for an invasion of the North**, Johnson opted for steady military escalation.
- **Despite massive American escalation**, the war remained stalemated in 1968 when the surprising force of the communists' **Tet Offensive** discredited American military leaders and led President Johnson to forego further escalation, open up peace negotiations with Hanoi, and then withdraw from his bid for reelection.

Years of Turmoil

Student radicals created campus unrest over free speech, war, racism, poverty, and a variety of other issues.

- **Opposition to the war in Vietnam** was a central theme for many students. To students the war seemed to symbolize all that was wrong with America.

- **Combined with the issues of war and race**, the youth of the country seemed to be **rejecting all the cultural values of middle-class, middle-aged Americans**.
- **Rock music and drugs** were key elements of this movement.
- **The civil rights movement** became more militant and less concerned with racial harmony. It also spawned a movement celebrating pride in one's culture.
- **The pride in ethnicity** included Mexican Americans and Native Americans.
- **The work of such authors as Betty Freidan** indicated that many **women** were not satisfied with housework and child rearing. Groups like **the National Organization for Women** served as a focus for these frustrations. In 1972 the **Equal Rights Amendment** was sent to the states.

The Return of Richard Nixon

Partially as a reaction to the turmoil, **Richard Nixon** made a remarkable comeback and sought the presidency in **1968**.

- **Without a clear candidate** the Democratic Party divided. After the assassination of **Robert Kennedy**, **Hubert Humphrey** became the heir apparent of the party, but divisions over the war deeply divided the party. These divisions became hardened at the tumultuous **Democratic convention in Chicago**.
- **With the wounded Democratic party foundering**, and a third-party candidate taking away much of the South, a traditional Democratic stronghold, the Republican nominee Richard Nixon easily won the presidency.

Multiple-Choice Questions

1. Critical to John F. Kennedy's victory in the election of 1960 was his
   - (A) success in televised debates against Richard Nixon.
   - (B) charge that Republicans had overstimulated the economy.
   - (C) rejection of United States participation in the Cold War.
   - (D) disavowal of his religious beliefs.
   - (E) stance as a war hawk.

2. John F. Kennedy's plan to balance out nuclear capability with conventional military strength was known as
   - (A) the New Look.
   - (B) the New Deal.
   - (C) flexible response.
   - (D) massive retaliation.
   - (E) total coverage.

3. The building of the Berlin Wall in 1961
   - (A) was a Soviet defensive measure.
   - (B) demonstrated East Germany's control of Berlin.
   - (C) was a joint effort by the United States and the Soviets.
   - (D) caused few problems for the Kennedy administration.
   - (E) was meant to keep East Germans from migrating to the West.

4. Kennedy's foreign policy approach to Latin America was known as the
   - (A) Domino Theory.
   - (B) "Banana Republic" Theory.
   - (C) Kennedy Doctrine.
   - (D) New Frontier.
   - (E) Alliance for Progress.

5. Why did Kennedy support the Bay of Pigs invasion?
   - (A) He believed it would thwart the aims of the Soviet Union.
   - (B) He felt pressure from Congress to support it.
   - (C) His advisers had proved the merit of the action.

(D) He felt committed by the actions of Eisenhower.

(E) He wanted to establish a U.S. missile base in Cuba.

6. One result of the Cuban Missile Crisis was the
   (A) "hot-line."
   (B) massive reduction of nuclear missiles.
   (C) successful invasion of Cuba by American forces.
   (D) de-escalation of the Cold War.
   (E) increase in Kennedy's international stature.

7. American foreign policy hawks believed that the outcome of the Cuban Missile Crisis
   (A) justified a policy of nuclear superiority.
   (B) proved that the Soviets were no real threat to the United States.
   (C) indicated the need for a secret invasion of Cuba.
   (D) supported their view of Kennedy's expertise in foreign policy.
   (E) inferred an ongoing policy of nuclear disarmament.

8. In the _____ decision, the Supreme Court ruled that state legislatures had to be reapportioned.
   (A) *Miranda v. Arizona*

(B) *Gideon v. Wainwright*
(C) *Yates v. U.S.*
(D) *Baker v. Carr*
(E) *Engle v. Vitale*

9. The Civil Rights Act of 1964
   (A) outlawed racial segregation in public facilities.
   (B) outlawed racial discrimination in employment.
   (C) protected the voting rights of African Americans.
   (D) included gender as an unacceptable basis for discrimination in hiring.
   (E) all of the above

10. Lyndon Johnson sought the Gulf of Tonkin Resolution
    (A) as a blank check for military escalation in Vietnam.
    (B) to jump-start the U.S. economy.
    (C) to place the blame for the war in Vietnam on the shoulders of North Vietnam.
    (D) to pacify the leadership of South Vietnam.
    (E) to demonstrate to the North Vietnamese and his political opponents his determination to take a tough stance in Vietnam.

Free-Response Question

The 1960s and 1970s was a period of conflict in South East Asia between U.S.-backed, anti-communist forces of South Vietnam and the Viet Cong, who were supported by North Vietnam's communist government and Soviet armaments. Using the sources below and your knowledge of this period, explain why the Cold War erupted into open conflict in Vietnam.

"The loss of any single country in South East Asia could lead to the loss of all Asia, then India and Japan, finally endangering the security of Europe.... You have a row of dominoes set up, you knock over the first one and what will happen to the last one is a certainty, that it will go over very quickly."

—*U.S. President Eisenhower*

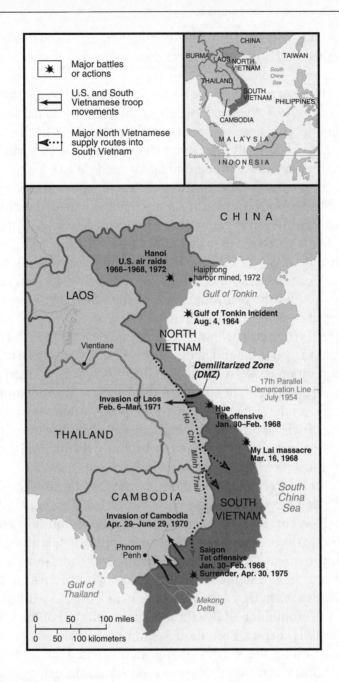

Legend:

- ✴ Major battles or actions
- ← U.S. and South Vietnamese troop movements
- ◄···· Major North Vietnamese supply routes into South Vietnam

CHINA
BURMA
LAOS
NORTH VIETNAM
TAIWAN
THAILAND
South China Sea
SOUTH VIETNAM
PHILIPPINES
CAMBODIA
MALAYSIA
Equator
INDONESIA

CHINA

Hanoi
U.S. air raids
1966–1968, 1972
Haiphong harbor mined, 1972

LAOS

Gulf of Tonkin

Gulf of Tonkin Incident
Aug. 4, 1964

Mekong R.

Vientiane

NORTH VIETNAM

Demilitarized Zone (DMZ)

17th Parallel
Demarcation Line
July 1954

Invasion of Laos
Feb. 6–Mar. 1971

Hue
Tet offensive
Jan. 30–Feb. 1968

THAILAND

Ho Chi Minh Trail

My Lai massacre
Mar. 16, 1968

South China Sea

CAMBODIA

Invasion of Cambodia
Apr. 29–June 29, 1970

SOUTH VIETNAM

Phnom Penh

Saigon
Tet offensive
Jan. 30–Feb. 1968
Surrender, Apr. 30, 1975

Gulf of Thailand

Mekong Delta

0   50   100 miles
0   50   100 kilometers

ANSWERS AND EXPLANATIONS

Multiple-Choice Questions

▌ **1. (A) is correct.** Kennedy's success in the televised debates, particularly the first debate which was watched by an estimated seventy-seven million, was a critical turning point in the 1960 election. His knowledge and use of statistics in responding to the questions, along with his calm and serene poise in listening to Nixon's responses, impressed much of the viewing public, who had seen him as too young and too inexperienced to be president prior to the televised debates.

▌ **2. (C) is correct.** Kennedy's nuclear strategy of Flexible Response allowed the United States the ability to choose between a number of operational plans in responding to communist moves.

▌ **3. (E) is correct.** Since the Soviet Union had taken control of East Germany after World War II, there had been a steady flight of skilled workers into West Berlin. Unable to negotiate a peaceful claim on West Berlin and fearing American nuclear superiority, the Soviet Union began the construction of the Berlin Wall to stop the flow of brains and talent to the West.

▌ **4. (E) is correct.** The Alliance for Progress was a massive economic aid package for the countries of Latin America that Kennedy had hoped would serve as a counter-offensive against any communist uprisings in these countries.

▌ **5. (A) is correct.** Kennedy's policy towards Cuba was generally a policy of preventing the Soviet Union from gaining and maintaining communist influence in the Western Hemisphere. The Bay of Pigs invasion was seen as a way to remove Castro and the communist supporters from Cuba and thus rid the Western Hemisphere of Soviet influence.

▌ **6. (A) is correct.** The "hot-line," a direct line from the White House to the Kremlin, was installed at the end of the Cuban Missile Crisis in an attempt to increase communication between Kennedy and Krushchev in an emergency situation.

▌ **7. (A) is correct.** The success of the American position during the Cuban Missile Crisis on the surface supported the policy of nuclear superiority as a means to deter Soviet expansion. In reality, however, this policy only served to increase the sense of urgency in the Soviet weapons program and a dramatic escalation in the arms race.

▌ **8. (D) is correct.** In 1962, the Supreme Court ruled that Tennessee had to redistribute its legislative seats to give citizens in Memphis equal representation.

▌ **9. (E) is correct.** The Civil Rights Act, signed on July 2 1964, made illegal the segregation of African Americans in public facilities, established an Equal Employment Opportunity Commission to lesson racial discrimination in employment, and protected the voting rights of African Americans. An amendment sponsored by segregationists in an effort to weaken the bill added gender to the prohibition of discrimination in Title VII of the act.

▌ **10. (E) is correct.** Even though Johnson had already ordered the retaliatory air strike against the North Vietnamese, he wanted the Gulf of Tonkin Resolution to demonstrate to North Vietnam the American determination to defend South Vietnam at any cost.

Free-Response Essay Sample Response

The 1960s and 1970s was a period of conflict in South East Asia between U.S.-backed, anti-communist forces of South Vietnam and the Viet Cong, who were supported by North Vietnam's communist government and Soviet armaments. Using the sources below and your knowledge of this period, explain why the Cold War erupted into open conflict in Vietnam.

> *"The loss of any single country in South East Asia could lead to the loss of all Asia, then India and Japan, finally endangering the security of Europe.... You have a row of dominoes set up, you knock over the first one and what will happen to the last one is a certainty, that it will go over very quickly."*
>
> —U.S. President Eisenhower

When the policy of containment was mixed in with Truman's "get tough" doctrine, the result was an offensive rather than defensive containment policy. It was made clear that the United States would do whatever was necessary to stop the spread of communism. This was first seen in the Korean War. When communists in North Vietnam started to harass the government of South Vietnam,

America became worried. The Americans feared a Domino Effect, in which one country after another would fall to communism if it could not be contained.

As a result of aggressive containment policies, America sent first military advisors, then troops to South Vietnam. At the same time, the U.S.S.R. wanted to expand Soviet influence by means of communism. It supported North Vietnam with supplies, arms and training. Now there existed two camps in South East Asia, as in the rest of the world. The North, backed by communist Russia, and the South, backed by democratic America. With both sides building up armies and being pushed by the two cold war countries, war between North Vietnam and South Vietnam was inevitable.

CHAPTER 31

To A New Conservatism, 1969–1988

The Nixon administration's inordinate **fear of political enemies** led to numerous illegal activities by Republican officials and campaign supporters.

The Tempting of Richard Nixon

While Nixon appeared more moderate and restrained than in the past, he remained exceptionally **sensitive to criticism**. He assembled a powerful White House staff whose main task was to **shield him from Congress and the press**.

- **Nixon streamlined the federal bureaucracy**. He also appointed **conservative judges to the Supreme Court** and shifted the responsibility for school integration to the federal courts as part of his **"southern strategy"** to build a Republican majority for **1972**.
- **Nixon inherited severe economic problems** that did not seem to respond to traditional remedies. **In 1971, however, he curbed inflation** with temporary wage and price freezes and improved the balance of trade with a **devaluation of the dollar and a 10 percent surtax on imports**.
- **Republicans sought to win new voters** among traditionally Democratic **blue-collar workers and southern whites** for 1972.
- **Vice-President Spiro Agnew** blamed Democratic liberals for such national social problems as drug abuse, sexual permissiveness, and crime in the streets.
- **Strongly influenced by National Security Adviser Henry Kissinger**, Nixon pursued a foreign policy of **détente**—a relaxation of tension—with the Soviet Union and with China. **A Strategic Arms Limitation Talks (SALT) treaty was** signed in 1972, followed by American sales of grain and computer technology to the Soviet Union.
- **Secret negotiations between Kissinger and North Vietnam's Le Duc Tho** produced a truce, signed in January 1973. Accepting what amounted to a **disguised surrender**, the United States agreed to remove its troops in return for the **release of all American prisoners of war**, and the American role in Vietnam was over.
- **Nixon's refusal to accept any blame** after the break-in at the **Watergate Hotel** was the first step in his fall from power.
- **Ironically, the Watergate break-in was hardly necessary** to guarantee an overwhelming reelection victory for Nixon in 1972.
- **The Democrats nominated George McGovern**, a candidate perceived as too liberal by most Americans.

- **It took over two years of painstaking investigation** to reveal the president's attempt to cover up the involvement of White House aides.
- **After the House Judiciary Committee** voted **three articles of impeachment** and the Supreme Court ordered the release of the tapes of presidential conversations, **Nixon chose to resign** on August 9, 1974.

The Economy of Stagflation

Though Nixon was occupied with the Watergate scandal, a war in the Middle East meant that oil and a national energy crisis was on the agenda as well.

- **In October 1973**, Arab nations imposed an **oil embargo** against the United States to **force American pressure on Israel to return Arab lands**.
- **Increased energy costs led to double-digit inflation**, rising **unemployment**, and a **decline in economic growth** for the United States. In 1979, the **Organization of Petroleum Exporting Countries (OPEC)** took advantage of the **Iranian Revolution** to embark on a new round of oil price increases.
- **Congress** could not agree on a coherent energy policy.
- **Republicans advocated removal of price controls** and increased production while the **Democrats wished to maintain price controls** and pursue conservation efforts.
- **The startling price increases of the 1970s** resulted from the Vietnam War, a worldwide shortage of food, and especially the six-fold increase in oil prices.
- **Wages for many Americans failed to keep pace**, and actions by the Federal Reserve Board increased interest rates.

Private Lives, Public Issues

American families and the private lives of individuals changed beginning in the 1970s and continued changing throughout the century.

- **Families became smaller and the divorce rate increased** in the seventies, while the number of **households headed by women** increased.
- **Women made dramatic strides** in the last third of the decade, but still faced discrimination and lower pay.
- **A new gay and lesbian pride movement**, in some ways modeled after the ethnic pride movements of the same time period, emerged as homosexual men and women across the country fought against discrimination based on sexual orientation.

Politics and Diplomacy after Watergate

Conflicts between the president and Congress meant that there would be ineffective leadership to handle the major crisis of the 1970s.

- **Gerald Ford's popularity rapidly declined with a pardon of Nixon** and a seeming ineptitude in dealing with Congress. When congressional investigations revealed **excesses by the CIA**, Ford approved reform of the agency and appointed **George Bush** as its new director.
- **Former Georgia Governor Jimmy Carter** won the Democratic nomination by portraying himself as an honest and candid "outsider," untainted by Washington politics.

- **Although an intelligent politician and a master of symbols**, Carter seemed to lack a clear sense of direction.
- American political power in the world declined in the 1970s because of both internal and external causes.
- **In 1974**, Congress cut military aid to **South Vietnam** and refused to grant additional aid the next year as communists seized control.
- **Carter signed two treaties in 1977** providing a gradual **return of the Panama Canal and zone** to Panama by the end of the century.
- **The Camp David accords of 1978** led ultimately to a peace treaty between **Egypt and Israel**, but left the problems of the **Palestinian Arabs** unsettled. In 1979, **Iranian mobs in Teheran seized the American embassy and fifty-eight American hostages**.
- **When the Soviets invaded Afghanistan** in December 1979, Carter banned sales of grain and high-tech equipment to the Soviet Union, reinstated registration for the draft, and ordered a **boycott of the 1980 Moscow Olympics**.

The Reagan Revolution

- A charismatic politician who stressed themes of reduced government, balanced budgets, protection of family values, and peace through increased military spending, **Ronald Reagan** was the perfect candidate for the Republicans at a time of growing national conservatism.
- Ronald Reagan and other conservatives took advantage of splits in the long-lasting liberal Democratic coalition and took power in a dramatic fashion in the 1980 election.
- **The failure of Carter's economic policies** and America's weak image abroad were issues seized by Reagan in the 1980 campaign. **Reagan** scored important points in a televised debate and **captured a decisive victory in the election**.
- **Reagan supported supply-side economics**, seeking to diminish the tax burden on the private sector and enhance investment-oriented growth. **Reduction of government spending** would hopefully ease inflation.
- **Under the direction of Reagan** and cabinet officials such as Interior Secretary **James Watt** and Transportation Secretary **Drew Lewis, deregulation** of the economy and restriction of federal activities became a major theme. Congress attempted to slow the rapid growth of Social Security benefits with legislative changes in 1983. Feminist groups and minorities found Reagan's policies disappointing as the Reagan administration appeared to move backwards on civil rights.
- The Reagan administration's sweeping economic changes gave rise to conflicting economic expectations.
- **After a temporary recession in 1981–1982** (which torpedoed the supply-side theory), the economy rebounded in 1983 with the automobile industry, consumer spending, and low inflation fueling economic growth.
- **The failure of supply-side economics** fed a huge and growing **federal deficit**.
- **Congress responded with the Gramm-Rudman Act**, a compromise that forced the president to give up further increases in the defense budget while Democrats sacrificed hopes for expanded social programs.

- **Under Reagan, the rich got richer**, the middle class scrambled to hold its own, and the poor stayed poor. Additionally, there was increasing income stratification.
- **Republicans convinced Americans that Reaganomics worked**, enabling the president to easily defeat **Democrats Walter Mondale and Geraldine Ferraro** in the election of **1984**.
- Complex social issues that would face the nation for the rest of the century began in the 1980s, causing concern in all sectors of the population.
- **AIDS** (acquired immune deficiency syndrome) is caused by **HIV** (human immunodeficiency virus) and spread by the exchange of bodily fluids. First noted in the U.S. in 1981, AIDS quickly reached epidemic proportions, ultimately affecting over 500,000 people by mid-1996 and killing over 345,000. The Reagan administration proved slow and halting in its response.
- **The 1980s witnessed the rapid spread of cocaine and crack use** and a consequent explosion of **urban crime** in America. Nancy Reagan urged an educational policy of **"Just Say No"** and the Reagan administration later sought to seal the nation's borders more effectively to prevent import of South American drugs.

Reagan and the World

Determined to alter America's shattered image abroad, Reagan continued the hard line adopted toward Russia and the massive military buildup begun by Carter and approved new offensive weapons systems.

- **Denouncing Soviet-sponsored terrorism and human rights violations**, Reagan depicted the Soviet Union as the **"evil empire"** and pushed for the deployment of additional missiles in European NATO locations. Prompted by Soviet intransigence on arms control, the United States quickened the pace of **Strategic Defense Initiative ("Star Wars")** research and development.
- **In Nicaragua**, the Sandinistas overthrew the Somoza regime in 1979. Although Carter had previously authorized economic aid for the Sandinistas, Reagan reversed that policy.
- **American forces** invaded the small Caribbean island of **Grenada** in October 1983 to confront Cuban workers and troops and prevent the communists from acquiring a strategic military base.
- **An initiative in 1985 aimed at improving American influence in the Middle East** by establishing contact with moderates in Iran deteriorated into an arms for hostages deal. Although Reagan was never personally tied to the diversion of funds, his popularity dropped rapidly.
- **The ascendancy of a more moderate Soviet leader in 1985, Mikhail Gorbachev**, offered hope for **improved U.S.-Soviet relations**. With Reagan hoping to rebound from the Iran-Contra affair and Gorbachev anxious to repair the Soviet economy, the two world leaders held a series of meetings during Reagan's second term.

1. The 1973 United States-North Vietnam agreement
   (A) was actually a disguised U.S. surrender.
   (B) guaranteed a future U.S. presence in Vietnam.
   (C) limited North Vietnamese control of South Vietnam.
   (D) dramatically reduced the size of the North Vietnam army in South Vietnam.
   (E) made Vietnam a protectorate of China.

2. The Watergate scandal
   (A) demonstrated the strength of America's basic governmental institutions.
   (B) allowed unchecked presidential authority.
   (C) involved a lust for money.
   (D) was conceived by Richard Nixon.
   (E) uncovered vast corruption in the U.S. Congress.

3. Which of the following was the greatest casualty of the Watergate scandal?
   (A) Richard Nixon
   (B) an independent judiciary
   (C) public confidence in the political system
   (D) the system of checks and balances
   (E) the U.S. Congress

4. The most grave consequence of the 1970s oil shock was
   (A) the collapse of several Arab states.
   (B) a glut of food world wide.
   (C) increased industrial growth.
   (D) initial failure of the fledgling computer industry.
   (E) inflation throughout America.

5. The women's movement
   (A) grew out of the civil rights and antiwar movements.
   (B) was hindered by the legislation of the New Frontier and Great Society.
   (C) had tremendous support from other protest groups.
   (D) quickly won the support of American society.
   (E) culminated in an amendment to the Constitution.

6. The birth of the gay liberation movement was
   (A) the founding of ACT UP.
   (B) at the Stonewall Inn.
   (C) the founding of the Gay Liberation Front.
   (D) the founding of the Gay Activist Alliance.
   (E) the Outing.

7. Reaganomics was a form of
   (A) Keynesian economics.
   (B) supply-side economics.
   (C) bear-bull marketing.
   (D) stock market investment policies.
   (E) futures-based economics.

8. Apparently _____ knew of the Iran-Contra affair before November 1986.
   (A) Oliver North
   (B) William Casey
   (C) John Poindexter
   (D) Robert McFarlane
   (E) all of the above

9. In responding to the burgeoning AIDS epidemic, the Reagan administration
   (A) showed great concern and compassion for its victims.
   (B) evidenced no concern at all.
   (C) generally ignored the problem.
   (D) committed billions of dollars to fight the dreaded disease.
   (E) proved slow and halting in its approach.

10. Mikhail Gorbachev's new policy included
   (A) *perestroika.*
   (B) *glasnost.*
   (C) the destruction of Lenin's tomb.
   (D) A and B
   (E) A and C

Free-Response Question

> *Explain how relationships between the Soviet Union and the Western powers led to an escalation of tensions between 1946 and 1989.*

ANSWERS AND EXPLANATIONS

Multiple-Choice Questions

▌ **1. (A) is correct.** In return for the release of all American political prisoners, the United States agreed to remove its troops from South Vietnam. At the same time, however, the agreement also allowed the North Vietnamese to keep its troops in South Vietnam, which virtually guaranteed a communist future for all of Vietnam. This reality meant that the agreement was largely a U.S. surrender to the North Vietnamese.

▌ **2. (A) is correct.** The ability of the Congress and the Supreme Court, two of the three branches of government, to operate independent of a corrupt White House (the third branch of government), demonstrated the strength of the government envisioned by the Founding Fathers and described in the Constitution.

▌ **3. (C) is correct.** While the American system of government and the independence of the three branches of it showed great strength during the Watergate scandal, the American people began a long mistrust with the political system and their political leaders that continues to the present day.

▌ **4. (E) is correct.** As a result of the oil shock of the 1970s, with only 6% of the world's population consuming 40% of the world's energy, the economy of the United States began to enter a period of inflation, with rising prices and falling purchasing power.

▌ **5. (A) is correct.** The Civil Rights Act of 1964 included gender as one of the classes against which discrimination was prohibited under Title VII. Many of the antiwar movements of the 1960s and early 1970s were from a newly liberated group of young women, primarily at universities and colleges across the United States. With the civil rights issues being left in the 1960s and the war ending, it was a natural extension for those who had been involved in both movements to take up the cause of equal rights during the 1970s.

▌ **6. (B) is correct.** Police arrests at the Stonewall Inn, a New York hotspot for "drag queens" and lesbians, became the focal point for the two-day riots known as the Stonewall Riots. Within days of the riots, two new organizations were formed to assist gays in affirming their sexual preference and demanding an end to discrimination against homosexuals.

■ **7. (B) is correct.** Supply-side economics believes that if private business is free from excessive government spending, it would invest its money in productive ventures that would stimulate the economy. This stimulation would lead to more jobs and increased purchasing power for the average citizen. This would then create a greater demand for goods, increasing productivity which would require businesses to expand and hire more people, thus beginning the cycle again.

■ **8. (E) is correct.** National Security Advisor Robert McFarlane initially conceived of the idea to trade weapons for American hostages being held by a group loyal to Iran. He relied upon Oliver North to work out the details at the National Security Council. North sought the assistance of Central Intelligence Agency director William Casey. By 1986, McFarlane had resigned and was replaced by John Poindexter, who eventually convinced the president to go ahead with the exchange.

■ **9. (E) is correct.** When HIV and AIDS first appeared in the United States in the early 1980s it was seen as a disease that affected only the homosexual community. As the nation was experiencing conservative sentiments and there was generally little sympathy for homosexuals during this time, the Reagan administration chose to fight the rising deficit and not to fund health-related research.

■ **10. (D) is correct.** In 1985, Mikhail Gorbachev began to introduce economic reforms in the Soviet Union itself. By 1986, he had introduced a policy of *perestroika* or economic restructuring that would see the Soviet Union start to end its state-sponsored socialist economic system and move towards a free-market system. That same year, he introduced a policy of *glasnost* or openness of personal freedoms and free exchange of the media. These two words, *glasnost* and *perestroika,* would become the words to mark the end of communism.

Free-Response Essay Sample Response

Explain how relationships between the Soviet Union and the Western powers led to an escalation of tensions between 1946 and 1989.

The Cold War was a period in which the two superpowers' conflicting ideologies gave way to disputes and ever-escalating tension which created a constant threat of war. The Soviet Union wanted to expand their influence globally. They targeted unstable countries which they could easily defeat and take over, thereby increasing communism around the world.

The United States opposed communism and communist expansion. The American policy of containment aimed at containing Soviet influence, and the Truman Doctrine aimed at abolishing it altogether. Fear and tension between the superpowers led to an arms race. The U.S. and the Soviet Union were constantly in competition to obtain a dominant military force against the opposing superpower. Both countries wanted to be perceived as a threat to the other in order to meet their goals.

Their conflicting goals led to armed conflicts on several occasions, for example, the Korean War, the Vietnam War, and the Soviet invasion of Afghanistan along with the American support of the rebels. There were also other periods of heightened alert such as the Berlin Blockade and the Cuban Missile Crisis, which never resulted in armed conflict but the potential certainly existed. These flashpoints increased tension between the East and West and further stimulated the arms race. A third world war never erupted as a result of the hostilities and tensions and arms race between the U.S. and the Soviet Union. "They talk about who won and who lost. Human reason won. Mankind won."

CHAPTER 32

To the Twenty-First Century

Many challenges faced Americans at the beginning of the twenty-first century. These included the war in Iraq and a variety of social, political, economic, and cultural issues.

The First President Bush

The Reagan presidency suffered some rough road in the middle of his second term as he changed staff. Reagan's continued successes, however, opened the door for **a George Bush victory** in the **1988** election.

- **Republican strategists effectively deflected public attention** from such issues as the **Iran-Contra affair** and budget woes by portraying the Democratic candidate, **Michael Dukakis**, as soft on crime and defense.
- **The majority of George Bush's early tenure** was taken by two pressing domestic problems: the clean-up of **the nation's savings-and-loan industry** and the challenge of stemming **the ever-growing federal deficits**.
- **An attempt at internal liberation by Chinese students** at Tiananmen Square proved tragically premature, while communist regimes in Eastern Europe collapsed with surprising speed in mid-1989 once it became apparent that Gorbachev would not use Soviet power to support them.
- **The end of the Cold War** did not mean a world free of violence. In December 1989, **the United States invaded Panama** to overthrow the regime of drug-trafficking **General Manuel Noriega**. In January 1991, the United States began an aerial assault leading to a ground offensive in the next month against **Iraq**, aiming to **free Kuwait** and protect the vital oil resources of the **Persian Gulf**.

The Changing Faces of America

- **In the 1970s and 1980s,** Americans moved internally at a significant rate, especially to the South and to the West.
- **The Sunbelt states of the South and West** began to flourish during World War II with the buildup of military bases and defense plants.
- **This growth continued with the Cold War** and the movement of industries attracted by lower labor costs and favorable climate.
- **Americans increasingly moved to urban areas,** enjoying better education and higher incomes, but also suffering rising crime rates, traffic congestion, and costs of living.
- **Another striking population trend** was the marked increase in the number of elderly Americans.
- **The numbers of immigrants rose sharply in the 1970s and 1980s,** as millions

arrived primarily from **Latin America and Asia**.

▌ **The largest of the nation's ethnic groups, African Americans** made some economic gains during the era, but still did not share proportionately in the nation's wealth.

▌ **National reaction against policies of affirmative action** and the acquittal of policemen who had beaten black motorist **Rodney King** led to frustration and the eruption of a bloody **race riot in South Central Los Angeles in 1992**.

▌ **Hispanics**, people with Spanish surnames, formed the nation's second largest ethnic group.

▌ **The large number of illegal immigrants** from Mexico also contributed to an exploited class of undocumented aliens who provided needed and desired cheap labor but who strained social services.

▌ **By the 1980s, Asian Americans became the nation's fastest-growing minority** group, although they still only comprised a little over 3 percent of the total population.

▌ **Rather than a melting pot** in which individual groups lose their distinctiveness, America in the latter twentieth century had become a "mosaic" in which ethnic groups retained their identities while also contributing to a more encompassing and diverse whole.

▌ **The stubborn recession of 1990** proved politically devastating for the Bush administration.

▌ **This economic stagnation** led many Americans to listen to new political voices promising to revitalize the American economy and way of life.

The New Democrats

Democrats campaigned hard on the issue of the economy, and were able to capture the White House in 1992 and keep it in 1996.

▌ **The Democratic party** gained political strength by moving away from its traditional reliance on big government, choosing moderate candidates, and tailoring programs to appeal to the middle class.

▌ **Democratic candidate Bill Clinton**, stressing investment in the nation's future, benefited when independent **H. Ross Perot** dropped out of the race, and Republican assaults on Clinton's character failed to sway voters disenchanted with the economic results of Republican policies.

▌ **Clinton was an adept politician** helped by his loyal wife and effective political partner, **Hillary Rodham Clinton**. Swayed by the advice of **Alan Greenspan**, chair of the Federal Reserve Board, Clinton cut federal spending and raised income taxes for the wealthy.

▌ **Clinton won approval of the North American Free Trade Association** in 1993, but effective opposition prevented the passage of Clinton's health care reform plan.

▌ **Clinton rebounded from the 1994 election** and scandals mainly because of the remarkable growth of the economy.

▌ **The economy was doing better than ever** before, but there were many issues that remained unsettled as the country moved into the new millennium.

- **The economy was the bright spot** in the last decade of the twentieth century—the country experienced its **longest period of sustained economic growth** in its history and unemployment and inflation were at all-time lows.
- **Amid the prosperity were some shocking signs** that all was not well in American society. The disasters at **Waco** and **Ruby Ridge**, the court house bombing in **Oklahoma City**, the **Unabomber** and increasing school violence all showed that there were some who wanted to solve their complaints with violence.
- **President Clinton's relationship with a White House intern** cast a shadow on the president and led to his impeachment by the Republican-controlled Congress. Clinton survived because of his shrewd political instincts and skills, but the presidency was badly damaged.

Clinton and the World

Clinton supported free-market reforms and nuclear non-proliferation in the former Soviet Union.

- **In Somalia**, American troops botched attempts to capture a local warlord and were withdrawn after eighteen American soldiers were killed.
- **In Haiti**, American troops helped restore a democratic government, but one that proved unable to handle economic woes.
- **In Bosnia**, Clinton's call for NATO air strikes on Serb forces contributed to a cease-fire and a shaky peace settlement, one supported by American troops.

Republicans Triumphant

Texas governor George W. Bush and Vice President Al Gore faced off in the 2000 election, and it was a close race, ending in a disputed election.

- New President George W. Bush faced a host of domestic problems including the collapse of several major corporations in the face of corporate fraud.
- **Terrorism** became the central focus of the United states in 2001 when hijacked passenger jets flew into the twin towers of the **World Trade Center** in New York and Washington D.C.'s **Pentagon**. Bush's proclaimed **"war on terrorism"** prompted the American invasion of **Afghanistan and Iraq** in the wake of suspect CIA intelligence.

Challenges of the New Century

- **Americans remained divided** on issues such as race and affirmative action. This was exemplified by the reaction to the *Hopwood* and *Bakke* cases. Abortion remained a controversial issue, as did gay rights and the conflict between science and religion.
- **The economy began to recover** in Bush's second term. However, economic disparaties grew. Globalization and rising oil prices contributed to a sense of economic unease.
- **Americans had some concerns about the future** as the new century began. People worried about the Social Security system as the baby boom generation began to retire. Health care costs continued to skyrocket. Immigration—particularly illegal immigration—was a major issue of the day.

Multiple-Choice Questions

1. By the late 1990s, the American Association of Retired Persons (AARP) represented approximately _____ million Americans.
   (A) 5
   (B) 10
   (C) 20
   (D) 30
   (E) 50

2. Asian Americans
   (A) have had few educational and economic opportunities.
   (B) have not found assimilation easy.
   (C) have had little interest in the American system.
   (D) were readily accepted by American society.
   (E) were viewed with suspicion by other ethnic groups.

3. In the presidential election of 1992, which one of the following individuals was NOT a candidate for president of the United States?
   (A) George Bush
   (B) Bill Clinton
   (C) Sam Nunn
   (D) Ross Perot
   (E) Joe Walsh

4. In 1991, Bush replaced Supreme Court Justice Thurgood Marshall with
   (A) Clarence Thomas.
   (B) Antonin Scalia.
   (C) William Rehnquist.
   (D) Earl Warren.
   (E) Ruth Bader Ginsberg.

5. The woman who accused Clarence Thomas of sexual harassment was
   (A) Betty Ford.
   (B) Anita Hill.
   (C) Carol Sims.
   (D) Hillary Thomas.
   (E) Donna Rice.

6. No economic issue had more political impact by 1992 than the
   (A) widespread belief in the decline of the middle class.
   (B) collapse of the Soviet Union.
   (C) end of the Cold War.
   (D) Gulf War.
   (E) campaign of Ross Perot.

7. The most controversial proposal of Bill Clinton's administration was
   (A) cutting off Cuban immigration.
   (B) the proposal to end discrimination against gays in the military.
   (C) health care.
   (D) tax cuts.
   (E) forced busing.

8. The consumer advocate who ran for president in 2000 with the Green Party was
   (A) Ross Perot.
   (B) Reverend Al Green.
   (C) Ralph Nader.
   (D) Bill Bradley.
   (E) Joe Perry.

9. Who was the special prosecuter appointed to investigate Whitewater and the Lewinsky scandal?
   (A) Linda Tripp
   (B) Paula Jones
   (C) Kenneth Starr
   (D) Joe Lieberman
   (E) Ralph Reed

10. The leading Republican proponent of the Contract With America was
    (A) Robert Reich.
    (B) Alexander Simmons.
    (C) Newt Gingrich.
    (D) Alan Greenspan.
    (E) Bob Dole.

Free-Response Question

Discuss the significance of the 1992 election.

ANSWERS AND EXPLANATIONS

Multiple-Choice Questions

▌ **1. (D) is correct.** One of the largest and most influential lobby groups in the United States, the American Association of Retired Persons represented approximately 30 million Americans by the late 1990s.

▌ **2. (B) is correct.** By the end of the 1990s, Asian Americans were the fastest-growing minority in the United States. While tending to be well educated with many economic opportunities, Asian Americans have not found assimilation into American culture to be easy. Difficulty in learning the English language, along with frequently being the target of racially provoked violence, have made life in America more difficult for Asian Americans than many of the other groups of immigrants to the United States.

▌ **3. (C) is correct.** George Bush and Bill Clinton ran for the Republican and Democratic parties respectively. Texas billionaire Ross Perot ran as an independent candidate. A former member of the rock band, The Eagles, Joe Walsh, ran for the second time (having run once before in 1980). Sam Nunn was the only person listed who was not involved in the 1992 presidential election.

▌ **4. (A) is correct.** In 1991, Bush nominated Clarence Thomas to replace Thurgood Marshall on the bench. While both men were African Americans, maintaining the racial make-up of the Supreme Court, Thomas was a conservative justice and was against programs such as affirmative action. This was in stark contrast to Marshall, who had gained national fame for arguing the *Brown* case before the Supreme Court.

▌ **5. (B) is correct.** While failing to block his confirmation, Antia Hill brought national attention to how women were treated in the workplace when she accused Supreme Court justice nominee Clarence Thomas of sexual harassment.

▌ **6. (A) is correct.** During the post-World War II period, the American middle class was born. Increased purchasing power for the working class allowed them to purchase homes in the same neighborhoods as doctors and lawyers (usually suburbs). By the 1980s and 1990s, the majority of Americans identified themselves as being in the middle class. The belief that there was a decline in the middle class was largely due to the fact that the median income for this group had declined in the 1970s, again in the 1980s and for a third time in the early 1990s.

▌ **7. (B) is correct.** One of the first measures that the Clinton administration undertook once in office was the proposal to end discrimination against gays in the military. This proved to be quite a controversial proposal and would be one of the many mishaps experienced by President Clinton in his first few months in office.

▌ **8. (C) is correct.** The decision of Ralph Nader, popular consumer advocate, to run as the presidential candidate for the Green Party in 2000 further complicated the Democratic candidate Al Gore's chances of winning the election by forcing Gore to move to the left of the political spectrum. This allowed

Republican challenger, George W. Bush to appeal to the more moderate among the electorate.

▎**9. (C) is correct.** Appointed in 1994 to investigate whether President Clinton had been involved in any illegal activities in a land development called Whitewater, Kenneth Starr began to investigate whether the president had a sexual affair with White House intern Monica Lewinsky and then encouraged her to lie about the affair in 1998.

▎**10. (C) is correct.** Political scandals such as Travelgate and the alleged sexual misconduct of the President with Paula Jones, along with his failure to deliver on his health care promises, allowed Republican Newt Gingrich to lead the way for the Republicans to capture both houses of Congress with his popular Contract With America.

Free-Response Essay Sample Response

Discuss the significance of the 1992 election.

According to political scientists, the election of 1992 was a negative referendum. This means that the typical American voter did not vote for a candidate, party or platform, but against one. In this instance, the American people had voted against the economic policies of the conservative administrations of Presidents Reagan and Bush.

In addition to a vote against the fiscal policies of Reagan and Bush, the election of 1992 was the first time in decades that the Democratic Party was able to capture popular support in the South and the West. Traditionally these areas were strong supporters of the Republican Party; however, in the election of 1992 only Texas and a few interior western states remained Republican strongholds.

This rejection of the fiscal policies of Reagan and Bush was evident in the fact that after the election there were still questions as to what form of fiscal policy the majority of Americans were looking for. It was unclear if they wanted responsible budgetary policies to reduce the deficit or federal spending programs to achieve jobs and economic growth. The only clear message was that they wanted an end to the conservative, trickle-down economics of the 1980s and early 1990s.

Part III

Sample Tests with Answers and Explanations

On the following pages are two sample exams. They mirror the actual AP* exam in format and question types. Set aside a time to take these exams, timing yourself as you will be timed when you take the real test, to prepare you for your actual test-taking experience.

AP* U.S. History
Sample Practice Test 1

U.S. History
Section I

Time: 55 Minutes
80 Questions

Directions: Each of the questions or incomplete statements below is followed by five suggested answers or completions. Select the one that is best in each case and then fill in the corresponding oval on the answer sheet.

1. Under the _____ system adopted by the Virginia Company in 1618, new immigrants received fifty acres.
   (A) headright
   (B) Toleration Act
   (C) charter
   (D) reformation
   (E) homestead

2. Most Native American tribes shared
   (A) the same language.
   (B) a society based on complex kinship systems.
   (C) the same religious beliefs.
   (D) the same economic patterns.
   (E) the same type of government.

3. Most Native American tribes
   (A) greatly preferred Christianity to their own religions.
   (B) rejected their own traditions immediately after learning of European values.
   (C) coveted European technology.
   (D) believed that white Europeans were superior to them.
   (E) refused to allow members to marry whites.

4. Which European nation-state was the first to colonize and exploit the riches and peoples of the Western Hemisphere?
   (A) France
   (B) England
   (C) Spain
   (D) Italy
   (E) Portugal

5. The men largely responsible for Spain's conquest of the New World were known as
   (A) *los conquistadores.*
   (B) *coureurs de bois.*
   (C) "sea dogs."
   (D) *condottiere.*
   (E) *comerciante.*

6. English settlers in seventeenth-century America could be characterized best in terms of their
   (A) striking social diversity.
   (B) similarity to French and Spanish migrants of the same period.
   (C) unity of purpose and motivation.
   (D) desire to help each other.
   (E) homogeneity.

7. Which one of the following was NOT a factor that stimulated English migration to the New World?
   - (A) religious disagreements in England
   - (B) poverty or fear of falling into poverty
   - (C) a desire for land ownership
   - (D) government laws that forced the migration of the poorer classes
   - (E) rapid population growth

8. Upon arriving in the New World, English settlers
   - (A) quickly abandoned English beliefs and values.
   - (B) generally adapted old beliefs to the new environment.
   - (C) rarely were forced to change significantly their old English ways.
   - (D) usually adopted the customs of the local Native American tribes as a way to survive.
   - (E) immediately focused on converting the Native Americans.

9. To resolve the problem of the vast expenses New World settlement required, English merchant-capitalists introduced the concept of
   - (A) proprietorship.
   - (B) primogeniture.
   - (C) the joint-stock company.
   - (D) feudalism.
   - (E) mercantilism.

10. The selection of a site for Jamestown was primarily based on the settlers'
    - (A) fear of diseases in the swamps.
    - (B) desire for a healthful place to live.
    - (C) belief that friendly native peoples lived nearby.
    - (D) need for close proximity to the open ocean.
    - (E) fear of surprise attacks.

11. By the end of the seventeenth century, Virginia could best be described as
    - (A) a plantation society, dominated by a slaveholding aristocracy.
    - (B) a diversified society and economy, with minimal social stratification.
    - (C) a society of small farmers, committed to multicrop agriculture.
    - (D) a successful commercial enterprise that returned large profits to the Crown.
    - (E) a society struggling with the question of slavery.

12. By the late 1600s, the gap between rich and poor in white Chesapeake society
    - (A) steadily shrank.
    - (B) steadily widened.
    - (C) remained unchanged.
    - (D) could not be estimated.
    - (E) was not commented on by contemporary chroniclers.

13. The Navigation Acts established the principle that
    - (A) certain American products could be sold only in England.
    - (B) only English or colonial merchants could engage in colonial trade.
    - (C) all foreign goods that were to be sold in England had to be shipped in England.
    - (D) all of the above
    - (E) none of the above

14. The intention of the Navigation Acts was to
    - (A) finance the British navy.
    - (B) promote English industrial development.
    - (C) keep the American colonies weak and dependent.
    - (D) stimulate colonial economic diversification.
    - (E) allow England to monopolize American trade.

15. Of the estimated 11 million African slaves carried to America, the great majority were sent to
    - (A) Chile.
    - (B) British North America.
    - (C) Brazil and the Caribbean.
    - (D) Argentina.
    - (E) Central America.

16. The so-called "triangular trade" in colonial America
    (A) involved commercial relations with China and Japan.
    (B) was formally prohibited by Great Britain in 1748.
    (C) was the key to American economic expansion.
    (D) was relatively insignificant.
    (E) took place in the Pacific.

17. The first large group of German immigrants moved to America seeking
    (A) free land.
    (B) religious tolerance.
    (C) an opportunity to become wealthy farmers.
    (D) markets for their craft products.
    (E) work.

18. The English leader whose policies brought a British victory in the Seven Years' War was
    (A) Lord North.
    (B) William Pitt.
    (C) George Grenville.
    (D) George II.
    (E) James Wolfe.

19. The major source of Anglo-French conflict in the colonies was
    (A) slavery.
    (B) international naval supremacy.
    (C) an ongoing argument about relations and treaties with Native Americans.
    (D) political grievances.
    (E) control of the Ohio Valley.

20. Colonial involvement with imperial wars began with
    (A) the French and Indian War.
    (B) King William's War.
    (C) King Philips's War.
    (D) the Thirty Years' War.
    (E) Queen Anne's War.

21. The central element in the Anglo-American debate over governance was known as
    (A) divine sovereignty.
    (B) *laissez-faire.*
    (C) parliamentary sovereignty.
    (D) absolute rule.
    (E) colonial sovereignty.

22. Central to the colonists' position in the Anglo-American debate over parliamentary powers was
    (A) their strong belief in the powers of their own provincial assemblies.
    (B) their unswerving support of the monarchy.
    (C) their willingness to defer to the wishes of Parliament.
    (D) their desire for an authoritarian government.
    (E) their desire for revolution.

23. The Declaration of Independence
    (A) stated that all men "are created equal."
    (B) blamed George III for much of the impasse.
    (C) was unanimously approved with no alterations.
    (D) both A and B
    (E) both A and C

24. Looking at the picture of George II's Coat of Arms, Colonists viewed it
    (A) with admiration and respect.

(B) emblematic of a monarch that neither understood nor cared about the colonies.

(C) on display throughout the American Colonies.

(D) as representing the monarchy in the absence of the monarchy.

(E) all of the above

25. Which of the following statements explains why England lost the war?
(A) The British government did not believe it could win the war.
(B) British finances could not support the war.
(C) British strategists did not understand how to fight the war.
(D) George III never supported the war effort.
(E) British soldiers sympathized with the Americans.

26. Which of the following was NOT a criticism of American government under the Articles of Confederation?
(A) It failed to deal with the nation's economic problems.
(B) It was unable to deal with the country's fiscal instability.
(C) It failed to adequately confront threats from Britain and Spain along American borders.
(D) It gave too much power to a central government.
(E) Its single legislative body gave some states an unfair advantage.

27. During the Confederation period, *nationalists* were people who
(A) supported the Articles of Confederation.
(B) believed the national government was too powerful.
(C) called for major constitutional reforms that would strengthen the national government.
(D) believed the states deserved more power.
(E) wanted to maintain close ties to England.

28. The European philosopher whose ideas supported the theory of state sovereignty was
(A) Locke.
(B) Montesquieu.
(C) Voltaire.
(D) Machiavelli.
(E) Rousseau.

29. The most brilliant American political theorist of the post-Revolutionary period was
(A) James Madison.
(B) George Washington.
(C) John Locke.
(D) John Adams.
(E) Thomas Jefferson.

30. *The Federalist* essays were written by
(A) Washington and Adams.
(B) Thomas Jefferson.
(C) Madison, Hamilton, and Jay.
(D) Randolph and Franklin.
(E) Madison, Jefferson, and Hamilton.

31. For many Americans, George Washington was
(A) a symbol of the new government.
(B) a routine, typical political leader.
(C) not a popular leader.
(D) a figurehead for the new government.
(E) a good general, but not necessarily a good politician.

32. During Washington's administration, policy was made by
(A) the cabinet.
(B) Alexander Hamilton.
(C) the president.
(D) the Congress.
(E) the secretary of state.

33. Which rebellion provided Washington with an opportunity to show the strength of the new nation?
(A) Whiskey Rebellion
(B) Shays' Rebellion
(C) Paxton Boys' Rebellion
(D) Bacon's Rebellion
(E) Stono Rebellion

34. This law was an infringement on the First Amendment rights of many Americans:
    (A) Naturalization Act
    (B) Sedition Act
    (C) Espionage Act
    (D) Smith Act
    (E) Kentucky Resolution

35. France attempted to directly interfere in American domestic politics through the actions of what man?
    (A) Jean Jacques Rousseau
    (B) Marquis de Lafayette
    (C) Francois Mitterand
    (D) Edmund Genet
    (E) Lord Baltimore

36. In the early 1800s, most Americans
    (A) developed a strong national identity.
    (B) identified themselves first by religious belief, then by region.
    (C) identified themselves primarily in terms of the city or town where they lived.
    (D) held on to a strong ethnic, as opposed to American, identity.
    (E) tended to identify themselves in terms of their regions.

37. In which section of the country did the most striking changes occur?
    (A) New England
    (B) South
    (C) Northeast
    (D) West
    (E) Southeast

38. Upon arriving in the West, many settlers
    (A) tried to transplant their Eastern customs.
    (B) had to adapt to a new environment.
    (C) were able to generate distinctive folkways.
    (D) depended on water transportation.
    (E) all of the above

39. The Treaty of Ghent
    (A) awarded part of Canada to the United States.
    (B) restored Quebec to France.

(C) gave the British navigation rights on the Mississippi River.
(D) did little more than end hostilities and postpone other issues for future negotiations.
(E) was negotiated quickly and quietly, since there were no real debates.

40. Which Native American leader attempted to unify the tribes against white settlement?
    (A) Sequoyah
    (B) White Horse
    (C) Chief Joseph
    (D) Sleeping Dog
    (E) Tecumseh

41. The most important decision of the Marshall Court was
    (A) *Gibbons v. Ogden.*
    (B) *McCulloch v. Maryland.*
    (C) *Dartmouth College v. Woodward.*
    (D) *Fletcher v. Peck.*
    (E) *Bakke v. California.*

42. The characteristic unit of western agriculture was a
    (A) family farm or owner-operated plantation.
    (B) small frontier settlement.
    (C) ranch devoted to raising beef cattle.
    (D) communally owned and operated farm.
    (E) large plantation farmed by sharecroppers.

43. Frontier pioneers
    (A) created new ways of living in the West.
    (B) quickly established a network of mercantilism.
    (C) relied on local government for the necessities of living.
    (D) failed to establish a self-sufficient lifestyle.
    (E) attempted to recreate the life they had left behind in the East.

44. The most spectacular engineering achievement of the young United States was the
    (A) Cumberland Trail.
    (B) Intercoastal Waterway.

(C) Erie Canal.
(D) Baltimore Turnpike.
(E) Washington Monument.

45. Between 1815 and 1820, the state banking systems
(A) represented an effective source of reliable currency.
(B) were the most important factor in expanding the market economy.
(C) were unreliable and often failed.
(D) supported the reestablishment of the national bank.
(E) were frequently the cause of currency depreciations.

46. The above picture is entitled *All Creation Going to the White House*. It is a celebration of the election of the "common man's" president. Who was that?
(A) Thomas Jefferson
(B) James Madison
(C) Tyler Jackson
(D) Andrew Jackson
(E) George Washington

47. The people represented in this painting could be described from what social classes?
(A) lower class
(B) middle class
(C) upper class
(D) all of the above
(E) A and B

48. By the 1830s, which of the following groups were NOT denied suffrage?
(A) African Americans
(B) white males
(C) Native Americans
(D) women
(E) indentured servants

49. The popular hero of the 1830s was
(A) the self-made man.
(B) an "Indian fighter."
(C) the privileged aristocrat.
(D) the working man.
(E) the American cowboy.

50. European observers believed the most evident feature of democracy in America was
(A) the American contribution.
(B) the decline in the spirit of deference.
(C) the participation of women in government.
(D) the American election process.
(E) the equality of former slaves.

51. An important change in the American family in the nineteenth century was
(A) the decreased importance of the extended family.
(B) the increase in the size of the family.
(C) the growing significance of mutual affection in marriage.
(D) the loss of some legal rights by men.
(E) the emergence of women as heads of households.

52. The sociological basis for the "Cult of True Womanhood" was
(A) an increasing division of labor between men and women.
(B) the accepted use of child labor.
(C) the growing urban population of the nation.
(D) the increasing acceptance of careers for women.
(E) the staggering number of women dying during childbirth.

53. The "proper" sphere for middle-class white women in the nineteenth century was
(A) home and family.
(B) education.
(C) family and career.
(D) labor outside the home.
(E) business or art schools.

54. As a result of changes in the middle-class family, nineteenth-century children
(A) left home sooner.
(B) became more available for labor.
(C) received more physical punishment than earlier generations.
(D) increasingly became viewed as individuals.
(E) were often offered up for adoption.

55. The most important function of the school in 1850 was seen as
(A) intellectual training.
(B) vocational training.
(C) moral indoctrination.
(D) child care.
(E) physical conditioning.

56. John Tyler initiated the politics of Manifest Destiny
(A) to win the support of his fellow Whigs.
(B) to bring together the Whig and Democratic parties.
(C) with the aid of Henry Clay.
(D) to build a base for his reelection in 1844.
(E) in hopes of identifying himself with James Monroe.

57. Opposition to Tyler's plan for the annexation of Texas came, primarily, from
(A) southern agricultural interests.
(B) Great Britain.
(C) northern antislavery Whigs.
(D) New England merchants.
(E) Mexican Catholics.

58. Manifest Destiny was based, in part, on
(A) the belief that God was on the side of American expansionism.

(B) the political needs of the Democratic party.
(C) the desire for new territory for slavery.
(D) the desire to drive Spain out of North America.
(E) simple greed.

59. The possibility of war with Great Britain over Oregon was increased by
(A) James Polk's aggressive foreign policy.
(B) the actions of American agents in the territory.
(C) American economic interests.
(D) the actions of Great Britain.
(E) direct pleas to Polk from the people who were living in Oregon.

60. _____, the hero of San Jacinto, became the first president of the Texas Republic.
(A) Stephen F. Austin
(B) W. B. Travis
(C) Frank Dallas
(D) William Becknell
(E) Sam Houston

61. Slavery would not have lasted as long as it did except for
(A) the constant supply of slaves from Africa.
(B) the South's lack of moral sensitivity.
(C) the willingness of slaves to submit to the system.
(D) the North's lack of interest in the problem.
(E) the place it held in the southern economy.

62. In the upper tier of southern states, the principal slave-produced commodity was
(A) cotton.
(B) tobacco.
(C) corn.
(D) wheat.
(E) indigo.

63. A major reason for the weaker hold of slavery in the upper South was the
(A) effectiveness of the abolitionist movement in the region.

(B) growing moral outrage against slavery in the region.

(C) passage of federal laws restricting slavery in the area.

(D) increasing industrialization and agricultural diversification in the region.

(E) lower slave birth rates.

The Compromise of 1850

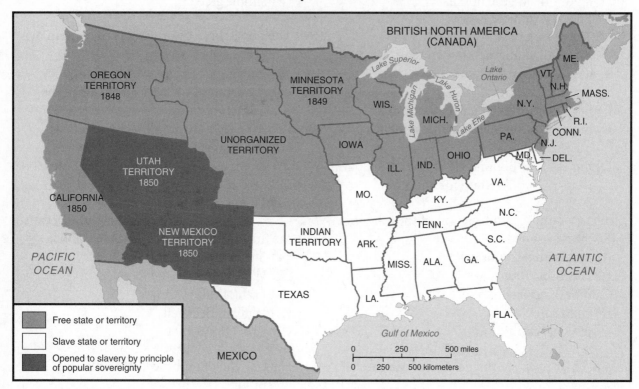

64. Based strictly on the Compromise of 1850, which territory would be admitted as a slave state?
(A) Oregon Territory
(B) Northern third of the Unorganized Territory
(C) Minnesota Territory
(D) New Mexico Territory
(E) All of the above would be admitted as slave states.

65. Based strictly on the Compromise of 1850, which territory would be admitted as a free state?
(A) California Territory
(B) Minnesota Territory
(C) Indian Territory
(D) New Mexico Territory
(E) All of the above would be admitted as free states.

66. Studies of the slave family reveal that _____ provided a model for personal relationships and the basis for a sense of community.
(A) kinship
(B) the nuclear family
(C) the extended family
(D) matriarchal family
(E) African family structures

67. The Free Soil movement supported the exclusion of slavery from the territories because of
(A) its belief in racial justice.
(B) its belief in the immorality of slavery.
(C) its desire to dominate the political process.
(D) racial prejudice and fear of labor competition from slaves.

(E) the land was unsuited for plantation agriculture.

68. According to the principle of popular sovereignty,
(A) Congress would determine whether a territory would have slavery.
(B) territorial legislatures would determine whether a territory would have slavery.
(C) settlers would determine whether a territory would have slavery.
(D) the Supreme Court would determine whether a territory would have slavery.
(E) the House of Representatives would determine whether a territory would have slavery.

69. Which of the following political parties did not run a presidential candidate in the election of 1848?
(A) Whig Party
(B) Republican Party
(C) Democratic Party
(D) Free Soil Party
(E) All of the above ran a presidential candidate.

70. In the *Dred Scott* case, the first question faced by the Supreme Court was
(A) whether slaves could be taken across state lines.
(B) the legality of slavery in Missouri.
(C) the constitutionality of inheritance laws involving slaves.
(D) whether or not Scott was a citizen.
(E) whether Scott's owner had the right to free him.

71. When Lincoln became president of the United States,
(A) he had more political experience than previous presidents.
(B) he was not able to command a leadership position in the Republican party.
(C) he was unable to convince congressional leaders to support his position on Southern secession.

(D) he identified wholeheartedly with the Southern cause.
(E) Northerners were convinced that his position on Southern secession was correct.

72. The border states
(A) all denounced slavery.
(B) divided amongst themselves and experienced several violent episodes.
(C) experienced bitter, internal division because of loyalty to the North and the South.
(D) all joined the Confederacy.
(E) remained loyal by a combination of local Unionism and federal intervention.

73. The term used to describe Confederate foreign policy was
(A) dollar diplomacy.
(B) gunboat diplomacy.
(C) King Cotton diplomacy.
(D) sugar and slaves diplomacy.
(E) corn cob diplomacy.

74. The first state to secede from the Union was

_____

(A) Texas.
(B) North Carolina.
(C) Virginia.
(D) Georgia.
(E) South Carolina.

75. The Emancipation Proclamation freed
(A) all African Americans.
(B) only slaves in the loyal border states.
(C) only slaves in the Confederacy.
(D) only slaves in the military occupation zones of the Union army.
(E) all slaves.

76. According to the map, Iowa was a
(A) slave state seceding before the fall of Fort Sumter.
(B) free state.
(C) slave state seceding after the fall of Fort Sumter.
(D) free territory.
(E) slave state loyal to the Union.

Secession

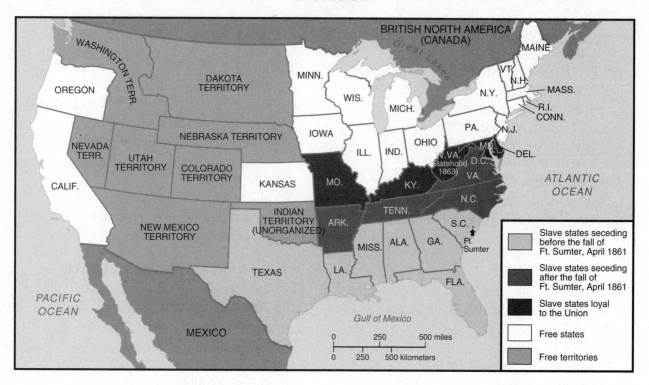

77. According to the map, Maryland was a
    (A) slave state seceding before the fall of Fort Sumter.
    (B) free state.
    (C) slave state seceding after the fall of Fort Sumter.
    (D) free territory.
    (E) slave state loyal to the Union.

78. Which one of the following Constitutional amendments abolished slavery?
    (A) Thirteenth
    (B) Fourteenth
    (C) Fifteenth
    (D) Sixteenth
    (E) Seventeenth

79. Black Codes showed that
    (A) Southerners were willing to allow African Americans legal equality.

(B) Southerners wanted African Americans to return to positions of servility.
(C) Southerners were interested in improving the education of the freedmen.
(D) the freedmen would be allowed to vote and participate in the political process.
(E) the idea of "separate but equal" was already established.

80. The initial government policy toward the Native Americans of the Plains was
    (A) to exterminate them.
    (B) to give each Native American "40 acres and a mule" for farming.
    (C) to define boundaries for each tribe and sign treaties with them.
    (D) to provoke intertribal warfare.
    (E) to ignore them and hope they would eventually die out.

U.S. History
Section II
Part A

Suggested Writing Time: 45 Minutes
Percent of Section II Score: 45

Directions: The following question is based on the accompanying Documents 1–10. (Some of the documents have been edited for the purpose of this exercise.) Write your answer on the pages of the essay booklet.

This question is designed to test your ability to work with historical documents. As you analyze the documents, take into account both the sources of the document and the authors' points of view. Write an essay on the following topic that integrates your analysis of the documents. **Do not simply summarize the documents individually.** You may refer to relevant historical facts and developments not mentioned in the documents.

Part A, Question 1

1. *Identify the major reform movements in the United States during the period 1820–1850. In your answer, make use of your knowledge of the time period as well as the data contained in the documents below.*

DOCUMENT 1   Source: *The Harbinger*, "Female Workers of Lowell," 1836

We have lately visited the cities of Lowell [Mass.] and Manchester [N.H.] and have had an opportunity of examining the factory system more closely than before. We had distrusted the accounts which we had heard from persons engaged in the labor reform now beginning to agitate New England. We could scarcely credit the statements made in relation to the exhausting nature of the labor in the mills, and to the manner in which the young women—the operatives—lived in their boardinghouses, six sleeping in a room, poorly ventilated.

The operatives work thirteen hours a day in the summer time, and from daylight to dark in the winter. At half past four in the morning the factory bell rings, and at five the girls must be in the mills. A clerk, placed as a watch, observes those who are a few minutes behind the time, and effectual means are taken to stimulate to punctuality. This is the morning commencement of the industrial discipline (should we not rather say industrial tyranny?) which is established in these associations of this moral and Christian community.

At seven the girls are allowed thirty minutes for breakfast, and at noon thirty minutes more for dinner, except during the first quarter of the year, when the time is extended to forty-five minutes. But within this time they must hurry to

261

their boardinghouses and return to the factory, and that through the hot sun or the rain or the cold. A meal eaten under such circumstances must be quite unfavorable to digestion and health, as any medical man will inform us. After seven o'clock in the evening the factory bell sounds the close of the day's work.

DOCUMENT 2   Source: Charles G. Finney, *What a Revival of Religion Is,* 1835

It is altogether improbable that religion will ever make progress among *heathen* nations except through the influence of revivals. The attempt is now making to do it by education, and other cautious and gradual improvements. But so long as the laws of mind remain what they are, it cannot be done in this way. There must be excitement sufficient to wake up the dormant moral powers, and roll back the tide of degradation and sin. And precisely so far as our own land approximate to heathenism, it is impossible for God or man to promote religion in such a state of things but by powerful excitements. This is evident from the fact that this has always been the way in which God has done it. God does not create these excitements, and choose this method to promote religion for nothing, or without reason. Where mankind are so reluctant to obey God, they will not obey until they are excited. For instance, how many there are who know that they ought to be religious, but they are afraid if they become pious they will be laughed at by their companions. Many are wedded to idols, others are procrastinating repentance, until they are settled in life, or until they have secured some favorite worldly interest. Such persons never will give up their false shame, or relinquish their ambitious schemes, till they are so excited that they cannot contain themselves any longer....

DOCUMENT 3   Source: Lyman Beecher, "Six Sermons on Intemperance," 1828

But of all the ways to hell, which the feet of deluded mortals tread, that of the intemperate is the most dreary and terrific. The demand for artificial stimulus to supply the deficiencies of healthful aliment, is like the rage of thirst, and the ravenous demand of famine. It is famine: for the artificial excitement has become as essential now to strength and cheerfulness, as simple nutrition once was. But nature, taught by habit to require what once she did not need, demands gratification now with a decision inexorable as death, and to most men as irresistible. The denial is a living death. The stomach, the head, the heart, and arteries, and veins, and every muscle, and every nerve, feel the exhaustion, and the restless, unutterable wretchedness which puts out the light of life, and curtains the heavens, and carpets the earth with sackcloth. All these varieties of sinking nature, call upon the wretched man with trumpet tongue, to dispel this darkness, and raise the ebbing tide of life, by the application of the cause which produced these woes, and after a momentary alleviation will produce them again with deeper terrors, and more urgent importunity; for the repetition, at each time renders the darkness deeper, and the torments of self-denial more irresistible and intolerable.

DOCUMENT 4   Source: Horace Mann, *Report of the Massachusetts Board of Education*, 1848

Without undervaluing any other human agency, it may be safely affirmed that the common school, improved and energized as it can easily be, may become the most effective and benignant of all the forces of civilization. Two reasons sustain this position. In the first place, there is an universality in its operation, which can be affirmed of no other institution whatever. If administered in the spirit of justice and conciliation, all the rising generation may be brought within the circle of its reformatory and elevating influences. And, in the second place, the materials upon which it operates are so pliant and ductile as to be susceptible of assuming a greater variety of forms than any other earthly work of the Creator....

According to the European theory, men are divided into classes—some to toil and earn, others to seize and enjoy. According to the Massachusetts theory, all are to have an equal chance for earning, and equal security in the enjoyment of what they earn. A republican form of government, without intelligence in the people, must be, on a vast scale, what a mad-house without superintendent or keepers would be on a small one....However elevated the moral character of a constituency may be, however, well-informed in matters of general science or history, yet they must, if citizens of a republic, understand something of the true nature and functions of the government under which they live....

DOCUMENT 5   Source: William Lloyd Garrison, first issue of *The Liberator*, 1831

Assenting to the "self-evident truth" maintained in the American Declaration of Independence "that all men are created equal, and endowed by their Creator with certain inalienable rights—among which are life, liberty, and the pursuit of happiness," I shall strenuously contend for the immediate enfranchisement of our slave population....In Park Street Church, on the Fourth of July, 1829, in an address on slavery, I unreflectingly assented to the popular but pernicious doctrine of gradual abolition. I seize this opportunity to make a full and unequivocal recantation, and thus publicly to ask pardon of my God, of my country, and of my brethren the poor slaves, for having uttered a sentiment so full of timidity, injustice, and absurdity....

DOCUMENT 6   Source: The Beecher family, in a Matthew Brady photograph

DOCUMENT 7   Source: Temperance Cartoon, *The Drunkard's Progress*

DOCUMENT 8   Source: Eastern State Penitentiary in Philadelphia

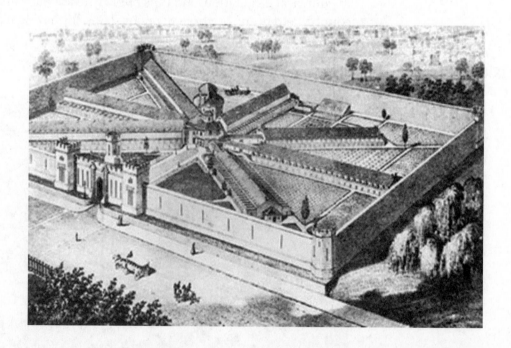

DOCUMENT 9   Source: Dorothea Dix

DOCUMENT 10   Source: Utopian Communities Before the Civil War

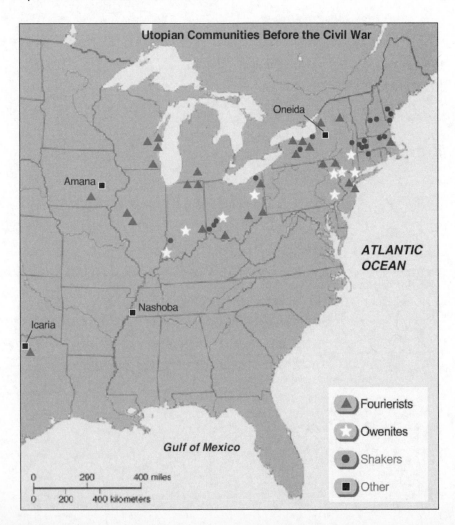

Utopian Communities Before the Civil War

Oneida

Amana

Nashoba

Icaria

ATLANTIC OCEAN

Gulf of Mexico

0   200   400 miles

0   200   400 kilometers

▲ Fourierists
★ Owenites
● Shakers
■ Other

U.S. History
Section II
Part B

Suggested Planning and Writing Time: 70 Minutes
Percent of Section II Score: 55

Directions: You are to answer the following two questions. You should spend 5 minutes organizing or outlining each essay. In writing your essays, *use specific examples to support your answer.* Write your answers to the questions on the lined pages of the essay booklet. If time permits when you finish writing, check your work.

Part B, Question 2

The suggested writing time for this question is 30 minutes. *You are advised to spend 5 minutes planning your answer.*

2. *Discuss how the literature of the Colonial Times to the Age of Westward Expansion was a reflection of the attitudes and feelings of the nation.*

Part B, Question 3

The suggested writing time for this question is 30 minutes. *You are advised to spend 5 minutes planning your answer.*

3. *Which President, Jefferson or Jackson, left the greatest impact on his country? Substantiate with proof.*

ANSWERS AND EXPLANATIONS

Sample Test 1

Section I: Multiple Choice

▌ **1. (A) is correct.** The headright system was to allow colonists an opportunity to move out in the correct direction once they reached the New World.

▌ **2. (B) is correct.** Most Native populations were interwoven familial units.

▌ **3. (C) is correct.** Once contact was made with the Europeans, the natives were in pursuit of trade for European technology.

▌ **4. (C) is correct.** The race for colonization began with the voyages of Columbus for the Spanish Crown. The Portuguese were quick to follow.

▌ **5. (A) is correct.** The *conquistadores* or conquerors were the Spanish explorers in search of wealth and fame.

▌ **6. (A) is correct.** English settlers came to America for a plethora of reasons. Some came seeking religious freedom, some for adventure, some to escape prosecution, some as a sentence, and others came because they were forced to travel.

▌ **7. (D) is correct.** England passed no laws directing poorer classes to settle. Many were offered their choice of debtor's prison or America and many made that choice.

▌ **8. (B) is correct.** The idea was try to find what had been comfortable and adopt it to the new situation.

▌ **9. (C) is correct.** The joint-stock company was designed as a profit-making venture to fund the expeditions across the Atlantic.

▌ **10. (E) is correct.** Cite selection was largely based on security and fear of attack.

▌ **11. (A) is correct.** This a true statement. Virginia had become predominately a colony of aristocratic landowners that held slaves.

▌ **12. (B) is correct.** In the 1600s the economic gap widened and divided the society.

▌ **13. (D) is correct.** All of the statements are true. The Navigation Acts insured that certain American products could be sold only in England. Only English or colonial merchants could engage in colonial trade. All foreign goods that were to be sold in England had to be shipped in England.

▌ **14. (E) is correct.** The Navigation Acts were a one-sided attempt to maintain the trade imbalance it had established with the Americans.

▌ **15. (C) is correct.** These two regions were rich in sugar plantations and were labor intensive. The African slave was in high demand in these two regions.

▌ **16. (D) is correct.** The Triangular trade route was of little significance in Colonial America as most of the farming came from small family farms. The Caribbean and South America were actually more important for the time frame.

▌ **17. (B) is correct.** The first large group of immigrants came seeking religious freedom. They were a sect of a religiously charged group of Mennonites.

▌ **18. (B) is correct.** King George II's minister, William Pitt, viewed the best way to attack France was to expel it from North America. Thus, the French and Indian War or Seven Years' War was fought on North American soil. This war had an unprecedented impact on American soil because they were forced to cooperate.

19. (E) is correct. The Ohio Valley was the source of major conflict and strife for Anglo-French relations. Both nations claimed regions of the Ohio Valley. This was part of the area fought for in the French and Indian War or Seven Years' War.

20. (B) is correct. King Williams' War was the first of the "Century of War." It started in 1689. Although the war was primarily fought on the European continent, there were skirmishes between French and British troops along the Frontier areas in New York and New England.

21. (C) is correct. This was the central concept that the colonists never shared with the homeland. The British believed supreme constitutional authority rested with Parliament. The Parliament was designed to protect rights and property from an arbitrary king.

22. (A) is correct. The colonists' position in the Anglo-American debate over parliamentary powers was their strong belief in the powers of their own provincial assemblies. The colonists believed these assemblies to be better and more directly represented their interests and beliefs.

23. (D) is correct. The Declaration of Independence was a document crafted to spell out the grievances with the king. The document also demonstrated the measures taken in good faith to stay loyal to the crown. When the two sides could no longer stay together, based on enlightened ideals, then the colonists were within their divine right to dissolve their bonds.

24. (E) is correct. All of the answers were true. How one viewed King George II depended on your interests. The Coat of Arms represented the monarchy in the absence of the monarchy and the Coat of Arms was displayed throughout the American Colonies. The loyalists viewed the king with admiration and respect. Opponents to the crown viewed him as emblematic of a monarch that neither understood nor cared about the colonies.

25. (C) is correct. The colonists had been engaging the British Redcoats in guerilla warfare. The colonial tactics were viewed as ungentlemanly and therefore beneath the proper British level of engagement. This and the fact that the British troops were largely untrained hindered the British in mounting an effective counterstrategy.

26. (D) is correct. The Articles of Confederation by its definition was a loose coupling of states. This would indicate there was very little central government. Even the institutions that were consolidated were weak and often ignored by the states.

27. (C) is correct. By definition, a nationalist would be for a strong national policy or government. These people viewed the Articles of Confederation as weak and a failure.

28. (B) is correct. The Baron de Montesquieu was the European philosopher who supported the theory of state sovereignty. He was an Anglophile and viewed the British system as the model government.

29. (A) is correct. James Madison was viewed by many as the most brilliant American political theorist of the post-Revolutionary period. The nation looked to Madison for leadership as the nation developed.

30. (C) is correct. All three were strong supporters of a strong Federal system.

31. (A) is correct. Washington was a victorious general who had repelled the

British. When the new Constitution called for a strong executive, the nation turned to him. To most, he was the embodiment of the American Spirit.

- **32. (C) is correct.** Washington was the final decision maker in his administration. The cabinet advised but Washington either took or rejected that advice.

- **33. (A) is correct.** This issue divided the cabinet between Federalist and Republicans. The rebellion was nothing more than a tax protest. Washington called out fifteen thousand militiamen and was embarrassed when all he could come up with was two mentally ill men that Washington would later pardon of their treason convictions. This was a challenge because the state failed to act and forced federal action.

- **34. (B) is correct.** The Alien and Sedition Act was an infringement on the First Amendment rights of many Americans because it used the weight of federal law to crush political dissent.

- **35. (D) is correct.** Edmund Genet and his subordinates tried to request bribes of U.S. envoys. This affair is known as the XYZ Affair.

- **36. (E) is correct.** The two largest regions were North and South. Americans were also identified by the other geographic regions or by state.

- **37. (D) is correct.** The West went from wild uninhabited land to civilized cities and states. All of this was facilitated by technological advances.

- **38. (E) is correct.** All of the answers are correct. This pattern is a repeat of the colonists arriving from Europe onto the North American continent.

- **39. (D) is correct.** The Treaty of Ghent was the treaty that ended the War of 1812. It essentially agreed to everything that was status quo before the war.

- **40. (E) is correct.** The Northwest Indians, under Tecumseh, had allied themselves with the British and had succeeded in capturing General Hull's personal baggage containing battle plans.

- **41. (B) is correct.** The decision of *McCulloch v. Maryland* on the surface was about taxes. However, this decision was important for two large Constitutional reasons. First, the decision was unanimous. The Supreme Court set forth the idea of "implied powers." The decisions therefore upheld that a national bank was constitutional and taxing a federal entity by a state was not.

- **42. (A) is correct.** The West was a patchwork network of small single-unit farms. This was a way for poorer families to flee the eastern life.

- **43. (E) is correct.** As already noted in Question 36, the pioneers of America's West tried to recreate their lifestyles and comforts.

- **44. (C) is correct.** In 1808, in order to open the country west of the Appalachian Mountains to settlers and to offer a cheap and safe way to carry produce to a market, Governor Dewitt Clinton proposed the construction of a canal. On July 4, 1817 he broke ground for the construction of the canal. In those early days, it was often sarcastically referred to as "Clinton's Big Ditch." When finally completed on October 26, 1825, it was the engineering marvel of its day. It included 18 aqueducts to carry the canal over ravines and rivers, and 83 locks, with a rise of 568 feet from the Hudson River to Lake Erie. It was 4 feet deep and 40 feet wide, and floated boats carrying 30 tons of freight. A ten foot wide towpath was built along the bank of the canal for horses, mules, and oxen led by a boy boat driver.

■ **45. (E) is correct.** The state banking systems were open to corruption and error during the period 1815 to 1820. Additionally, the country was in the tail end of a depression caused by the Embargo of Jefferson.

■ **46. (D) is correct.** Andrew Jackson was viewed as the "common man's" president because he did not have the aristocratic pedigree of his predecessors. He possessed no political experience when he was elected, but he had been a famous general.

■ **47. (D) is correct.** The picture clearly depicts all social classes being represented at the inauguration. In the lower left corner appears to be upper middle or upper class business men conversing. Next to them appears to be a yeoman family. In the right hand corner appears to be women of the middle class.

■ **48. (B) is correct.** By 1830 Universal Manhood Suffrage was extended to all white males.

■ **49. (A) is correct.** During the Jacksonian era, the self-made man was the every-man's hero. The self-made man was the inspiration to generations who wanted more than they had.

■ **50. (B) is correct.** Europeans viewed the Americans as boorish and ill-mannered. They felt the American democratic ways were at the core of this decline in civility.

■ **51. (C) is correct.** Mid-nineteenth century parents had less control over children's marriage plans. Romantic novels had started to popularize the idea of love in marriage.

■ **52. (A) is correct.** While men were gaining rights women were being left behind. Women, however, were beginning to take notice of this disparity.

■ **53. (A) is correct.** The "proper" place for a nineteenth-century woman was at home tending to the house and the children.

■ **54. (D) is correct.** With requirements for education and less need to have them work the family farm, middle class children were viewed more as individuals.

■ **55. (C) is correct.** All curriculum material dealt with teaching morals, right from wrong.

■ **56. (D) is correct.** The West was a great potential for votes. Tyler sees this and pushes the idea of Manifest Destiny.

■ **57. (C) is correct.** Those in opposition to slavery feared Texas would enter the Union as a slave state. Thus, they opposed the annexation of Texas.

■ **58. (A) is correct.** The idea that God destined the United States for its position to rule over all of North America was used all the way into the early twentieth century.

■ **59. (A) is correct.** Polk's policy decisions gave a realistic potential of war over Oregon.

■ **60. (E) is correct.** Sam Houston, the hero of San Jacinto, became the first president of the Texas Republic.

■ **61. (E) is correct.** Slavery was the backbone of the Southern economy. Slavery would have ended much sooner had it not been for its entrenchment in the Southern economy.

■ **62. (B) is correct.** Tobacco was king in the "Border States." These states were more suitable for the raising of tobacco rather than cotton.

■ **63. (D) is correct.** The economy of the "Border States" was stronger. This left the institution of slavery in a weaker state.

■ **64. (D) is correct.** New Mexico was south of the slave line and if it were to come into the Union it would have been as a slave state.

■ **65. (B) is correct.** Minnesota was north of the slave line and if it were to come into the Union it would have been as a free state.

■ **66. (A) is correct.** Kinship was the stabilizing factor because families were often torn apart by slavery.

■ **67. (D) is correct.** This was the tenant of the Free Soil Movement.

■ **68. (C) is correct.** Settlers in territories would be allowed to decide between free and slave. The problem was this opened many up to corruption because territorial lines were blurred and many crossed over these lines when elections were held.

■ **69. (B) is correct.** The Republican Party came into existence on the national level after the Election of 1848. This coincides with the death of the Whig Party.

■ **70. (D) is correct.** In the *Dred Scott* case the Justices first had to decide if Scott had legal standing to file in court. This standing meant that he was a U.S. Citizen. The court ruled he did not have legal standing to sue in court.

■ **71. (E) is correct.** Northerners believed that Lincoln's position was correct. He was the type of candidate that the average man could aspire to become. He in essence was the epitome of the American Ideal.

■ **72. (E) is correct.** The Border States were in a precarious position. They were torn between succession and loyalty to the union. These states were kept in the union by a combination of coercion and loyalty.

■ **73. (C) is correct.** King Cotton was the name of the Confederate Diplomacy. The Confederate States tried to use the only thing they had, cotton, as a tool to be recognized as a state by a foreign nation, in particular England.

■ **74. (E) is correct.** South Carolina was the first state to secede from the Union.

■ **75. (C) is correct.** Because there were no slaves in the North, the Emancipation Proclamation freed only slaves in the South. Unfortunately, the Emancipation Proclamation freed no slaves for two more years as the war raged on for that long.

■ **76. (B) is correct.** Iowa was a free state. It was above the "slave line."

■ **77. (E) is correct.** Maryland was a border state that stayed loyal to the Union.

■ **78. (A) is correct.** The Thirteenth Amendment abolished the institution of slavery where it existed at the time of ratification. This meant the Southern States would have to ratify the amendment to be readmitted to the Union.

■ **79. (B) is correct.** Black Codes were often clandestine ways of forcing freedmen back into servitude. This mindset remained in the South for the next century.

■ **80. (C) is correct.** Initial western policy was to negotiate to the reservation. This policy worked with some tribes. Many of the Plains Tribes did not cooperate with this plan and were thus hunted by frontier armies.

1. *Identify the major reform movements in the United States during the period 1820–1850. In your answer, make use of your knowledge of the time period as well as the data contained in the documents below.*

Many reform movements were active in the United States during this time period. Of these, the most potent was the abolitionist anti-slavery movement.

The country was going through the early Industrial Revolution at the time, and many women went to work in the factories of New England. While the conditions were often difficult, for many women these jobs also represented the opportunity to get away from the family farm and find some measure of independence in the city. Still, work at the factories was rigidly regulated and often very harsh. **(DOCUMENT 1)**

The country had experienced a religious revival during the colonial period, and a second Great Awakening swept the country at this time. **(DOCUMENT 2)** Another major reform movement was the temperance, or anti-alcohol, movement. This re-surfaced after the Civil War and ultimately led to Prohibition during the 1920s. **(DOCUMENTS 3 AND 7)** Education was another major reform movement, and Horace Mann of Massachusetts was a critical part of establishing a free public education system for all. **(DOCUMENT 4)** Other important reforms included treatment of the mentally ill and prison reform. **(DOCUMENTS 8 AND 9)** The Beecher family was active in many reform movements, including anti-slavery and women's rights. **(DOCUMENT 6)** Other important reforms included the various Utopian communities such as the Shakers, who used various methods to try and improve life for their adherents.

The most important movement of the time was the anti-slavery movement, which began in earnest in the 1830. William Garrison's *The Liberator* was a prime motivator of the early anti-slavery movement. **(DOCUMENT 5)** Ultimately this issue was not resolved until the Civil War of the 1860s and the passage of the Thirteenth Amendment banning slavery in the United States.

Section II
Part B

Sample Student Responses

2. *Discuss how the literature of the Colonial Times to the Age of Westward Expansion was a reflection of the attitudes and feelings of the nation.*

The literature of the day was a reflection of the society at that time. Better essays will show specific examples. All of these pieces of literature were stories that had a subplot that was a commentary on American life. The authors listed below were recognized for enhancing or creating the controversy that fueled great public debate.

Here is a sample list: *Common Sense* was a pamphlet that was to inform and persuade the colonial citizenry of the perils of the British Empire. Ben Franklin's autobiography was designed to inform and motivate a generation. George Washington's autobiography helped to establish and create a nation through its first leader. *Moby Dick* by Herman Melville was about carving out one's own destiny. Harriet Beecher Stowe wrote *Uncle Tom's Cabin*, which was designed to alarm and inform about the conditions of southern plantation slaves. Mark Twain wrote about the naiveté of the American society.

3. *Which President, Jefferson or Jackson, left the greatest impact on his country? Substantiate with proof.*

Many writers will select Jefferson. Jefferson probably had a greater impact before he was President. He was the author of the Declaration of Independence. He engaged in the debates over policy in the Washington Administration with Alexander Hamilton. He was responsible for one or both of today's major political parties. All of these accomplishments occurred outside the scope of his tenure as President. As President perhaps his greatest contribution was the Louisiana Purchase and the commissioning of the Lewis and Clark Expedition. By the time Jefferson left office he had stagnated or crippled the economy. Jefferson's Administration had crippled foreign policy through a series of blunders.

Writers who would select Jackson will also write about his being a war hero and his success at New Orleans. This is outside the scope. Jackson as President is largely responsible for shaping the idea of modern democracy. He was attractive to the common man and therefore opened politics up to them. Jackson granted the idea of "the voice of the people."

AP* U.S. History
Sample Practice Test 2

U.S. History Section I

**Time: 55 Minutes
80 Questions**

Directions: Each of the questions or incomplete statements below is followed by five suggested answers or completions. Select the one that is best in each case and then fill in the corresponding oval on the answer sheet.

1. Industrial growth was concentrated in the
   (A) Southwest.
   (B) Northeast.
   (C) Pacific.
   (D) Southeast.
   (E) Midwest.

2. The development of a national railway system
   (A) provided needed jobs for an overabundant labor supply.
   (B) had little effect on the economic changes of the late nineteenth century.
   (C) led to an integrated national economic system.
   (D) had little help from the political system.
   (E) was not completed until the early twentieth century.

3. Rapid rail construction after the Civil War was possible because
   (A) there was little competition between the builders.
   (B) the rail companies managed their money and land wisely.
   (C) federal and state governments provided important incentives.
   (D) the western half of the nation was uninhabitable.
   (E) the South was eager to participate.

4. Which of the following was NOT a prominent labor union in late nineteenth-century America?
   (A) Teamsters Union
   (B) Congress of Industrial Organizations
   (C) American Federation of Labor
   (D) Union of Iron and Steel Workers
   (E) Union of Sleeping Car Porters

5. Unlike the Knights of Labor, the American Federation of Labor
   (A) believed workers would rise in stature.
   (B) organized skilled and unskilled workers.
   (C) emphasized economic goals for workers.
   (D) organized a majority of the workers.
   (E) hoped all workers could eventually become self-employed.

6. In the Victorian code of morality,
   (A) children were active participants in family life.
   (B) wives were to be acknowledged as equal partners to their husbands.
   (C) moral values were less important than economic values.
   (D) strict standards of behavior should be followed.
   (E) young women could finally go out without a chaperone.

7. Public schools in the 1870s and 1880s
   (A) placed greater value on educating females.
   (B) vigorously stressed discipline and routine.
   (C) ignored moral, religious education.
   (D) emphasized egalitarianism between students and teachers.
   (E) were considered better than factories by most students.

8. A major difference between northern and southern schools was
   (A) more students attended school in the South.
   (B) most southern schools had compulsory school laws.
   (C) southern states could not finance their schools.
   (D) northern states provided segregated school systems.
   (E) southern schools provided better curricula.

9. W.E.B. Du Bois
   (A) supported the views of Booker T. Washington.
   (B) advocated revolutionary tactics for African Americans.
   (C) was popular with African Americans and white society.
   (D) believed educational advancement was the key to success.
   (E) was the author of the "Atlanta Compromise."

10. The model for the modern American research university came from
    (A) Germany.
    (B) Russia.
    (C) Great Britain.
    (D) France.
    (E) New England.

11. The Interstate Commerce Commission
    (A) was designed to protect railroads.

(B) had little effect on interstate commerce.
(C) was designed to strengthen states' rights.
(D) had little support from the American consumer.
(E) was the first attempt at federal regulation.

12. The Pendleton Act
    (A) eliminated presidential appointments.
    (B) provided a merit system for the national government.
    (C) allowed Congress greater power in appointing government jobs.
    (D) gave the judiciary greater power in the national government.
    (E) established the Secret Service.

13. Grover Cleveland
    (A) increased federal activities.
    (B) was committed to higher tariffs.
    (C) curtailed federal activities.
    (D) brought the Democratic Party dishonor.
    (E) was reelected in a landslide in 1888.

14. Those who supported the free coinage of silver
    (A) were convinced it would help the agrarian sectors.
    (B) were primarily found in the North and East.
    (C) wanted to keep the monetary power from the national government.
    (D) found little support for their views in Congress.
    (E) thought it would deflate the currency.

15. The Sherman Silver Purchase Act
    (A) assured that the nation would have a bimetallic system.
    (B) allowed the government to demonetize silver in favor of gold.
    (C) kept limited silver coinage in circulation.
    (D) allowed for the free coinage of silver.
    (E) recognized the continuing scarcity of silver in the United States.

16. The Samoan Islands
    (A) evoked brutal American aggression.
    (B) provided the United States with its initial outpost in the Pacific.
    (C) were completely insignificant to American interests.
    (D) forced the United States into a military alliance with Germany.
    (E) belonged exclusively to the United States by 1899.

17. According to the theories of Alfred T. Mahan,
    (A) large armies would protect American interests around the globe.
    (B) American greatness would be recognized through industrial output.
    (C) little would be gained from American expansion abroad.
    (D) a two-ocean navy was an integral part of America's wealth and power.
    (E) standing armies were dangerous.

18. One consequence of General Weyler's policy in Cuba was
    (A) to generate public sympathy for the Cuban people among Americans.
    (B) the ending of the Cuban rebellion.
    (C) strong support from the American government.
    (D) an alliance between the Cuban rebels and the American government.
    (E) the end of "reconcentration."

19. Yellow journalism
    (A) printed lurid stories of Spanish atrocities.
    (B) was actually a cause of the war.
    (C) was led by such prominent authors as Mark Twain and Bret Harte.
    (D) portrayed a totally impartial view of world events.
    (E) had been around for years, but became popular during the war.

20. At the outset of the Spanish-American War,
    (A) there was little public support for the war in the United States.
    (B) the American military was well-prepared to fight a war.
    (C) it was difficult to find the necessary volunteers for the American military.
    (D) the American army was composed of soldiers well-trained in quelling uprisings among Native Americans.
    (E) the American army was 200,000 strong.

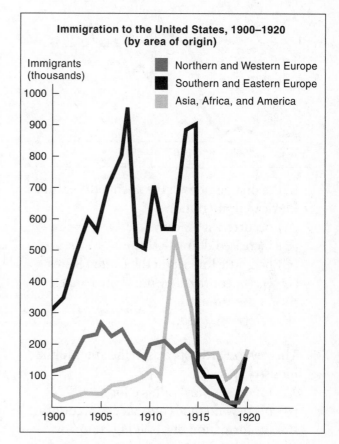

21. Between 1901 and 1914, the majority of immigrants were from
    (A) Asia.
    (B) Africa.
    (C) Scandinavian countries.
    (D) southern and eastern Europe.
    (E) Mexico.

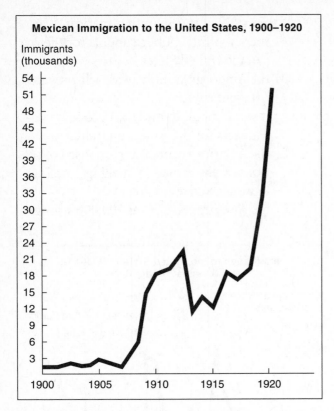

Mexican Immigration to the United States, 1900–1920

Immigrants (thousands)

54
51
48
45
42
39
36
33
30
27
24
21
18
15
12
9
6
3

1900   1905   1910   1915   1920

22. In the first decades of the twentieth century, Mexican immigration
    (A) occurred at a steady rate.
    (B) increased dramatically.
    (C) had little impact on the United States.
    (D) was encouraged by the United States government.
    (E) rarely occurred.

23. The key to Ford's success in the automobile industry was
    (A) union support for his efforts.
    (B) his new methods of financial accounting.
    (C) his formation of a holding company.
    (D) mass production.
    (E) vertical integration of supplies.

24. Which one of the following individuals was NOT a prominent American writer of the Progressive Era?
    (A) T. S. Eliot
    (B) Carl Sandburg
    (C) Isadora Duncan
    (D) Ezra Pound

(E) Robert Frost

25. The Niagara Movement was headed by
    (A) W. E. B. Du Bois.
    (B) Booker T. Washington.
    (C) William Walling.
    (D) Marcus Garvey.
    (E) William Lloyd Garrison.

26. The Supreme Court's decision in the *Northern Securities* case
    (A) paved the way for several other antitrust actions.
    (B) had little effect on the overall problem of trusts.
    (C) was opposed by Roosevelt.
    (D) affected only the smaller American trusts.
    (E) was unanimous.

27. The most famous reform governor of the Progressive period was
    (A) Robert W. La Follette.
    (B) "Golden Rule" Jones.

(C) Hiram Johnson.
(D) Lincoln Steffens.
(E) Richard Ely.

28. The Hepburn Act of 1906
 (A) was aimed, primarily, at the mining industry.
 (B) lessened government regulation of industry.
 (C) strengthened the power of the Interstate Commerce Commission.
 (D) raised the tariff.
 (E) banned child labor.

29. The Underwood Tariff of 1913
 (A) was the first tariff cut in nineteen years.
 (B) continued the tradition of raising the tariff.
 (C) was opposed by Wilson.
 (D) required little skill for passage by Congress.
 (E) kept tariff rates constant for two years.

30. The commission form of government was pioneered in
 (A) New York City.
 (B) Philadelphia.
 (C) Galveston.
 (D) Boston.
 (E) Chicago.

31. Using your own knowledge and the political cartoon above, the Roosevelt Corollary
 (A) reflected America's increasing trust in the motives of Europe.

(B) indicated a new American spirit of cooperation with Latin America.
(C) resulted from America's fear that Latin American debts to Europe invited intervention.
(D) had relatively little influence on American foreign policy.
(E) stated "speak softly and carry a big stick."

32. The immigration restrictions of the 1920s
 (A) were a realistic response to the problem of immigrants.
 (B) reflected the strength of nativism in America.
 (C) did little to stem the tide of immigrants.
 (D) did not favor immigrants from any one country.
 (E) were the first, though not the last, of their kind.

33. As secretary of state, William Jennings Bryan
 (A) relied heavily on State Department experts.
 (B) opposed many of Wilson's policies.
 (C) believed international disputes should be settled on the battlefield.
 (D) brought a practical approach to the position.
 (E) embarked on a campaign to negotiate arbitration treaties.

34. With respect to Latin America, Wilson
 (A) continued the policies of Roosevelt and Taft.
 (B) showed little interest in the area.
 (C) refused to intervene in the region.
 (D) intervened militarily in the region.
 (E) adopted a policy of shared wealth.

35. The *Sussex* pledge
 (A) renounced American bank loans to the Allies.
 (B) indicated Germany's intention to yield to Wilson's demands.
 (C) marked an intensification in the use of submarines.
 (D) was opposed by Great Britain.

(E) was viewed by most Americans as a call to arms.

36. The Ku Klux Klan
    (A) was exclusively a movement against African Americans.
    (B) had little strength outside the deep South.
    (C) attacked anyone who seemed different to them.
    (D) was open to any American who agreed with their ideas.
    (E) in the 1920s was exactly the same as the Reconstruction Klan.

37. In the 1920s, the automobile
    (A) was just a passing fancy.
    (B) had little effect on American life.
    (C) profoundly changed American life.
    (D) had little effect on the rest of the economy.
    (E) was a novelty since most people could not afford to own one.

38. The leading social critic of the 1920s was
    (A) Jane Addams.
    (B) H. L. Mencken.
    (C) Ezra Pound.
    (D) Theda Bara.
    (E) John Dos Passos.

39. An indicator of the future strength of the Democratic Party was
    (A) its success in the presidential race of 1924.
    (B) the shift of urban voters to the party.
    (C) an increase in the number of rural Democrats.
    (D) the unpopularity of Republican presidents.
    (E) a large number of women voters.

40. Beneath the surface, the two candidates in the election of 1928
    (A) were strikingly similar.
    (B) were radically different.
    (C) were somewhat alike.
    (D) had little in common.
    (E) despised each other.

41. In the presidential campaign of 1932, Hoover
    (A) announced that he had been irresponsible in his attitude toward the Depression.
    (B) conducted an upbeat, optimistic campaign.
    (C) announced his support for public relief.
    (D) was haunted by the public's memory of the Bonus March.
    (E) announced he would take more bold action in the future.

42. Labor issues in Roosevelt's National Recovery Administration were addressed in
    (A) Section 14b.
    (B) the Wagner Act.
    (C) Section 7a.
    (D) Article 14.
    (E) Sub-Section 7.

43. Under the Agricultural Adjustment Act, the federal government paid subsidies to farmers who
    (A) reduced their crop production.
    (B) increased their output.
    (C) bought more efficient equipment and fertilizers.
    (D) donated their surplus to the urban unemployed.
    (E) ceased all production.

44. The National Recovery Administration
    (A) prohibited collective bargaining by labor.
    (B) set parity prices for farm produce.
    (C) encouraged increased farm production.
    (D) established guidelines for big business and fair trade codes.
    (E) forced big business to cooperate with government.

45. Francis Townsend advocated that the federal government pay $200 each month to
    (A) all Americans over the age of 60.
    (B) dispossessed farmers.
    (C) veterans of World War I.
    (D) widows with two or more children.
    (E) unemployed urban workers.

46. During the war, U.S.-Soviet relations were
    (A) close and tranquil.
    (B) constantly strained by significant ideological differences.
    (C) totally uncooperative.
    (D) hurt by the United States' refusal to extend recognition to the Soviet Union as a cobelligerent.
    (E) influenced by Roosevelt's personal dislike for Stalin.

47. The United States' strategy against Japan in the Pacific can be described as
    (A) island hopping.
    (B) human wave assaults.
    (C) a traditional naval blockade.
    (D) a battleship "slugfest."
    (E) guerilla warfare.

48. United States troops first went into combat against German troops in
    (A) Italy.
    (B) France.
    (C) Greece.
    (D) Poland.
    (E) North Africa.

49. During World War II, Japanese Americans
    (A) were essentially ignored by the American public.
    (B) were systematically slaughtered by the thousands in concentration camps.
    (C) were forced to live as prisoners in concentration camps.
    (D) experienced about the same amount of discrimination as German Americans.
    (E) were asked to voluntary leave their homes if they lived near the Pacific coast.

50. The Supreme Commander of Allied forces in Europe was
    (A) George Patton.
    (B) Chester Nimitz.
    (C) George C. Marshall.
    (D) Dwight D. Eisenhower.
    (E) Douglas MacArthur.

51. American policy toward Japan after World War II
    (A) allowed shared U.S.-Soviet responsibility for the Japanese islands.
    (B) emphasized the continuation of traditional Japanese institutions.
    (C) was aimed at preventing the recovery of the Japanese economy.
    (D) brought the transition of the Japanese government into a constitutional democracy.
    (E) was similar to American policy in Europe.

52. Despite many advantages, the ability of Chiang Kai-shek to maintain control of China was eroded by
    (A) the refusal of the United States to support his cause.
    (B) widespread government corruption and high inflation.
    (C) his refusal to take aggressive action against the Communists.
    (D) lack of recognition from the United States.
    (E) the appeal of communism to large numbers of Chinese citizens.

53. At the beginning of the Korean War, North Korea was
    (A) a colony of Japan.
    (B) a colony of China.
    (C) strongly supported by the Soviet Union.
    (D) a trustee state of the United Nations.
    (E) still recovering from the devastation of World War II.

54. In the final analysis, the most significant result of the Korean War was
    (A) its final solution: the division of Korea.
    (B) the fact that it inhibited the Soviet Union's further expansionism.
    (C) that it reinforced Truman's popularity with the American people.
    (D) that it humiliated the United States in the eyes of the world.
    (E) that it brought about massive American rearmament.

55. The leading figure of the Red Scare of the early 1950s was
    (A) Dwight D. Eisenhower.
    (B) Senator Joseph McCarthy.
    (C) Dean Acheson.
    (D) Richard Nixon.
    (E) Roy Cohn.

56. As a result of *Brown v. Board of Education of Topeka,*
    (A) segregation in the South ended almost immediately.
    (B) segregation was allowed to continue for ten years.
    (C) the slow process of desegregating schools was begun.
    (D) African-American protests against discrimination began to decline in number.
    (E) martial law was immediately imposed in most southern states.

57. The Deep South responded to court-ordered desegregation
    (A) with massive resistance.
    (B) by moving immediately to end discrimination in schools.
    (C) with grudging acceptance of the decisions.
    (D) by closing all of its schools.
    (E) with bloody race riots.

58. Martin Luther King, Jr.'s philosophy of protest stressed
    (A) massive demonstrations in the streets.
    (B) acceptance of discrimination until the courts could act.
    (C) acceptance of discrimination until African Americans could form a more solid economic base.
    (D) intensive, radical action.
    (E) nonviolent, passive resistance.

59. The organization founded by Martin Luther King, Jr. to promote civil rights was the
    (A) Student Nonviolent Coordinating Committee.
    (B) National Association for the Advancement of Colored People.
    (C) Southern Christian Leadership Conference.
    (D) Fair Employment Practices Committee.
    (E) Black Panther Party for Self-Defense.

60. By 1960, the most racially integrated institution in American society was
    (A) the public high school system.
    (B) the private university system.
    (C) corporate America.
    (D) the military.
    (E) professional hockey.

61. In the long run, the Gulf of Tonkin Resolution can be evaluated as
    (A) a costly victory for Lyndon Johnson.
    (B) a relatively minor event in the long history of war in Vietnam.
    (C) a significant and positive victory for Lyndon Johnson.
    (D) having significantly elevated Lyndon Johnson's standing with Congress.
    (E) a dismal failure for the Johnson administration.

62. Using your own knowledge and the following map, one of the immediate consequences of the Tet offensive in 1968 was that
    (A) President Johnson completed the process of Vietnamization.
    (B) popular support for the war declined in the United States.
    (C) the South Vietnamese government was overthrown.
    (D) Congress gave greater support to President Johnson's war policies.
    (E) was a blank check for military escalation in Vietnam.

CHINA

Hanoi
U.S. air raids
1966–1968, 1972

Haiphong
harbor mined, 1972

LAOS

Gulf of Tonkin

Gulf of Tonkin Incident
Aug. 4, 1964

NORTH
VIETNAM

Vientiane

Mekong R.

Demilitarized Zone
(DMZ)

17th Parallel
Demarcation Line
July 1954

Invasion of Laos
Feb. 6–Mar. 1971

Hue
Tet offensive
Jan. 30–Feb. 1968

THAILAND

Ho Chi Minh Trail

My Lai massacre
Mar. 16, 1968

CAMBODIA

SOUTH
VIETNAM

South
China
Sea

Invasion of Cambodia
Apr. 29–June 29, 1970

Phnom
Penh

Saigon
Tet offensive
Jan. 30–Feb. 1968
Surrender, Apr. 30, 1975

Gulf of
Thailand

Mekong
Delta

0   50   100 miles
0   50   100 kilometers

(D) was more committed to the implementation of containment policy than his predecessors had been.

(E) took funding away from the war effort to prop up his Great Society programs.

64. A major critic of Lyndon Johnson's foreign policies was
(A) William Fulbright.
(B) Walter Rostow.
(C) Robert McNamara.
(D) Daniel Ortega.
(E) William Westmoreland.

65. Lyndon Johnson's political downfall resulted primarily from
(A) his Latin American policy.
(B) his obsession with the Vietnam War.
(C) the failure of his Great Society.
(D) his refusal to be a Cold Warrior.
(E) his advocacy of welfare programs.

66. In the election of 1976, Jimmy Carter defeated
(A) Ronald Reagan.
(B) Gerald Ford.
(C) Richard Nixon.
(D) Spiro Agnew.
(E) George Bush.

67. In 1979 revolutionaries in _____ took U.S. diplomats hostage.
(A) Iraq
(B) Israel
(C) Pakistan
(D) Iran
(E) Afghanistan

68. Which foreign policy would lessen tensions with the Soviet Union?
(A) containment
(B) brinkmanship
(C) detente
(D) rapprochement
(E) "one-upsmanship"

63. Lyndon Johnson must bear great responsibility for the American problems in the Vietnam War because he
(A) failed to confront the American people with the stark truth of the war.
(B) was the first president to commit U.S. military personnel to Vietnam.
(C) was the first U.S. leader to commit American financial resources to fighting the Communists in Vietnam.

69. The SALT treaties involved
    (A) the United States' withdrawal from Vietnam.
    (B) reductions in the number of offensive ballistic missiles.
    (C) removal of Soviet nuclear weapons from Cuba.
    (D) preventing war in the Middle East.
    (E) the collapse of the former Soviet Union.

70. The SALT I agreements
    (A) were more important as symbols than concrete events.
    (B) forced the United States to take a secondary position in the arms race.
    (C) were never accepted by the Soviet and American governments.
    (D) provided China with military support along its border with the Soviet Union.
    (E) limited the two superpowers to one thousand anti-ballistic missiles each.

71. The only clear-cut triumph that Reagan achieved in the Western Hemisphere came in
    (A) Nicaragua.
    (B) Lebanon.
    (C) El Salvador.
    (D) the Caribbean.
    (E) Mexico.

72. The central tenet of Reagan's approach to foreign policy was the belief that
    (A) the Palestine Liberation Organization (PLO) represented a serious threat to the United States.
    (B) trading arms for hostages was an effective way to quietly negotiate with terrorists.
    (C) The Soviet Union was a deadly enemy that threatened the United States.
    (D) Central America needed United States intervention to achieve freedom.
    (E) Israel could not be trusted.

73. The Cold War had been dormant throughout the 1970s until
    (A) the United States invaded North Vietnam.
    (B) the Soviet Union invaded Afghanistan.
    (C) the Chinese attacked Korea.
    (D) the Soviet Union attacked China.
    (E) the Soviet Union invaded Pakistan.

74. In the election of 1988, Bush carried all of the following states EXCEPT
    (A) the South.
    (B) the West.
    (C) Michigan.
    (D) Massachusetts.
    (E) Pennsylvania.

75. Reagan was able to please feminists with his appointment of _____ to the Supreme Court.
    (A) Anita Hill
    (B) Madeline O'Hara
    (C) Sandra Day O'Connor
    (D) Clarence Thomas
    (E) Ruth Bader Ginsberg

76. Which of the following was NOT a foreign policy problem for the Clinton administration?
    (A) Bosnia
    (B) Somalia
    (C) Kosovo
    (D) Western Europe
    (E) Haiti

77. In 1994, Clinton sent U.S. troops to which one of the following Caribbean countries?
    (A) Jamaica
    (B) Grenada
    (C) Haiti
    (D) the Dominican Republic
    (E) Puerto Rico

78. The police beating of _____ precipitated the Los Angeles riots of 1992.
    (A) Rodney King
    (B) Ruth Ginsberg
    (C) Len Bias
    (D) Henry Cisneros
    (E) O.J. Simpson

79. The vice president of the United States during the Clinton administration was
    (A) Janet Reno.
    (B) Lloyd Bentsen.
    (C) Al Gore.
    (D) Alan Greenspan.
    (E) Dan Quayle.

80. Which one of the following individuals ran for president in 1992 and 1996 as a third-party candidate?
    (A) Ross Perot
    (B) Jerry Falwell
    (C) Orville Faubus
    (D) Janet Reno
    (E) John Anderson

U.S. History
Section II
Part A

Suggested Writing Time: 45 Minutes
Percent of Section II Score: 45

Directions: The following question is based on the accompanying Documents 1–10. (Some of the documents have been edited for the purpose of this exercise.) Write your answer on the pages of the essay booklet.

This question is designed to test your ability to work with historical documents. As you analyze the documents, take into account both the sources of the document and the authors' points of view. Write an essay on the following topic that integrates your analysis of the documents. **Do not simply summarize the documents individually.** You may refer to relevant historical facts and developments not mentioned in the documents.

Part A, Question 1

1. *What were the major issues, events, and ideas of the period 1960–1969? In your answer, draw upon your knowledge of the time period in addition to the information contained in the documents.*

DOCUMENT 1   Source: John F. Kennedy, inaugural address, 1961

We dare not forget today that we are the heirs of that first revolution. Let the word go forth from this time and place, to friend and foe alike, that the torch has been passed to a new generation of Americans—born in this century, tempered by war, disciplined by a cold and bitter peace, proud of our ancient heritage—and unwilling to witness or permit the slow undoing of those human rights to which this nation has always been committed, and to which we are committed today.

Let every nation know, whether it wish us well or ill, that we shall pay any price, bear any burden, meet any hardship, support any friend or oppose any foe in order to assure the survival and success of liberty.

DOCUMENT 2   Source: Lyndon Johnson, The War on Poverty, 1964

I have called for a national war on poverty. Our objective: total victory. There are millions of Americans—one fifth of our people—who have not shared in the abundance which has been granted to most of us, and on whom the gates of opportunity have been closed.

What does this poverty mean to those who endure it?

It means a daily struggle to secure the necessities for even a meager existence. It means that the abundance, the comforts, the opportunities they see all around them are beyond their grasp.

Worst of all, it means hopelessness for the young.

DOCUMENT 3   Source: Tonkin Gulf Resolution, 1964

Resolved by the Senate and House of Representatives of the United States of America in Congress assembled, that the Congress approves and supports the determination of the President, as Commander in Chief, to take all necessary measures to repel any armed attack against the forces of the United States and to prevent further aggression.

SEC. 2. The United States regards as vital to its national interest and to world peace the maintenance of international peace and security in southeast Asia. Consonant with the Constitution of the United States and the Charter of the United Nations and in accordance with its obligations under the Southeast Asia Collective Defense Treaty, the United States is, therefore, prepared, as the President determines, to take all necessary steps, including the use of armed force, to assist any member or protocol state of the Southeast Asia Collective Defense Treaty requesting assistance in defense of its freedom.

SEC. 3. This resolution shall expire when the President shall determine that the peace and security of the area is reasonably assured by international conditions created by action of the United Nations or otherwise, except that it may be terminated earlier by concurrent resolution of the Congress.

DOCUMENT 4   Source: Students for a Democratic Society, The Port Huron Statement, 1962

We are the people of this generation, bred in at least modest comfort, housed now in the universities, looking uncomfortably to the world we inherit.

When we were kids the United States was the wealthiest and strongest country in the world; the only one with the atom bomb, the least scarred by modern war, an initiator of the United Nations that we thought would distribute Western influence throughout the world. Freedom and equality for each individual, government of, by, and for the people—these American values we found good, principles by which we could live as men. Many of us began maturing in complacency.

As we grew, however, our comfort was penetrated by events too troubling to dismiss.

First, the permeating and victimizing fact of human degradation, symbolized by the Southern struggle against racial bigotry, compelled most of us from silence to activism.

Second, the enclosing fact of the Cold War, symbolized by the presence of the Bomb, brought awareness that we ourselves, and our friends, and millions of abstract "others" we knew more directly because of our common peril, might die at any time. We might deliberately ignore, or avoid or fail to feel all other human problems, but not these two, for these were too immediate and crushing in their impact, too challenging in the demand that we as individuals take the responsibility for encounter and resolution.

DOCUMENT 5   Source: National Organization for Women, Statement of Purpose, 1966

NOW is dedicated to the proposition that women, first and foremost, are human beings, who, like all other people in our society, must have the chance to develop their fullest human potential. We believe that women can achieve such equality only by accepting to the full the challenges and responsibilities they share with all other people in our society, as part of the decision-making mainstream of American political, economic, and social life.

DOCUMENT 6   Source: Student Nonviolent Coordinating Committee, Statement of Purpose, 1960

We affirm the philosophical or religious ideal of nonviolence as the foundation of our purpose, the presupposition of our faith, and the manner of our action. Nonviolence as it grows from Judaic-Christian tradition seeks a social order of justice permeated by love. Integration of human endeavor represents the crucial first step toward such a society.

Through nonviolence, courage displaces fear; love transforms hate. Acceptance dissipates prejudice; hope ends despair. Peace dominates war; faith reconciles doubt. Mutual regard cancels enmity. Justice for all overthrows injustice. The redemptive community supersedes systems of gross social immorality.

Love is the central motif of nonviolence. Love is the force by which God binds man to Himself and man to man. Such love goes to the extreme; it remains loving and forgiving even in the midst of hostility. It matches the capacity of evil to inflict suffering with an even more enduring capacity to absorb evil, all the while persisting in love.

By appealing to conscience and standing on the moral nature of human existence, nonviolence nurtures the atmosphere in which reconciliation and justice become actual possibilities.

DOCUMENT 7   Source: John Lewis, Address at the March on Washington, 1963

We march today for jobs and freedom, but we have nothing to be proud of, for hundreds and thousands of our brothers are not here—they have no money for their transportation, for they are receiving starvation wages…or no wages, at all.

For the first time in 100 years this nation is being awakened to the fact that segregation is evil and it must be destroyed in all forms. Our presence today proves that we have been aroused to the point of action.

We are now involved in a serious revolution. This nation is still a place of cheap political leaders who build their careers on immoral compromise and ally themselves with open forms of political, economic, and social exploitation....The party of Kennedy is also the party of Eastland. The party of Javits is also the party of Goldwater. Where is our party?

I want to know—which side is the federal government on?

The revolution is at hand, and we must free ourselves of the chains of political and economic slavery. The non-violent revolution is saying, "We will not wait for the courts to act, for we have been waiting hundreds of years. We will not wait for the President, nor the Justice Department, nor Congress, but we will take matters into our own hands, and create a great source of power, outside of any national structure that could and would assure us victory."...We cannot be patient, we do not want to be free gradually, we want our freedom, and we want it now. We cannot depend on any political party, for both the Democrats and Republicans have betrayed the basic principles of the Declaration of Independence....

DOCUMENT 8   Source: The Civil Rights Act of 1964

Sec. 101 (2). No person acting under color of law shall—

(A) in determining whether any individual is qualified under State law or laws to vote in any Federal election, apply any standard, practice, or procedure different from the standards, practices, or procedures applied under such law or laws to other individuals within the same county, parish, or similar political subdivision who have been found by State officials to be qualified to vote;...

(C) employ any literacy test as a qualification for voting in any Federal election unless (i) such test is administered to each individual wholly in writing; and (ii) a certified copy of the test and of the answers given by the individual is furnished to him within twenty-five days of the submission of his request made within the period of time during which records and papers are required to be retained and preserved pursuant to Title III of the Civil Rights Act of 1960....

Sec. 201. (a) All persons shall be entitled to the full and equal enjoyment of the goods, services, facilities, privileges, advantages, and accommodations of any place of public accommodation, as defined in this section, without discrimination or segregation on the ground of race, color, religion, or national origin. Sec. 601. No person in the United States shall, on the ground of race, color, or national origin, be excluded from participation in, be denied the benefits of, or be subjected to discrimination under any program or activity receiving Federal financial assistance.

DOCUMENT 9 Source: Anti-war protest at the Pentagon, 1967

DOCUMENT 10 Source: Poster for the Woodstock Music Festival, 1969

U.S. History
Section II
Part B

Suggested Planning and Writing Time: 70 Minutes
Percent of Section II Score: 55

Directions: You are to answer the following two questions. You should spend 5 minutes organizing or outlining each essay. In writing your essays, *use specific examples to support your answer.* Write your answers to the questions on the lined pages of the essay booklet. If time permits when you finish writing, check your work.

Part B, Question 2

The suggested writing time for this question is 30 minutes. *You are advised to spend 5 minutes planning your answer.*

2. *From mid-July to early August 1945, Truman, Stalin, and Clement Attlee, the new British Prime Minister, met at Potsdam in Germany. Here, the Allied leaders warned the Japanese, without being specific, that if they did not agree to unconditional surrender, Japan would suffer "complete and utter destruction."*

Use the source below and relevant historical information to explain the effectiveness of the Allied warning and the consequences which resulted.

Unfortunately the declaration was not an explicit (clearly expressed) warning that the United States possessed nuclear weapons and would use them....Perhaps because the warning was only a general statement, the Japanese responded with something approaching contempt. The prime minister chose to ignore it, employing the ambiguous (not clear) word mokusatu, which means literally "to kill with silence"....Tokyo radio used the word, saying the government would mokusatu the declaration and fight on. The English translation became "reject," and the president took it as a rebuff (blank rejection).

In addition to being unaware that the United States possessed nuclear weapons, the Japanese leaders also believed, foolishly, that they could negotiate with the Americans, even though the Japanese were thoroughly aware of the rapine (plundering) and butchery associated with their nation's troops as they fought across East Asia....As the war was coming to an end the Americans, British, and Soviets were publicly stating that they would arraign (bring before a court for trial) war criminals, but Tokyo officials deluded themselves into believing it would be possible to bargain to save the people involved....

Truman and the Bomb, a Documentary History
Ch. 7: The Potsdam Declaration, July 26
Edited by Robert H. Farrell

Part B, Question 3

The suggested writing time for this question is 30 minutes. *You are advised to spend 5 minutes planning your answer.*

3. *Assess how the opposing political plans of the Soviet Union and Western powers (United States and Great Britain) affected political developments in Europe during the period 1945–1949.*

ANSWERS AND EXPLANATIONS

Sample Test 2

Section I: Multiple Choice

▌ **1. (B) is correct.** By 1890, more than 85 percent of America's manufactured goods originated in the Northeast.

▌ **2. (C) is correct.** With the advantages of speed and safety, along with more direct routes, the development of a national railway system allowed the economy of the United States to become more fully integrated. While the United States possessed a fine system of interior waterways, it was the railway that transformed the way that raw materials were brought to manufacturers and then how goods were brought to market.

▌ **3. (C) is correct.** With significant donations of land and capital, the local, state and federal government provided railroad companies with the ability to expand rapidly after the Civil War.

▌ **4. (A) is correct.** The Teamsters Union was not founded until 1903.

▌ **5. (C) is correct.** Unlike other unions, the American Federation of Labor accepted the fundamental nature of the capitalist system and was only interested in achieving a greater piece of the capitalist pie for the worker.

▌ **6. (D) is correct.** The code of Victorian morality, named after the British queen during this period, prescribed strict standards of dress, manners and sexual behavior. Children were to be seen and not heard, young couples who were courting were to be chaperoned.

▌ **7. (B) is correct.** Public schools were seen as a way to train people for life and work in the industrial economy. This meant that the curriculum would be a discipline and routine consideration of the basic skills, such as reading, mathematics and obedience.

▌ **8. (C) is correct.** With families that averaged twice the size of their northern counterparts and much of the population spread out in very rural communities, many southern states were unable to finance their public schools.

▌ **9. (D) is correct.** Unlike Booker T. Washington, who believed that the key to African American success was simply through education and jobs in the workplace, W. E. B. Du Bois believed that educational advancement was key to securing professional careers for African Americans. He argued that only through established professions would the African American be able to improve their place in society.

▌ **10. (A) is correct.** Using the model that had become popular in Germany, the United States began to found specialized research universities. One of the first of these new model universities was John Hopkins University in Baltimore, Maryland, which opened the nation's first separate graduate school.

▌ **11. (E) is correct.** Created by the Congress in 1887 in reference to the case of *Wabush, St. Louis, & Pacific Railway Co. v. Illinois*, it was the first attempt that the federal government made at regulation of the railway and became a modern model for regulation of the economy.

12. (B) is correct. Passed in 1883 as a measure to reform the civil service, the Pendleton Act created a bipartisan Civil Service Commission to administer competitive examinations and appoint officeholders on the basis of merit.

13. (C) is correct. The first Democratic president in twenty-three years, Grover Cleveland curtailed federal activities by vetoing more than two-thirds of the legislation that was sent to him by Congress.

14. (A) is correct. Support for free coinage of silver was particularly strong in the South and the West, both areas whose economies were predominantly based upon agriculture. In addition, many of those who supported the free coinage of silver felt that it would inflate crop prices.

15. (C) is correct. Fearing having to coinage all silver presented to its mints, the Sherman Silver Purchase Act allowed for the Treasury to purchase 4.5 million ounces of silver a month and to issue Treasury notes as the form of payment. This measure limited the amount of silver coinage in circulation, but was enough of a compromise to keep both sides happy.

16. (E) is correct. After tense moments with warships from the United States, Britain and Germany all posed near the Samoan Islands, an agreement was signed that allowed the United States to maintain its military installations at the harbor in Pago Pago.

17. (D) is correct. In his books *The Influence of Sea Power Upon History, 1660–1783* (1890) and *The Interest of America in Sea Power* (1897), Alfred Mahan outlined his belief that industrialization created an excess of goods and that a two-ocean navy would provide the United States with the protection it needed to exploit distant seaport markets in both the Atlantic and the Pacific.

18. (A) is correct. General Weyler gave the rebels ten days to lay down their arms. He then put into effect a "reconcentration" policy designed to move the native population into camps and destroy the rebellion's popular base. Herded into fortified areas, Cubans died by the thousands from unsanitary conditions, overcrowding and disease. This mistreatment generated public sympathy for the Cuban people among Americans.

19. (A) is correct. In order to sell newspapers to the public before and during the Spanish-American War, publishers William Randolph Hearst and Joseph Pulitzer engaged in blatant sensationalization of the news, which became known as "yellow journalism." Althought it did not cause the war with Spain, it helped turn U.S. public opinion against Spain's actions in Cuba.

20. (D) is correct. The United States army was unprepared due to the fact that it had been thirty years since the Civil War had ended. Many of the soldiers who had remained in the army had been stationed at western outposts and were better equipped in fighting Native Americans than they were at fighting against soldiers who used conventional weapons.

21. (D) is correct. Based upon the graph, the line for "Southern and Eastern Europe" is larger than the lines that would include any of the other grouped nationalities.

22. (B) is correct. The graph indicates that the immigration rate was steady from 1900 to 1905, then rose slightly from 1905 to about 1913. It decreased from about 1913 to 1915, when it again began to increase, quite dramatically during the last few years before 1920.

23. (D) is correct. While it was Ransom E' Olds' company that first began using the system of mass production and the assembly-line system to make automobiles, Henry Ford's success came from his drive to enable every American to own an automobile. By slashing the price of automobiles and a nonstop flow from raw material to finished product, the workers at Ford's assembly plants were able to assemble a car in 93 minutes in 1925, one-tenth the time it had taken only eight months earlier.

24. (C) is correct. Isadora Duncan and Ruth St. Denis transformed dance by departing from traditional ballet steps to a form of dance that was based upon improvisation, emotion and the human form.

25. (A) is correct. After meeting on the Canadian side of Niagara Falls, because no American hotel would rent them a room, W.E.B. Du Bois formed the Niagara Movement to focus upon equal rights and education for African American youth.

26. (A) is correct. The success of the *Northern Securities* decision against corporate giants such as Morgan and Rockefeller allowed lawmakers to pursue other antitrust actions under the Sherman Antitrust Act. In a 5 to 4 decision, the Supreme Court had ordered the massive railroad trust Northern Securities Company to be dissolved.

27. (A) is correct. After being elected governor in 1901, Robert W. La Follette put together the "Wisconsin Idea." This reform program established an industrial commission to regulate factory safety and sanitation; improved education, worker's compensation, public utility controls and resource conservation; and lowered railroad rates and raised railroad taxes.

28. (C) is correct. The Hepburn Act empowered the Interstate Commerce Commission to fix reasonable maximum railroad rates and broadened its jurisdiction to include oil pipelines, express and sleeping car companies.

29 (A) is correct. The Underwood Tariff of 1913 lowered rates about 15 percent and removed duties from sugar, wool and several other consumer goods. This victory for President Wilson and the Democratic Party represented the first tariff since 1894.

30. (C) is correct. A form of municipal government in which a commission of experts, rather than elected officials, ran the city was pioneered in Galveston, Texas in 1900.

31. (C) is correct. After the Dominican Republic defaulted on its debts in 1904, the United States introduced the Roosevelt Corollary to the Monroe Doctrine. Designed to allow the United States to intervene in any Latin American country if it could not maintain its finances, it also prevented European countries from interfering in Latin America.

32. (B) is correct. The restrictions that were placed upon immigration during the 1920s reflected that American society was concerned with the perceived flood of immigration that was coming to America from the war-torn countries of Europe.

33. (E) is correct. William Jennings Bryan, inexperienced in foreign relations, believed that he could negotiate a series of "cooling off" treaties, which would provide for parties to submit all international disputes to a permanent commission of investigation. As such, he embarked upon an idealistic campaign to negotiate treaties of arbitration throughout the world.

34. (A) is correct. While an idealist by nature, Wilson was distracted by other problems and impatient with the results of his own approach. This forced the president to maintain roughly the same policies that Roosevelt and Taft had held towards Latin America.

35. (B) is correct. Made by the Germans on May 4, 1916, the *Sussex* pledge agreed to allow American passenger ships not to be subject to the unrestricted submarine warfare that the Germans had begun in February of that same year.

36. (C) is correct. The Ku Klux Klan was an organization that was originally created to terrorize and intimidate former slaves. However, during the 1920s, it found new support from Anglo-Saxon Protestant men who were concerned about the lack of morals in American society. This threat to American culture, as they perceived it, came from blacks and immigrants to the United States.

37. (C) is correct. Filling stations appeared on the main streets, replacing the smithies and stables of the past. Shopping centers were built, followed by suburban developments. Rubber factories boomed with the demand for tires, and paint and glass suppliers had more business than ever before. These are just some of the ways in which the automobile had a profound effect upon American life.

38. (B) is correct. Mencken is best known for his coining of the term "flapper," a term to refer to young women who cut their hair short, raised their skirts above their knee and bound their breasts. Mencken, who founded *American Mercury* in 1923, mocked everything that he found distasteful in American society.

39. (B) is correct. During the elections of 1928, the shift of urban voters to the party threatened to tear it apart. It drove a wedge between the traditional Democrats of the South and West and the new Democrats from the emerging metropolitan areas of the North and Midwest. A hindrance in 1928, it showed promise for the future as the population and number of potential voters in these emerging metropolitan areas of the North and Midwest continued to increase.

40. (A) is correct. After the different views on prohibition, both Al Smith (Democrat) and Herbert Hoover (Republican) were quite similar. Both were self-made men who embodied the American belief in freedom of opportunity and upward mobility. Neither advocated any significant degree of economic change nor any redistribution of national wealth or power.

41. (D) is correct. In the summer of 1932 some twenty-two thousand World War I veterans marched on Washington to demand immediate payment of a bonus for military service that was due to them in 1945. Hoover's failure to convince Congress to honor the wishes of these veterans and the rather brutal means used to disperse the veterans remained in the public's memory during the 1932 presidential campaign.

42. (C) is correct. Section 7a of the enabling act mandated protection for labor in all the codes by establishing maximum hours, minimum wages, and the guarantee of collective bargaining by unions.

43. (A) is correct. The Agricultural Adjustment Act would allocate acreage among individual farmers, encouraging them to take land out of production by paying them subsidies. This meant that the overall crop production of farmers would be reduced and that the production that was maintained should have an inflated price.

44. (D) is correct. The National Recovery Administration attempted to achieve economic advances through planning and cooperation among government, business and labor. This would be achieved through the use of written codes of fair competition.

45. (A) is correct. Francis Townsend, a 67-year-old physician, came forward in 1934 with a scheme to assist the elderly, who were suffering greatly during the Depression. The Townsend Plan proposed giving everyone over the age of 60 a monthly pension of $200 with the proviso that it must be spent within thirty days.

46. (B) is correct. The relationship between all of the wartime Allied powers and the Soviet Union was less than perfect. Distrustful over the initial Nazi-Soviet Pact, along with the Soviet support of communist activities in the other Allied nations, the United States had a particularly strained relationship with the Soviet Union. Diametrically opposed both on political and economic ideology, neither nation trusted the other.

47. (A) is correct. After winning the Battle of Midway, the United States began to attack the Japanese positions, island by island throughout the Pacific Ocean, starting with the Solomon Islands. Next came the Gilbert, Marshall and Caroline Islands, then the Philippines.

48. (E) is correct. In order to have American troops engage the German army prior to an invasion of continental Europe, Roosevelt sent American troops into North Africa in November 1942.

49 (C) is correct. After the attack on Pearl Harbor, more than 120,000 Japanese Americans were forcibly re-located from the west coast of the United States due to racial fears. These relocated individuals were sent to concentration camps in the interior until the end of the war, when the camps were finally closed in March of 1946.

50. (D) is correct. It was George C. Marshall, the British Army Chief of Staff, who placed a relatively junior general, Dwight D. Eisenhower, in charge of the Allied invasion of continental Europe.

51. (D) is correct. Under the control of General Douglas McArthur, the Japanese government was transformed into a constitutional democracy based upon western models after World War II.

52. (B) is correct. While Chiang Kai-shek had the backing of the United States, widespread corruption in high government, along with inflation that reached levels of 100% per year devastated the Chinese middle class and much of Chiang Kai-shek's support. Along with military mistakes when it came to Manchuria, Chiang Kai-shek was not able to hold back the communist forces.

53. (C) is correct. After having occupied the northern portion of the Korean peninsula for four years, the Soviet Union had left behind a well-trained and supplied army in North Korea.

54. (E) is correct. The Korean War allowed the United States to put NSC-68, its national defense policy, into action. This increased the size of the American army to more than 3.5 million men, increased the defense spending budget and provided the United States with bases on foreign soil all around the world.

55. (B) is correct. The Red Scare came about through the speeches and congressional hearings of Senator Joseph McCarthy, who became obsessed with exposing those who were members of or who sympathized with the communist party. These actions created a fear in the American population, who were concerned that the United States would lose the Cold War to the Soviet Union because of these subversives.

56. (C) is correct. While Chief Justice Warren called for the process of desegregation to begin "with all deliberate speed," in reality the process was quite slow and met with strong resistance, particularly from states deeper in the South.

57. (A) is correct. In the Deep South, local white citizens' councils organized to fight for retention of racial separation; 101 representatives and senators signed a Southern Manifesto in 1956 that denounced the *Brown* decision as "a clear abuse of judicial power." School boards, encouraged by this show of defiance, found a variety of ways to evade the Court's ruling, such as pupil placement laws.

58. (E) is correct. A follower of Mahatma Gandhi's philosophy of passive resistance, King's first major protest against the segregated seating laws on buses in Montgomery, Alabama was a boycott of the city's bus system where blacks organized car pools to avoid needing to use the bus system.

59. (C) is correct. In the late 1950s, Martin Luther King Jr. created the Southern Christian Leadership Conference to direct the crusade against segregation.

60. (D) is correct. By 1960, the education system (both the high school and university systems) were still largely racially segregated due to the resistance of the Deep South to the *Brown* decision. Even still today, the world of corporate America and professional hockey remain largely a white community. However, for a number of decades the American military had been admitting blacks into its ranks and these African Americans had been serving with valor and distinction.

61. (A) is correct. The Gulf of Tonkin Resolution was worded broadly enough that it could be used to wage a complete American war against the North Vietnamese. While this was not Johnson's intention at the time, the fact that the war was escalated to this level during his tenure in office made it seem like he had misled Congress from the very beginning.

62. (B) is correct. The Tet Offensive was one of the reasons that Lyndon Johnson withdrew from the 1968 presidential race. This indicates the lack of support that President Johnson had during this time period and how widely unpopular the war in Vietnam had become.

63. (A) is correct. When CBS-TV newscaster Walter Cronkite visited Saigon to see what was happening in the war, he remarked "What the hell is going on? I thought we were winning the war." This statement speaks to the manner in which Johnson misled the American people about the true nature of the war in Vietnam.

64. (A) is correct. After the election of a conservative government in the Dominican Republic in 1966, William Fulbright published *The Arrogance of Power*, a critical analysis of the policy of containment and, in particular, Lyndon Johnson's foreign policy actions in that regard.

65. (B) is correct. The resistance to and lack of public support for the war in Vietnam was the primary reason for the unpopularity of Lyndon Johnson. His concentration on that war and the misinformation that he provided to the American public, eventually led the anti-war movement in America and his own party to force him out of the 1968 presidential race and politics in general.

■ **66. (B) is correct.** After being selected by Richard Nixon to replace Spiro Agnew (after he had been forced to resign in order to avoid prosecution), Vice-President Gerald Ford had assumed the presidency upon Nixon's resignation at the conclusion of the Watergate scandal. The legacy of Watergate, along with Ford's own lackluster record, allowed Democratic candidate Jimmy Carter to win the election of 1976.

■ **67. (D) is correct.** Militant Muslims came to power in Tehran and the United States allowed the exiled shah to come to American soil to receive medical treatment. In retaliation, revolutionaries in Iran seized the American embassy and took fifty-eight Americans prisoner.

■ **68. (C) is correct.** The period or policy that reflected an easing of relations between the United States and the Soviet Union (along with other countries) was known as détente. This included such American actions as the end of the Vietnam War, Nixon's visit to China and the SALT agreements.

■ **69. (B) is correct.** The SALT treaties were a series of agreements between the United States and the Soviet Union to limit the number of antiballistic missiles and offensive ballistic missiles that each country possessed. Beginning in 1969, the final agreements were finally signed in 1972.

■ **70. (A) is correct.** While many of the actual reduction targets in the SALT I agreements were never reached, it marked an important symbolic agreement. This was the first initiative undertaken by the United States and the Soviet Union to try and reduce the number of nuclear weapons in the world and it showed that both parties were willing to look for peaceful means to settle their differences.

■ **71. (D) is correct.** Reagan's only clear-cut military victory in the Western Hemisphere came with the 1983 invasion of Grenada, an island in the Caribbean. American forces, while met with spirited resistance from about eight hundred Cuban workers and troops, were able to claim victory with only eighteen lives being lost.

■ **72. (C) is correct.** The basic principle of Reagan's foreign policy was the fact that the Soviet Union threatened the security of the United States. Military excursion in Lebanon, Nicaragua, El Salvador and Grenada, along with funding defense programs such as the B-1 bomber and the Strategic Defense Initiative, were all designed to prevent the Soviet Union from gaining influence beyond its current satellite states.

■ **73. (B) is correct.** In 1979, the Soviet Union invaded Afghanistan in an attempt to gain influence into southwest Asia and start to gain a foothold in the Middle East. After ten years of unsuccessful conflict, the Soviet forces withdraw in 1989.

■ **74. (D) is correct.** Democratic presidential candidate Michael Dukakis was the former Governor of Massachusetts and carried the state in the 1988 presidential election.

■ **75. (C) is correct.** In 1981, President Reagan nominated Sandra Day O'Connor to be the first woman to serve on the Supreme Court.

■ **76. (D) is correct.** The United States was involved in United Nation peacekeeping missions in Somalia and Bosnia and a North Atlantic Treaty Organization involvement in Kosovo. The Clinton administration also decided to use force in Haiti to return the overthrown government of Jean-Bertrand Aristide to power.

77. (C) is correct. In September 1984, President Clinton sent U.S. troops into Haiti (after former President Jimmy Carter had worked out a compromise that allowed U.S. troops to land unopposed). The overthrown government of Jean-Bertrand Aristide returned to power, but it wasn't until 1996 that the democratically elected successor was able to take power from Aristide.

78. (A) is correct. After a bystander caught the police beating of African American Rodney King on video tape, riots began in Los Angeles that saw more than fifty people die and more that $1 billion in property damage.

79. (C) is correct. Claiming to have "invented the Internet," Clinton vice president Al Gore was saddled with the Clinton scandals during the 2000 presidential election and unable to use the successful economy that he had helped manage over the past eight years as an effective component of his campaign.

80. (A) is correct. As an independent candidate in 1992 and as the Reform Party candidate in 1996, Texas billionaire Ross Perot ran for president twice, without winning a single state in either election.

Section II
Part A

1. *What were the major issues, events, and ideas of the period 1960–1969? In your answer, draw upon your knowledge of the time period in addition to the information contained in the documents.*

The 1960s was in many ways a difficult period in American history. There were many issues that drove this turbulent time of change.

The election of John Kennedy in 1960 signaled some of this. He was the first president born in the 20th century and one of the youngest to assume the office. He was clearly of a different generation than President Eisenhower, whom he was replacing. His Inaugural Address was energetic and forward looking, but also addressed many of the Cold War issues that still dominated American politics. **(DOCUMENT 1)**

Americans made many efforts to grapple with other issues of the day. Poverty was still an issue in America at the time, and President Lyndon Johnson identified that problem for many Americans and made solving it a national priority. **(DOCUMENT 2)** The Civil Rights Movement was in its heyday, and it drove much of the events of that period. The early part of the Movement was dominated by Martin Luther King and SNCC. Their basic philosophy was that of non-violent, peaceful resistance. **(DOCUMENT 6)** The culminating event of the early part of the Civil Rights Movement was the 1963 March On Washington. Many of the speakers of the day pointed out the ills of American society on the issue of race and demanded justice. **(DOCUMENT 7)** Although the government did not solve every problem, the Johnson Administration did address many of them, most notably with the Civil Rights Act of 1964 which prohibited discrimination in any place of public accommodation or in anything that receives Federal funds. **(DOCUMENT 8)** The Civil Rights Movement was also the catalyst for the modern women's rights movement, which began in the 1960s. The formation of NOW is the biggest symbol of this. **(DOCUMENT 5)**

The over-riding issue of the day was the war in Vietnam. This war slid up on us slowly and was never formally declared. The Congress did authorize the

President to take military action after some incidents that may have been attacks by the North Vietnamese took place in the Gulf of Tonkin. **(DOCUMENT 3)** While Americans initially supported the war, it eventually became tremendously controversial as thousands of Americans were killed. Young people, in particular, often protested the war and spoke out against other things in American society that bothered them. **(DOCUMENTS 4 AND 9)** Many young people became disenfranchised from and disillusioned with American society. They often turned to drugs and music as a way of expressing themselves. The Woodstock Music Festival was the culminating event of this aspect of the 1960s.

Section II
Part B

Sample Student Responses

2. *From mid-July to early August 1945, Truman, Stalin, and Clement Attlee, the new British Prime Minister, met at Potsdam in Germany. Here, the Allied leaders warned the Japanese, without being specific, that if they did not agree to unconditional surrender, Japan would suffer "complete and utter destruction."*

Use the source below and relevant historical information to explain the effectiveness of the Allied warning and the consequences which resulted.

Unfortunately the declaration was not an explicit (clearly expressed) warning that the United States possessed nuclear weapons and would use them....Perhaps because the warning was only a general statement, the Japanese responded with something approaching contempt. The prime minister chose to ignore it, employing the ambiguous (not clear) word mokusatu, which means literally "to kill with silence"....Tokyo radio used the word, saying the government would mokusatu the declaration and fight on. The English translation became "reject," and the president took it as a rebuff (blank rejection).

In addition to being unaware that the United States possessed nuclear weapons, the Japanese leaders also believed, foolishly, that they could negotiate with the Americans, even though the Japanese were thoroughly aware of the rapine (plundering) and butchery associated with their nation's troops as they fought across East Asia....As the war was coming to an end the Americans, British, and Soviets were publicly stating that they would arraign (bring before a court for trial) war criminals, but Tokyo officials deluded themselves into believing it would be possible to bargain to save the people involved....

Truman and the Bomb, a Documentary History
Ch. 7: The Potsdam Declaration, July 26
Edited by Robert H. Farrell

The Allied message was unclear. The Americans did not come out and directly say they planned to use an atomic weapon. The Japanese obviously chose to ignore this threat. The Japanese did not want to be shamed with surrender and would try to negotiate with the Americans. Obviously the Japanese did not know that the Americans had atomic weapons. The United States had threatened Japan before and had even fire-bombed Tokyo, but the Japanese did not believe that the United States would drop an atomic bomb. Japan also underestimated how much America valued its soldiers. The war was dragging on and resulted in thousands of American casualties. Americans wanted to end the war quickly, before more men died. So when Japan ignored the Potsdam declaration, the United States decided to drop an atomic bomb on the city of Hiroshima. The Japanese did not respond so two days later the city of Nagasaki was also bombed. After that, the Japanese agreed to unconditional surrender.

The use of an atomic weapon in combat had many consequences. First was the moral question—not only were so many civilians killed, but the radiation caused cancers and birth defects for decades after. Secondly, this show of force proved that the United States was the most powerful nation on earth. This created a new world order and a new role for America. No longer could it be the isolationist society it had been before. The use of atomic weapons also brought about the nuclear era. Now the world would see the dawning of a new threat to global security. The U.S. show of force also acted as a subtle threat to the U.S.S.R. America had the technological advantage over the Soviets for four years. However, eventually the U.S.S.R. developed nuclear weapons. This brought about the nuclear arms race, which threatened to destroy the world. Other countries soon developed their own nuclear weapons despite attempts by the Soviets and America to stop proliferation. The Americans' use of atomic weapons on Japan signalled the end of a war and the beginning of a new, and more dangerous, atomic age. Had Japan better understood the Allied threat, had the Allies been clearer, perhaps the atomic age would have been delayed.

3. *Assess how the opposing political plans of the Soviet Union and Western powers (United States and Great Britain) affected political developments in Europe during the period 1945–1949.*

During the Yalta conference of 1945, where Stalin, Roosevelt and Churchill were present, the fate of post-war Europe (particularly East Europe and Germany) was to be decided. After much negotiation, the West and the Soviet Union settled upon the idea of spheres of influence. This meant that they were each in charge of their own "sphere" to maintain peace until later elections were made for independence and self-determination. The United States and Britain both generally agreed that the countries within their spheres would eventually "be free to elect their own governments." However, Stalin had a different view. He believed that "whoever occupies the territory also imposes his own social system." This was a concern to the West because it meant the spread of communism or communist influence.